PUNISH AND EXPEL

CLARENDON STUDIES IN CRIMINOLOGY

Published under the auspices of the Institute of Criminology, University of Cambridge; the Mannheim Centre, London School of Economics; and the Centre for Criminology, University of Oxford.

RECENT TITLES IN THIS SERIES:

Speaking Truths to Power: Policy Ethnography and Police Reform in Bosnia and Herzegovina
Jarrett Blaustein

Prisoners, Solitude, and Time
Ian O'Donnell

Criminal Careers in Transition: The Social Context of Desistance from Crime
Stephen Farrall, Ben Hunter, Gilly Sharpe, and Adam Calverley

Hate Crime and Restorative Justice: Exploring Causes, Repairing Harms
Mark Austin Walters

Policing the Waterfront: Networks, Partnerships, and the Governance of Port Security
Russell Brewer

Punish and Expel

Border Control, Nationalism, and the New Purpose of the Prison

EMMA KAUFMAN

OXFORD
UNIVERSITY PRESS

OXFORD
UNIVERSITY PRESS

Great Clarendon Street, Oxford, OX2 6DP,
United Kingdom

Oxford University Press is a department of the University of Oxford. It furthers the University's objective of excellence in research, scholarship, and education by publishing worldwide. Oxford is a registered trade mark of Oxford University Press in the UK and in certain other countries

First Edition published in 2015
Impression: 1

Published in the United States of America by Oxford University Press
198 Madison Avenue, New York, NY 10016, United States of America

British Library Cataloguing in Publication Data
Data available

Library of Congress Control Number: 2015931233

ISBN 978-0-19-871260-2

Printed and bound by
CPI Group (UK) Ltd, Croydon, CR0 4YY

General Editor's Introduction

Clarendon Studies in Criminology aims to provide a forum for outstanding empirical and theoretical work in all aspects of criminology and criminal justice, broadly understood. The Editors welcome submissions from established scholars, as well as excellent PhD work. The *Series* was inaugurated in 1994, with Roger Hood as its first General Editor, following discussions between Oxford University Press and three criminology centres. It is edited under the auspices of these three centres: the Cambridge Institute of Criminology, the Mannheim Centre for Criminology at the London School of Economics, and the Centre for Criminology at the University of Oxford. Each supplies members of the Editorial Board and, in turn, the Series Editor or Editors.

Emma Kaufman's book *Punish and Expel: Border Control, Nationalism, and the New Purpose of the Prison* is light on the eye but hard on the heart. It is a book based on a year of fieldwork in and around five men's prisons, including interviews with 200 prisoners and prison staff. It takes as its subject the 14 per cent of the British prison population who are foreign nationals. This figure alone testifies to one of Kaufman's arguments that the British prison has become a site for border control and is no longer exclusively about punishment, deterrence, or rehabilitation; or indeed about returning the reformed to the population at large. Rather prisons have oriented themselves in important ways towards the goals of nationalism and migration control. Foreign national prisoners can only leave prison once immigration officers have approved their release; and for many this means deportation. This further tier of bureaucracy in turn leads to a category of people detained beyond the terms of their punishment in some nether world of uncertainty, anxiety, and intense sadness about their futures, prisoners who can be neither readily removed nor released. Kaufman captures their lived experiences through extensive reporting of their words and through an analysis which is profound in its implications. Her focus on how imprisonment feels is one from which all criminologists could learn and on which everyone involved in the debates on migration and nationality should reflect.

Definitions of nationality clearly lie at the centre of this book, yet defining nationality is no easy task. Kaufman argues that the new 'hubs and spokes' policy—introduced in 2006 as a response to a political scandal that led to the resignation of Home Secretary Charles Clarke—has resulted in a definition by exclusion from citizenship. Stereotyping amongst prisoners, staff and, ironically, foreign prisoners themselves infuse the analysis. But as Kaufman powerfully illustrates the 'hubs and spokes' policy is as much about race, ethnicity, sexuality, and gender as it is about nationality. For how people define themselves almost defies explication. Some born in this country associate themselves with the communities amongst whom they have lived, leading to a self-definition that formally would classify them as foreign nationals; others born in former colonial countries, holding British passports and schooled in former colonial schools, think of themselves as British and feel British, yet get defined otherwise; in short, as non-citizens. The documenting of the fluidity of this process is one of the many strengths of this book. Her work is, moreover, tellingly informed by Stuart Hall's concept of collective amnesia, a coordinated mechanism for forgetting our past, and by his notion that the concept of a transcendent Britishness—of free speech, the welfare state, and the NHS—has only emerged as a result of hard-won struggles between different versions of what it is to be British. It is only coherent with the benefit of hindsight. So if there have always been many different ways of being British there is unlikely to be one version that holds good: the version Kaufman documents, which is deeply problematic, is that whether or not prisoners are foreign nationals depends on whether the prison service counts them in that way. Yet people's lives hang on this determination.

The book also takes up Lucia Zedner's argument that sociologists studying punishment have lost sight of the political implications of their writings. Kaufman's stated goal is to pursue a more normative and politically explicit account of punishment, framing punishment as a political act and advancing this through a form of political activism. As she says, she is less committed to outing the state. Thus, one learns about punishment by asking how it feels. And asking how it feels places a focus on people's bodies and their capacity both to experience pain and to be the site of feelings of hope and empathy. Detailing how prisoners self-harm, both intentionally and unintentionally, brings to these notions of pain an acute reality. Her book will undoubtedly generate amongst its readers a shared capacity for feeling with respect to this largely hidden population. It should also make criminologists reflect on the coherence of their understanding of punishment as going beyond concepts of rehabilitation, retribution, and the nation state. As she asserts, and going back to Foucault's famous words that even 'lenient' methods of incarceration put the body at issue, imprisonment is always about the body; or as she and Mary Bosworth put it in 2012, 'whether it is tarred and feathered, incarcerated, or electronically tagged' it is about the body. Focusing on the bodily aspects of penal practices explicitly revisits the core of criminology's methodological concerns and provides one way into thinking about systemic claims relating to imprisonment and how the notions of state power and sovereignty manifest themselves in practice. Focusing on testimonies thus demystifies the realities of prisons.

Where 40 per cent of the black and ethnic minority prison population is made up of foreign nationals, and some prisons hold only prisoners facing deportation, the conception of what imprisonment means in contemporary British society needs serious adjustment, and in particular for the most of us not subject to imprisonment or privy to its organization. Emma Kaufman has remarkably achieved the production of a vehicle for attaining this. Her book is both accessible and transformative.

As Editors we commend this book as making significant contributions to the fields of criminology and penology. It is a book to be most warmly welcomed to the *Clarendon Studies in Criminology Series*.

Jill Peay and Tim Newburn
London School of Economics
and Political Science
January 2015

For Eric

Acknowledgements

I owe thanks to my teachers. A decade ago, Christia Mercer introduced me to the themes that guide this book. Marianne Hirsch taught me to borrow from different disciplines and to care about how people choose to speak. Jack Beck took me on my first prison visit. Gayatri Spivak led the most challenging seminar I have ever taken. I have also learned from Ian Loader, Coretta Phillips, and Lucia Zedner, three incisive and kind readers, and from Mike Wishnie and Judith Resnik, who believe that law can make the world more humane. Above all, I am grateful to Mary Bosworth, my supervisor and my friend. Mary helped me conceive, research, and write every one of the pages that follow.

I was able to spend four years on this book because of the Marshall Scholarship, the Clarendon Fund, and New College, Oxford. I am immensely lucky to have found institutions that offered equal parts freedom and support as I imagined and undertook this project. It is not lost on me that a book about the treatment of non-citizens in the United Kingdom relied on British funds. This study could not have happened in the United States, my home country, and I am indebted to the British government for its openness to my work.

At different stages in the process, a number of people read drafts, gave interviews, and offered me their time. Policymakers in the Her Majesty's Prison Service and the UK Border Agency answered questions they could have ignored. Hindpal Bhui, who knows more about foreign national prisoners than anyone else in the United Kingdom, helped get my research off the ground. Yale Law School and the Center for Comparative Immigration Studies at the University of California, San Diego provided support at key moments, as did Sally Tarshish and Jo Borrill. Conversations with Hope Metcalf, Megan Quattlebaum, Sia Sanneh, and Anna Arons changed the way I saw prisons. Various parts of the book came to life in workshops with Katja Aas, Keramet Reiter, Alexa Koenig, Jackie Stevens, Anil Kalhan, and Alessandro di Giorgi.

Ultimately, this monograph belongs to the prisoners and staff who shared their lives with me. Given the tensions that pervade penal institutions, most of the people who were part of this project chose to remain anonymous. I hope anonymity will not obscure their contributions. Many prison staff members participated in this project and two in particular made my research possible. I appreciate their curiosity and self-reflection.

I also owe thanks, on a level that exceeds articulation, to the prisoners whose testimonies constitute this book. More than a hundred people, living with anxieties I can at best try to understand, allowed me to come into their homes and ask questions about the most painful part of their lives. Prisoners had very little to gain in speaking to me, and yet they spoke. This book aims to do some measure of justice to that generosity.

Finally, I thank the people that I love. Wendy Moffat made me a feminist and a writer. Donald Kaufman gave me the law. Lucy Kaufman taught me to care about history by caring about people. Matt Lockwood thinks punishment is as odd and interesting as I do. Nancy Dalva has been an ear, an eye, and a shoulder for a decade. Barbara Cate, Tracy Cate, Donald Moffat, Gwen Arner, and Annie Murray have provided encouragement and support. Andrew Hammond, Bonnie Ernst, and Danny Altabef are the family I have built.

And then there is Eric Gardiner, who has done more than anyone else, and more than anyone could ask, to help me write this book. Eric drove me to prisons in the snow, camped out in British motels, edited 700 footnotes, and listened to every chapter out loud many times over. He continues to show me what it means to live with empathy. For that I am grateful.

Emma Kaufman
New York
August 2014

Contents

And what exotic part of the world do you come from?
—Prince Phillip, to Lord Taylor of Warwick,
the son of Jamaican immigrants[1]

Birmingham.
—Lord Taylor of Warwick, to Prince Phillip

Shit, I can't go to Somalia. I haven't been there in twenty years. My father and mother live in Birmingham.
—Said, HMP Canterbury[2]

I see it feelingly.
—Gloucester, *King Lear*, Act IV, Scene 6

[1] 'Ninety Gaffes in Ninety Years', *The Independent*, 28 May 2011, <http://www.independent.co.uk/news/uk/home-news/ninety-gaffes-in-ninety-years-2290148.html>.

[2] All names used in this book are pseudonyms chosen by prisoners.

Introduction

Patrick was born in Zaire in the early 1980s.[1] He was six years old when a group of men from the Mobutu regime kidnapped his father. Patrick does not remember the night his father disappeared, but he does recall leaving home a few days later. Alongside his mother and three brothers, Patrick travelled more than 6,000 kilometres to London, where his family hopscotched between friends' houses. After a year, Patrick and his family settled in Croydon. There, in the shadow of Britain's immigration headquarters, Patrick began his life as a British man.

By age ten, Patrick was attending British schools and speaking in an English accent. He played football and made a tight-knit group of friends. Shortly after Patrick's twentieth birthday, police arrested him for robbing a post office. He was tried, convicted, and sentenced to six years' imprisonment. Patrick served the bulk of his time just outside London in a prison close enough for his family to visit. On the last day of his sentence, as he prepared to go home, Patrick met with a man from the UK Border Agency. The man told Patrick that he would not be released at the end of the day. Instead, he would soon be deported.

For the next seventeen months, Patrick remained in a high-security men's prison under a deportation order. During that time, two of his three brothers died—one collapsed on the football field, and the other, his youngest brother, was murdered in London. After nearly a year and a half waiting in prison, Patrick received bail and went home for the first time in close to a decade. He began to live as a free man, albeit one under strict supervision. Patrick's bail conditions required him to check in with an immigration agent, which he did every month. One day, without warning, a routine meeting resulted in Patrick's arrest. Deportation to

[1] The Republic of Zaire was renamed the Democratic Republic of the Congo on 17 May 1997.

the Congo had begun again, his supervisor explained. Patrick had to be 'removed'.

This time Patrick was sent to an immigration detention centre to await his expulsion. He lived there much as he had in the prison, in a cell, on a block, with hundreds of other men. Life in detention was monotonous and indefinite. Information about deportation dates was scarce. After seven months with no movement in his case, Patrick signed a petition and joined a hunger strike to protest his ongoing incarceration. A week later, officials transferred him back to prison, where he remained on suicide watch for four months. Then, four years after the end of his criminal sentence, Patrick was released on bail for the second time.

Noishime was born in a Rwandan village. He was nine years old when the genocide began. Noishime's entire family died in Rwanda, but he escaped with a friend to the Kenyan border, where he lived for eight months. Noishime turned ten in a border camp. Eventually, he moved to a site inside Kenya run by missionaries. When he turned eighteen, Noishime migrated to Britain and began a decade of asylum applications, denials, and appeals.

Time and again, immigration authorities told Noishime that he had to provide documents proving his identity as a Rwandan national. Time and again, he replied that those documents had been destroyed. As a failed asylum-seeker, Noishime could neither work legally nor claim benefits. Instead, he volunteered at a refugee organization and leaned on his partner, a fellow asylum-seeker with two young daughters. He also began drinking. Noishime was arrested for public drunkenness in early 2009. When he encountered immigration officials at reception into the penal system, he failed, yet again, to prove his identity.

Said was born in Somalia.[2] He migrated with his parents at age eight, first to Italy and then to Holland, where his extended family lived. Said liked Holland, and along with his parents and siblings, he became a Dutch national. He was fifteen when his aunt decided to move to the United Kingdom for work. Said went with his aunt, and upon arriving in London, received leave to remain and began using a British name. After a few years, Said was arrested, tried, and convicted for drug possession. When he arrived in prison, he

[2] This is a different person than the Said quoted in the epigraph.

met immigration agents, who interview every person coming into the system.

Said told the border agents that he was from Somalia. He did not want to return to Holland and he had heard from other prisoners that foreign nationals could not be deported to countries they had fled. To avoid 'removal', Said changed his name again, to a different Somali name, and started an asylum application. He thought this plan would prevent his expulsion from the United Kingdom. Instead, the British government issued a deportation order pending a determination about where Said could go. He served his sentence in this ambiguous state, thinking less of his time in prison than of his imminent deportation. Four months after the end of his criminal sentence, Said remained in the same prison, waiting for a flight.

Said, Noishime, and Patrick are three of the approximately 11,000 foreign nationals imprisoned in England and Wales.[3] Noishime is one of the many failed asylum-seekers in these ranks. Said and Patrick are among the more than 1,000 people who are living in prisons beyond the length of their criminal sentences as immigration detainees.[4] These men are part of a significant change

[3] National Audit Office (NAO), *Managing and Removing Foreign National Offenders* (London: NAO, 2014); see also *Ministry of Justice, Offender Management Statistics Quarterly Bulletin: January to March 2013, England and Wales* (London: Ministry of Justice, 2013); Ministry of Justice (2013), *Table 1.6: Population in Prison by Nationality and Sex, 30 June 2013, England and Wales* (London: Ministry of Justice, 2013). The precise number of foreign nationals in the British penal estate is difficult to calculate. As of 22 October 2014, the National Audit Office had identified 10,650 prisoners as foreign nationals and another 1,600 people as foreign nationals 'serving in prison or living in the community after prison, pending removal'. NAO, *Managing and Removing Foreign National Offenders*, p. 4. In an official poll from 2013, prison officials listed 10,786 prisoners as foreign nationals and another 877 prisoners as 'nationality not recorded'. Ministry of Justice, *Offender Management Statistics Quarterly Bulletin*. Both my own research and Hindpal Bhui's work for the Prison Reform Trust suggest that 'unidentified' prisoners are often foreign nationals, which would put the number of non-British citizens in the prison estate as high as 11,663 in 2013, and possibly higher today. See Hindpal Singh Bhui, *Going the Distance: Developing Effective Policy and Practice with Foreign National Prisoners* (London: Prison Reform Trust, 2004). However, prisoners identified as foreign nationals can also be misidentified British nationals, a phenomenon described in Chapters 4 and 5. The inaccuracy in these statistics reflects a broader problem with the attempt to determine prisoners' nationalities.

[4] The number of post-sentence immigration detainees in British prisons is notoriously difficult to find. The *Vine Report*, which was published by the

in the British prison population. In the past decade, the number of non-citizens in British prisons has more than doubled, while the number of British nationals in prison has declined.[5] Today's penal estate holds a vastly increased number of prisoners under deportation orders, many of whom are deported directly from their cells. As of mid-2014, foreign nationals constituted 14 per cent of Britain's total prison population and a full 40 per cent of the black and minority ethnic penal population.[6] For a growing number of people, 'removal' rather than release is the conclusion of time behind bars.

The foreign nationals who end up in British prisons come from all over the world. People from Vietnam, Moldova, the United States, Sri Lanka, Jamaica, and Italy live in English and Welsh penal facilities. According to official polls, imprisoned non-citizens hail from 161 different countries.[7] Former colonies figure heavily in these statistics: Jamaica, Ireland, and Nigeria are among the top four nations represented in the prison system and nearly half of the 'foreigners' in British prisons were born in countries with colonial ties

Chief Inspector of the UK Border Agency, stated that 760 people were being detained under immigration powers in prisons in early 2012. John Vine, *Thematic Inspection of How the UK Border Agency Manages Foreign National Prisoners: February–May 2011* (London: HMSO, 2012), p. 19 (hereinafter the *Vine Report*). More recently, a 2013 newspaper article cited the number 1,500. Matt Chorley, 'Revealed: British Prisons Holding 1,500 Foreign Offenders beyond the End of their Sentence because They Can't Be Sent Home', *Daily Mail*, 15 January 2013, <http://www.dailymail.co.uk/news/article-2262791/Revealed-British-prisons-holding-1-500-foreign-offenders-end-sentence-sent home.html>.

[5] In 1999, there were 5,388 foreign nationals in British prisons. Ministry of Justice, *Offender Management Caseload Statistics 2009* (London: Ministry of Justice, 2010). Today that number lies somewhere between 10,700 and 11,700, depending on the source of the statistics and the definition of foreign nationality. See note 3; see also James Banks, 'Foreign National Prisoners in the UK: Explanations and Implications', *Howard Journal of Criminal Justice* 50, no. 2 (May 2011): pp. 184–98.

[6] NAO, *Managing and Removing Foreign National Offenders*; see also Bhui, *Going the Distance*; Hindpal Bhui, 'Alien Experience: Foreign National Prisoners after the Deportation Crisis', *Probation Journal* 54, no. 4 (December 2007): pp. 368–82.

[7] The 161 locations listed in Prison Service polls on nationality include not only countries but also disputed territories such as Western Sahara. Ministry of Justice, *Table 1.6*; see also Ministry of Justice, *Offender Management Caseload Statistics 2009*.

to the British state.[8] Some of these prisoners, like Patrick, conceive of themselves as British. Others do not. Some imprisoned foreign nationals migrated to England as infants; others were arrested at Heathrow. Some of these prisoners want to return to their home countries. Others vow to appeal their deportation no matter how long it takes.

What these prisoners have in common is that they face a new kind of prison. Over the past several years, British prisons have become part of the country's migration control apparatus. In 2009, in the wake of a government scandal, the British government began to use its penal institutions to identify and deport non-citizens.[9] Today, the British Prison Service and the UK Border Agency share information, training, and staff. Under a new penal policy, certain prisons serve as 'all-foreign' facilities and foreign nationals cannot leave any British penal institution, even if they have completed their sentences, until immigration officials approve their release.[10] Prison staff are also obliged to identify non-citizens to immigration authorities and prisons hold people, sometimes for years, as immigration detainees.[11] The penal institution is one border of the British state.

[8] At the time of my study, prisoners born in countries whose colonial ties to Britain formally ended in the twentieth century constituted 45 per cent of the foreign national prisoner population and 8 per cent of the total prison population. Ministry of Justice, *Offender Management Caseload Statistics 2009*. Those numbers include both sentenced and remand (unsentenced) prisoners. They exclude prisoners whose nationalities are not recorded, as well as prisoners born in nations whose colonial relations with Britain concluded before the twentieth century, such as the United States, or were never formally colonial, such as Somalia. Hindpal Bhui has noted that the unrecorded prison population likely includes foreign nationals. Bhui, *Going the Distance*. That claim, not to mention a more expansive definition of nations that have colonial relations with Britain, suggests that the estimate of 45 per cent is low.

[9] This effort is documented in a 2009 agreement between the Prison Service and the UK Border Agency, which was leaked to the press shortly after it was signed. Ministry of Justice (MoJ) and UK Border Agency (UKBA), *Service Level Agreement to Support the Effective and Speedy Removal of Foreign National Prisoners* (London: MoJ and UKBA, 2009).

[10] MoJ and UKBA, *Service Level Agreement*. See also Haroon Siddique, 'Foreign-Only Prisons Used to Speed Deportation', *The Guardian*, 24 October 2007, <http://www.theguardian.com/uk/2007/oct/24/ukcrime.prisonsandprobation>.

[11] MoJ and UKBA, *Service Level Agreement*; see also the *Vine Report*, which describes the ongoing detention of more than 760 immigration detainees in British prisons.

This is the prison that Noishime faced when he failed to produce documents proving he was born in Rwanda. It is the system that Patrick navigated as he was twice imprisoned and released. This is the place where Said's choice to change his name resulted in months of additional detention. The contemporary British prison is a precarious and human place. The stories that emerge from inside it challenge our understanding of what prisons do, both to the people in them and for society as a whole. In popular culture and academic literature, prisons are typically understood as domestic institutions. We tend to think of prisons as spaces whose boundaries are defined by the criminal code. Incarcerated foreign nationals tell a very different story: they portray imprisonment as a process of boundary-drawing as much as a practice of punishment. Foreign nationals depict the prison as a site for the construction and contestation of citizenship. When you focus on the non-citizen penal population, the prison begins to look like one place where the nation is made.

The stories told by foreign national prisoners also give life to claims about globalization. Since the late nineties, some of the most exciting writing in political theory, law, and sociology has developed around the concept of globalization.[12] Under this heading, scholars have grappled with the emergence of a world order in which information, capital, and some people move freely, while the nation-state recedes in both clarity and import. The collective energy directed towards understanding these social changes has produced provocative theories and a new set of academic themes, including risk, mobility, and managerialism.[13] The term

[12] See, e.g., Katja Franko Aas and Mary Bosworth, eds, *The Borders of Punishment: Migration, Citizenship, and Social Exclusion* (Oxford: Oxford University Press, 2013); Zygmunt Bauman, *Globalization: The Human Consequences* (Cambridge: Polity Press, 1998); Ulrich Beck, *World Risk Society* (Cambridge: Polity Press, 1999); Seyla Benhabib and Judith Resnik, eds, *Migrations and Mobilities: Citizenship, Borders, and Gender* (New York, NY: NYU Press, 2009); Wendy Brown, 'At the Edge', *Political Theory* 30, no. 4 (August 2002): pp. 556–76.

[13] For writing on mobility, see Aas and Bosworth, *The Borders of Punishment*; and Benhabib and Resnik, *Migrations and Mobilities*. For scholarship on risk, see Beck, *World Risk Society*; and Pat O'Malley, *Risk, Uncertainty, and Government* (London: Glasshouse Press, 2004). For accounts of managerialism, see Pat Carlen, 'Governing the Governors: Telling Tales of Managers, Mandarins and Mavericks', *Criminology and Criminal Justice* 2, no. 1 (February 2002): pp. 27–49; Malcolm Feeley and Jonathan Simon, 'Actuarial Justice: The Emerging New Criminal Law', in David Nelkin, ed., *The Futures of Criminology*

globalization has also prompted scholars to revisit classic concepts of social theory such as democracy, citizenship, and modernity to ask whether they fit in a transnational frame.[14] This body of work poses serious questions about the relevance and future of the sovereign state.

Wading into this theoretical space, and merging it with concerns about the meaning of punishment, this book examines the treatment of non-citizens in British prisons. Drawing on a year of fieldwork in and around five men's prisons, I make three claims.

First, this book presents a theoretical argument about the purpose of the British prison. Over the course of seven chapters, I contend that recent legislative and policy shifts have transformed prisons into sites for border control. Prisons are always institutions onto which societies graft their collective anxieties. Penal institutions have served multiple purposes throughout their short history and they continue to do so today. This book argues that, in the face of increasingly acute fears about sovereignty, prisons have become a staging ground for migration control and a mechanism for the assertion of a British national identity. In a deeper and more systemic way than we typically realize, penal institutions are part of the national border. Indeed, they produce it.

While I hope it will find readers across the spectrum of globalization studies, this account is written with scholars of punishment in mind. Since Foucault wrote *Discipline and Punish* in the 1970s, criminologists and legal academics have mounted a sustained critical examination of the relationship between prisons and state power.[15] This body of scholarship asks what role

(London: Sage Publications Ltd, 1994): pp. 173–201; Eugene McLaughlin and Karim Murji, 'Lost Connections and New Directions: Neo-Liberalism, New Managerialism and the Modernisation of the British Police', in Kevin Stenson and Robert Sullivan, eds, *Crime, Risk and Justice* (Cullompton: Willan, 2000): ch. 6; and Pat O'Malley, 'Volatile and Contradictory Punishment', *Theoretical Criminology* 3, no. 2 (May 1999): pp. 175–96.

[14] See, e.g., Brown, 'At the Edge'; David Garland, 'The Limits of the Sovereign State: Strategies of Crime Control in Contemporary Society', *British Journal of Criminology* 36, no. 4 (Winter 1996): pp. 445–71.

[15] For two famous examples of this approach to punishment, see David Garland, *Punishment and Modern Society: A Study in Social Theory* (Chicago, IL: University of Chicago Press, 1990); and Jonathan Simon, *Governing through Crime* (Oxford: Oxford University Press, 2007). For a compilation of work in this field, which is generally called either the sociology of punishment or punishment and society, see Jonathan Simon and Richard Sparks, eds, *The SAGE Handbook of Punishment and Society* (London: Sage Publications Ltd, 2012).

prisons play in societies that aim to punish those who transgress. This book begs rather than answers that question; I argue that, in a globalizing world, punishment and imprisonment are decreasingly aligned. Contemporary prisons are less domestic, less tied to crime, and less oriented towards returning offenders to the polity than they ever have been. These developments warp the meaning of punishment and blur the line between civil and criminal law.

My second claim is ethnographic. One way to read this book is as a case study of a penal policy called hubs and spokes, which the British government introduced in 2006. On paper, the hubs and spokes policy imported the goals of border control into the British penal estate. In practice, it led to a series of perverse consequences, including the indefinite detention of hundreds of prisoners who can be neither deported nor released and the widespread profiling of black British citizens. This book draws on interviews with the people who manage, work, and live in British prisons to argue that the new policy on non-citizens has changed the character of the penal system. I contend that hubs and spokes has altered the meaning of race in prison, amplified the gender dynamics in men's penal institutions, and encouraged an exclusionary notion of British citizenship.

When told from inside multiple institutions, this ethnographic story becomes a lesson in twenty-first-century governance. Since its debut less than a decade ago, the British policy on non-citizen prisoners has changed several times. The government has altered details of the policy and has altogether abandoned some of its key components, including one 'foreign-only' prison where I conducted fieldwork.[16] As a result, my research has become the record

[16] Chapter 3 describes the origins and development of the British policy on incarcerated non-citizens. The first version of that policy was created in a 2009 Service Level Agreement between the Prison Service and the UK Border Agency. See MoJ and UKBA, *Service Level Agreement*. The most recent version of the policy is a November 2011 Prison Service Instruction (PSI). Ministry of Justice, National Offender Management Service (NOMS), *PSI 52/2011: Immigration, Repatriation, and Removal Services* (London: Ministry of Justice, 2011). I conducted fieldwork at HMP Canterbury, one of the prisons designated as an all-foreign national facility after the 2009 Service Level Agreement. That prison closed in January 2013 and has since been sold. See Ministry of Justice, 'Changes to Prison Capacity Announced', 10 January 2013, <https://www.gov.uk/government/news/changes-to-prison-capacity-announced>.

of a particular and fleeting moment in British prison management. The book that follows describes what happens to the criminal justice system, and to the idea of punishment, when two large and historically situated agencies respond to a perceived crisis. This is a study of bureaucracy in flux.

My third claim is methodological. In recent years, the foremost scholars of punishment have wondered aloud what criminology is, whether its project is coherent, and what studies of criminal justice aim to do.[17] One part of that conversation is a debate about the value of sweeping critiques of justice systems, or as they are often called in the field, grand narratives of penality.[18] While it takes many forms, this debate is at its heart about how academics represent and relate to state power. On one hand, penal institutions reveal social trends and reflect cultural beliefs about justice and condemnation. On the other, punishment is a practice that has concrete and often wrenching effects on people's lives.

The question is how to capture these two aspects of imprisonment—how, in other words, to make a systematic claim about prisons without forgetting the people inside them. This book argues that a focus on the affective dimension of prison life, on how concepts like state power and sovereignty feel and become real in practice, can help scholars achieve this goal. Focusing on prisoners' testimonies is one way to demystify the prison and to prioritize its lived effects. This methodological approach can also ground a theoretical critique of penality. When you start from the story of a person like Patrick, when you study incarceration in his words, it quickly becomes clear that the prison is both a collection of cells where real people live and an institution whose purpose has fundamentally changed.

[17] See, e.g., Mary Bosworth and Carolyn Hoyle, eds, *What Is Criminology?* (Oxford: Oxford University Press, 2011); John Braithwaite, 'What's Wrong with the Sociology of Punishment?', *Theoretical Criminology* 7, no. 1 (February 2003): pp. 5–28.

[18] See, e.g., Lucia Zedner, 'Dangers of Dystopias in Penal Theory', *Oxford Journal of Legal Studies* 22, no. 2 (Summer 2002): pp. 341–66; see also Braithwaite, 'What's Wrong with the Sociology of Punishment?'.

Shape of the Book

The structure of this book tracks its main claims. I begin on a theoretical note with questions about how and why scholars study prisons. The first two chapters examine the goals of prison research and lay the conceptual groundwork for the middle of the book, which describes how immigration-focused penal policies have changed the purpose of the prison. Drawing on ethnographic research, Chapters 3 and 4 argue that governments use prisons to make good citizens. Chapters 5 and 6 expound on this theme by exploring how the project of making citizens relates to the histories of race and colonialism in Great Britain. The final chapter ties my theoretical and empirical arguments together to imagine a more transnational, phenomenological approach to prison studies. As a whole, the book proceeds from theory, through ethnography, to method.

To offer a slightly more granular sketch of this progression, Chapter 1 begins with an examination of the guiding assumptions in prison theory. Building from a review of sociological and legal scholarship on prisons, the first chapter traces current accounts of the penal institution to their roots in the political theories of Weber, Marx, and Foucault.[19] Chapter 1 asks how these theories of the social world—and in particular, their distinct approaches to the concept of legitimacy—shape the conceptual divisions in prison studies. I argue that the field is roughly divided between liberal and critical approaches to the state, each of which produces a different picture of the prison. This bifurcation obscures the link between imprisonment and border control and leaves prison theory ill equipped to address the changes wrought by globalization. The implicit claim in Chapter 1 is that scholars cannot adequately critique punishment without revising our relationship to the nation-state.

Chapter 2 asks whether the limitations of prison studies can be understood as a problem of method. In the last decade, scholars

[19] Michel Foucault, *Discipline and Punish: The Birth of the Prison*, trans. Alan Sheridan (New York, NY: Vintage Books, 1977); Karl Marx, *Capital, Volume I: A Critique of Political Economy*, trans. Ben Fowkes (London: Penguin Press, 1992); Max Weber, *Economy and Society: An Outline of Interpretive Sociology*, 4th edn., eds Guenther Roth and Claus Wittich (Berkeley, CA: University of California Press, 1978).

have decried the tendency to view the nation-state as 'the natural and necessary representation of modern society'.[20] Sociologists call this practice 'methodological nationalism'.[21] Nancy Fraser refers to it as the 'Westphalian blindspot' of social theory.[22] In both iterations of the argument, the concern is that academics are wedded to outmoded and internally incoherent conceptions of citizenship and sovereignty. Chapter 2 examines how the blind spots of prison theory develop from our methodological mores. Borrowing from oral history and literary theory, I argue that ethnography focused on testimony—on the language that people use to describe incarceration—can deliver an account of the prison that is less tied to the contours of the nation-state.[23] Chapter 2 also recounts my own effort to bear witness to imprisonment over the course of one year and more than 200 interviews with prisoners, immigration agents, prison guards, and penal policymakers.

Chapter 3 shifts gears to examine the origins of the hubs and spokes policy. The current British policy on foreign national prisoners grew from a political scandal so vivid it feels contrived. The short story, which Chapter 3 elaborates, is that the policy developed from an incident in which a Somali national who had recently been released from prison shot a female police officer and then fled the United Kingdom by cross-dressing in his sister's niqab. This episode dominated newspaper headlines and dovetailed with a political campaign to reform the Prison Service.[24] Behind closed

[20] Daniel Chernillo, 'The Critique of Methodological Nationalism: Theory and History', *Thesis Eleven* 106, no. 1 (August 2011): p. 99; see also Zsuzsa Gille and Seán Ó Riain, 'Global Ethnography', *Annual Review of Sociology* 28, (August 2002): pp. 271–95. For the broader critique of sociological methods, see Neil Smelser, *Problematics of Sociology* (Berkeley, CA: University of California Press, 1997); and Peter Wagner, *A Sociology of Modernity: Liberty and Discipline* (London: Routledge, 1994).

[21] Chernillo, 'The Critique of Methodological Nationalism'.

[22] Nancy Fraser, *Scales of Justice: Reimagining Political Space in a Globalizing World* (Cambridge, Polity Press), p. 85.

[23] Chapter 3 draws heavily on the work of the anthropologists, literary theorists, oral historians, and trauma theorists who have developed the concept of witnessing in recent years. See, e.g., Aleida Assmann, 'History, Memory, and the Genre of Testimony', *Poetics Today* 27, no. 2 (Summer 2006): pp. 261–74; Martha Minow, *Between Vengeance and Forgiveness: Facing History after Genocide and Mass Violence* (Boston, MA: Beacon Press, 1999); Annette Wieviorka, *The Era of Witness* (Ithaca, NY: Cornell University Press, 2006).

[24] For examples of sensationalist newspaper accounts of the prisoner scandal, see Sam Greenhill, Michael Seamark, and Paul Sims, 'The Killer Asylum Seekers',

doors, the scandal also led to a reorganization of the country's migration control machinery. Chapter 3 examines the agency-level response to the 'problem of foreign criminals' and asks what it can tell scholars about the bureaucratic practice of punishment.

After situating prison policies in this political context, the book turns to lived experience. In Chapter 4, I take up the claim that prisons counteract the diminution of national sovereignty. Scholars of punishment have made several versions of this claim in recent years. In 2008, Mary Bosworth argued that penal institutions 'write the nation-state' by clarifying and reaffirming national borders.[25] Wendy Brown has advanced a similar argument about proposals to build a wall at the United States–Mexican border.[26] Chapter 4 asks what it means, in practice, for the prison to determine the boundaries of the polity. Drawing on observations of citizenship classes in British prisons, I argue that contemporary penal institutions not only divide citizens from foreigners, but also work to establish what being British really means.

Chapters 5 and 6 raise questions about race, gender, and colonialism, topics that surface somewhat belatedly given their import. These chapters lean heavily on prisoners' testimonies to assess how the British policy on 'foreign criminals' has affected identity dynamics in British prisons. Chapter 5 reports that the effort to identify foreign nationals is often an exercise in profiling, or to put it more mildly, a practice based on racialized assumptions about what foreignness looks, sounds, and seems like to prison staff. This chapter argues that the implementation of a border-focused penal policy has complicated the meaning of race and, at least in some cases, has hardened gender and sexuality norms. Chapter 5 also examines prisoners' nuanced methods of resistance to migration control.

Daily Mail Online, 19 December 2006, <http://www.dailymail.co.uk/news/article-423813/The-killer-asylum-seekers.html>; and Phillip Johnston, 'Veil Escape "Exposes Chaos in Border Controls"', *The Telegraph*, 21 December 2006, <http://www.telegraph.co.uk/news/uknews/1537514/Veil-escape-exposes-chaos-in-border-controls.html>.

[25] Mary Bosworth and Mhairi Guild, 'Governing through Migration Control: Security and Citizenship in Britain', *British Journal of Criminology* 48, no. 6 (Fall 2008): p. 715.

[26] Wendy Brown, *Walled States, Waning Sovereignty* (Cambridge, MA: Zone Books, 2010).

In examining the meaning of race behind bars, Chapter 5 is an attempt to come to terms with two related sets of ideas: on one hand, the now classic readings of race in Stuart Hall's *Policing the Crisis* and Paul Gilroy's *There Ain't No Black in the Union Jack*; and on the other, both authors' more recent writing on race in twenty-first-century Britain.[27] In their earlier incarnations, Hall and Gilroy argued that racialized responses to crime produce the 'problems' of criminal justice. More recently, both theorists have noted the changing and perhaps diminishing degree to which their critiques of race resonate in an increasingly multicultural Britain. Chapter 5 asks how the history of British racism relates to contemporary prisons.

Chapter 6 explores the legacy of British conquest. Prisoners like Patrick and Noishime often struggle to understand why they can be identified as foreign and deported from the United Kingdom when the British government once colonized their home countries. Many of the prisoners I interviewed were educated in British colonial schools. Some of them were old enough to have had British passports as colonial subjects. These people's testimonies challenge scholars to explain the prison's part in producing a postcolonial reality. Taking up that challenge, Chapter 6 argues that the hubs and spokes policy can be understood as an exercise in what Stuart Hall calls colonial 'amnesia'.[28] I contend that the late modern penal project depends on a wilful dissociation of colonial politics and prison practices.

The seventh and final chapter considers how scholars might return politics, and in particular the politics of identity, to discussions of prison policy. One of the concerns underlying this book is that questions about identity often get cast as subthemes of prison research. People who do empirical work on prisons tend to write

[27] Stuart Hall, Chas Critcher, Tony Jefferson, John N. Clark, and Brian Roberts, *Policing the Crisis: Mugging, the State, and Law and Order* (London: Palgrave MacMillan, 1978); Paul Gilroy, *There Ain't No Black in the Union Jack: The Cultural Politics of Race and Nation* (Abingdon: Routledge, 1987). For more recent writing, see Paul Gilroy, *There Ain't No Black in the Union Jack: The Cultural Politics of Race and Nation* (Abingdon: Routledge, 2002), pp. xi–xxxix; Paul Gilroy, *Postcolonial Melancholia* (New York, NY: Columbia University Press, 2006); and Stuart Hall, 'Conclusion: The Multicultural Question', in Barnor Hesse, ed., *UN/Settled Multiculturalisms: Diasporas, Entanglement, Transruptions* (London: Zed Books, 2001): pp. 209–41.

[28] Hall, 'Conclusion: The Multicultural Question', p. 219.

about race *in* prisons, nationality *in* prisons, and so on.[29] Chapter 7 contends that these aspects of identity are less secondary features of the prison experience than structural principles of imprisonment. My claim, in other words, is that prisons are motivated by the project of identity creation and that we ought to be studying them as such. Chapter 7 proposes that scholars turn to 'the bodily remainder' of penal policy—to stories told by the people who literally, physically remain in prisons with nowhere to go when laws and penal policies take effect.[30] These people's narratives demonstrate that, in the twenty-first century, the prison can no longer be conceived as a domestic space. In stark and often deeply personal terms, their stories portray the stakes of incarceration in an age of mass mobility.

Two Caveats

This book requires two qualifications. The first is that, while my argument is critical, it emerges from a place of curiosity and openness to aspects of the British penal system. This is a book about foreignness written by a foreigner, specifically, an American whose main point of reference is the conditions in American prisons and jails.[31] From that perspective, it bears mentioning that British prisons are relatively humane places. The conditions in the five British prisons I studied are nowhere near as viscerally unpleasant as those in many American penal institutions. Happily, this book is not a report on extreme brutality, prolonged sensory deprivation,

[29] For another version of the argument that race, gender, and other facets of identity are most often cast as subthemes rather than principles of imprisonment, see Mary Bosworth and Emma Kaufman, 'Gender and Punishment', in Jonathan Simon and Richard Sparks, eds, *The SAGE Handbook of Punishment and Society* (London: Sage Publications Ltd, 2012), pp. 186–204.

[30] The term 'bodily remainder' is borrowed from a line in Judith Butler's book *The Psychic Life of Power*. Judith Butler, *The Psychic Life of Power: Theories in Subjection* (Palo Alto, CA: Stanford University Press, 1997), p. 92. Chapter 7 examines and develops this phrase.

[31] To provide a specific account of my subjective perspective: I came to this study of British prisons having worked with two organizations that visited and reported on conditions in American prisons and jails. I have toured and interviewed prisoners in many of the prisons and jails in New York State, in one juvenile detention centre, and in the Baltimore City Detention Centre. This, too, is a limited perspective, as the conditions in American custodial institutions vary widely between states and even between particular facilities.

or dismal health care of the sort seen in some American prisons.[32] But this is a study scattered with accounts of self-harm, racism, and life-changing sadness. When it comes to the treatment of non-citizens and to their rates of incarceration, Britain leads rather than trails the United States.[33] The chapters that follow explore the legacy of xenophobia in a penal system that prides itself on its 'decency agenda'.[34] This is an account of the 'forgotten prisoners' in the British penal estate and of the oddly banal character of an exclusionary social project.[35]

The second qualification is that this book both is and isn't British. As a straightforward matter, it is inaccurate to talk about 'British

[32] For an example of the conditions in one of America's worst prison systems, see the American Civil Liberties Union (ACLU) National Prison Project's lawsuit against the Mississippi Department of Corrections (MDOC). *Complaint, Dockery et al. v. Epps et al.*, (S. D. Miss. 2013) (No. 13-326), <https://s3.amazonaws.com/s3.documentcloud.org/documents/710104/emcf-complaint-filed-5-30-13.pdf>. That complaint describes officer beatings, rampant prisoner self-harm, deficient health care, and deplorable environmental conditions including inadequate ventilation, flooding, and loose-hanging electrical wires.

[33] For a comparative account of the treatment and rates of incarceration for non-citizens in the United States and United Kingdom, see Mary Bosworth and Emma Kaufman, 'Foreigners in a Carceral Age: Immigration and Imprisonment in the United States', *Stanford Law and Policy Review* 22, no. 1 (May 2011): pp. 429–54. There is also a growing body of comparative writing on the treatment of non-citizens in European prison systems. See, e.g., Hans van Kooten, *Conference Report: Foreigners in European Prisons—From 'Good Practices' to 'Good Policy'*, (Nieuwersluis, Netherlands: Ministry of Justice, 2008), <http://www.cepprobation.org/uploaded_files/Report%20Nieuwersluis%20E.pdf>; Thomas Ugelvik, 'Imprisoned on the Border: Subjects and Objects of the State in Two Norwegian Prisons', in Barbara Hudson and Synnove Ugelvik, eds, *Justice and Security in the 21st Century: Risks, Rights, and the Rule of Law* (Abingdon: Routledge, 2012), pp. 64–82.

[34] Alison Liebling has analysed the Prison Service's 'decency agenda', a purportedly systematic approach to British prison management that Prison Service Director General Martin Narey introduced in 1999. See Alison Liebling, *Prisons and Their Moral Performance: A Study of Values, Quality, and Prison Life* (Oxford: Oxford University Press, 2005), p. 478. Chapter 3 examines the decency agenda.

[35] Prison Reform Trust, *Forgotten Prisoners: The Plight of Foreign National Prisoners in England and Wales* (London: PRT, 2004). Note, however, that foreign national prisoners have garnered increasing attention from academics in recent years.

prisons' when I mean facilities in England and Wales. The United Kingdom is home to three distinct legal jurisdictions and both Scotland and Northern Ireland operate their own prison systems. The prisons I visited, and the facilities I often describe as British for brevity's sake, are technically governed by policies that are English and Welsh but not Scottish or Northern Irish. This terminological wrinkle reflects a much deeper reality about the state of punishment in the United Kingdom. It is not possible to write a simple or apolitical sentence about prisons, in Britain or anywhere else.

The book is also un-British in another sense. While my fieldwork took place in England, and neither can nor should be disconnected from that context, my argument finds obvious analogues in other penal practices. Detention without an end or a clear legal basis is not unique to Britain, nor is the claim that a country's penal system reinforces its racialized history of inequality. My hope is that a local story about British policy will prompt reflection on the consequences of detaining non-citizens in any penal space.

This book explicitly encourages academics to incorporate concerns about our own purpose into that reflection. If the next seven chapters have one clarion theme, it is that criminologists and legal scholars should be thinking about why we study penal institutions. Serious barriers to prison access often inhibit ethnographic prison research.[36] At the same time, criminologists debate whether the politicization of crime policy over the past several decades has rendered academic scholarship on punishment a futile or even wholly counterproductive effort.[37] These concerns merit

[36] For accounts of the barriers to ethnographic research in prisons, see Kelly Hannah-Moffat, 'Criminological Cliques: Narrowing Dialogues, Institutional Protectionism, and the Next Generation', in Mary Bosworth and Carolyn Hoyle, eds, *What Is Criminology?*, pp. 440–52; Beth Richie, 'Feminist Ethnographies of Women in Prison', *Feminist Studies* 30, no. 2 (Summer 2004): pp. 438–50; and Jennifer Schlosser, 'Issues in Interviewing Inmates: Navigating the Methodological Landmines of Prison Research', *Qualitative Inquiry* 14, no. 8 (December 2008): pp. 1500–25.

[37] See, for example, the 2004 exchange between Kevin Haggerty and Michael Jacobsen regarding the utility (or futility) of criminological theory. Michael Jacobsen, 'Reply to Kevin D. Haggerty', *Theoretical Criminology* 8, no. 2 (May 2004): pp. 223–38; Kevin Haggerty, 'Displaced Expertise: Three Constraints on the Policy Relevance of Criminological Thought', *Theoretical Criminology* 8, no. 2 (May 2004): pp. 211–31.

serious consideration. Yet the fact remains that in writing about the prison, scholars constitute its role and place in society.

Not everyone knows what it feels like to be inside a prison. Both prisoners and prison staff members are rarely heard on their own terms. Prisons are by definition set apart from free society. They are presented more often as metaphors and imagined worlds than as concrete spaces where thousands of people live and work. Prison scholars have an opportunity to counteract this trend. Empirical research on prisons can highlight the unexpected dimensions of incarceration and can foreground the tensions that inhere in penal institutions. It can also recast questions about the prison's basic purpose. By connecting prisons to the worlds outside them, scholars can help to explain—and resist—the impulse to punish and expel.

1

The Prison and The State

Prison scholarship has reached an impasse. Roughly divided between empirical and theoretical work, contemporary scholarship on imprisonment has cohered around an entrenched set of questions and methodologies.[1] At the same time, the concepts that have motivated critical writing about prisons over the last three decades—legitimacy, governmentality, discipline—seem less compelling than they once did, somehow less applicable to the social world they seek to explain.

Globalization has much to do with this predicament. As the shape and import of the nation-state has shifted over the last thirty years, academic paradigms for understanding punishment and state power have often struggled to follow suit. While academics have faithfully and insightfully documented the Anglo-American punitive turn and the rise of the penal state, scholars have given less thought to the theories and methods that such a 'new' state demands.[2] The developments commonly collected under the

[1] For examples of empirical work in criminology, see Ben Crewe, *The Prisoner Society: Power, Adaptation, and Social Life in an English Prison* (Oxford: Oxford University Press, 2009); Elaine Genders and Elaine Player, *Grendon: A Study of Therapeutic Prison* (Oxford: Clarendon Press, 1995); and Alison Liebling, *Prisons and Their Moral Performance: A Study of Values, Quality, and Prison Life* (Oxford: Oxford University Press, 2004). For examples of theoretical scholarship on imprisonment, see Vanessa Barker, *The Politics of Imprisonment: How the Democratic Process Shapes the Way Americans Punish Offenders* (New York, NY: Oxford University Press, 2009); David Garland, *The Culture of Control: Crime and Social Order in Contemporary Society* (Oxford: Oxford University Press, 2001); and Loïc Wacquant, *Punishing the Poor: The Neoliberal Government of Social Insecurity* (Durham, NC: Duke University Press, 2009).

[2] Scholars have written thoughtful accounts of the punitive turn. See Ian Loader, 'For Penal Moderation: Notes Toward a Public Philosophy of Punishment', *Theoretical Criminology* 14, no. 3 (August 2010): pp. 349–67; see also Garland, *The Culture of Control*; Pat O'Malley, 'Volatile and Contradictory Punishment', *Theoretical Criminology* 3, no. 2 (May 1999): pp. 175–96; Wacquant, *Punishing the Poor.*

heading globalization—the increased movement of information, capital, and certain classes of people; the introduction of worldwide forms of communication, trade, and travel—have changed what scholars study.[3] But they have not always changed the way critics approach justice systems. Criminologists have spent less time than we might considering how the challenges of globalization go all the way down to the basic questions of sociological inquiry: What are the boundaries of our project? How are we studying the social world? Why study justice at all?

These questions are particularly pressing in prison studies. In the past three decades, changes in the nature of sovereignty have transformed the prison's purpose and undermined the traditional rationales for punishment. This book tracks these developments and argues in favour of a new approach to prison research. To ground that argument, I begin with a critical survey of prison scholarship. Drawing on classic criminological texts, I examine how theories of punishment work or fail to explain the prison's role in an increasingly transnational society. I conclude that the dominant theories of prison warp and stall in the face of a newly global state of affairs.

The first part of the chapter is dedicated to mapping the intellectual terrain of prison studies. The chapter starts by tracing

[3] Contemporary criminology is distinctly more global than in decades past. Today, the field encompasses everything from transnational policing and border control to environmental crime and human trafficking. For examples of writing on transnational crime and policing, see Benjamin Bowling, 'Transnational Policing: The Globalization Thesis, a Typology, and a Research Agenda', *Policing* 3, no. 2 (April 2009); and Benjamin Bowling, 'Transnational Criminology and the Globalization of Harm Production', in Mary Bosworth and Carolyn Hoyle, eds, *What Is Criminology?* (Oxford: Oxford University Press, 2011), pp. 361–76. For examples of criminological scholarship on border control, see Katja Aas, 'Analysing a World in Motion: Global Flows Meet "Criminology of the Other"', *Theoretical Criminology* 11, no. 2 (May 2007): pp. 283–303; and Mary Bosworth and Mhairi Guild, 'Governing through Migration Control: Security and Citizenship in Britain', *British Journal of Criminology* 48, no. 6 (Fall 2008): p. 715. For writing on environmental crime, see Reece Walters, 'Environmental Crime', in Hazel Croall, Gerry Mooney, and Mary Munro, eds, *Criminal Justice in Scotland* (Cullompton: Willan, 2010). For criminological work on trafficking, see Maggy Lee, 'Human Trade and the Criminalization of "Irregular Migration"', *International Journal of the Sociology of Law* 33, no. 1 (March 2005): pp. 1–15. For more on the definition of globalization, a broad and often fraught term, see Zygmunt Bauman, *Globalization: The Human Consequences* (New York, NY: Columbia University Press, 1998).

the development of prison sociology from the abolitionist movements of the 1970s to the empirical research of scholars such as Pat Carlen, Ben Crewe, Alison Liebling, and Elaine Genders.[4] The first section examines some of the most influential writing on the prison's legitimacy, as well as the now classic work on 'the problem of order' that evolved from British prison riots during the 1990s.[5] The second section compares empirical writing on prison legitimacy to critical scholarship on penal power.[6] This body of writing, which is often called the sociology of punishment, differs

[4] See, e.g., Pat Carlen, *Women's Imprisonment: A Study in Social Control* (London: Routledge, 1983); Crewe, *The Prisoner Society*; Alison Liebling, *Suicides in Prison* (London: Routledge, 1992); Liebling, *Prisons and Their Moral Performance*; Genders and Player, *Grendon*.

[5] For writing on legitimacy, see Elaine Genders, 'Legitimacy and Accountability in Private Prisons', *Punishment and Society* 4, no. 3 (July 2002): pp. 285–303; and Richard Sparks, 'Can Prisons Be Legitimate? Penal Politics, Privatization, and the Timeliness of an Old Idea', in Roy D. King and Mike Maguire, eds, *Prisons in Context* (Oxford: Clarendon Press, 1994), pp. 14–28. There is also a large body of work on riots and 'the problem of order' in British prisons. See, e.g., Michael Cavadino and James Dignan, *The Penal System: An Introduction* (London: Sage Publications Ltd, 1992); Eamonn Carrabine, *Power, Discourse, and Resistance: A Genealogy of the Strangeways Prison Riot* (Aldershot: Ashgate Publishing, 2004); Elaine Player and Michael Jenkins, *Prisons after Woolf: Reform through Riot* (London: Routledge, 2004); Richard Sparks, A. E. Bottoms, and Will Hay, *Prisons and the Problem of Order* (Oxford: Clarendon Press, 1996); see also Lord Justice Harry Woolf and Judge Stephen Tumim, *Prison Disturbances April 1990: Report of an Enquiry by the Rt. Hon. Lord Justice Woolf (Part I and II) and His Honor Judge Stephen Tumim (Part III)* (London: Home Office, 1991) (hereinafter *The Woolf Report*).

[6] For examples of critical scholarship on penal power, see Vanessa Barker, 'The Politics of Punishing: Building a State Governance Theory of American Imprisonment Variation', *Punishment & Society* 8, no. 1 (January 2006): pp. 5–33; Malcolm Feeley and Jonathan Simon, 'The New Penology: Notes on the Emerging Strategy of Corrections and Its Implications', *Criminology* 30, no. 4 (November 1992): pp. 449–74; Jonathan Simon, *Governing through Crime* (Oxford: Oxford University Press, 2007); Garland, *The Culture of Control*; Kelly Hannah-Moffat, *Punishment in Disguise? Penal Governance and Federal Imprisonment of Women in Canada* (London: University of Toronto Press, 2001); Adrian Howe, *Punish and Critique: Towards a Feminist Analysis of Penality* (New York, NY: Routledge, 1996); Joe Sim, *Punishment and Prisons: Power and the Carceral State* (London: Sage Publications Ltd, 2009); Wacquant, *Punishing the Poor*. See also Jonathan Simon and Richard Sparks, eds, *The SAGE Handbook of Punishment and Society* (London: Sage Publications Ltd, 2012).

from prison sociology in its focus on the wider cultural effects of imprisonment.

There are many points of overlap between prison sociology and critiques of penal power. Scholars concerned with riots, order, and the legitimacy of penal institutions are often highly attuned to the prison's part in reproducing social inequities, while academics who write about penality are committed to less violent prisons. It can be problematic and even counterproductive to overstate divisions in any academic field. Yet it is also useful to link philosophies of punishment to genres of prison study.[7] In distinguishing between institutional sociologies and broad critiques, this chapter aims to connect the questions that motivate prison research to the way academics write about prisons. Prison studies find their roots in the political philosophies of Emile Durkheim, Max Weber, and Michel Foucault.[8] These philosophies deliver divergent pictures of what the prison is, how scholars should study it, and whether the institution is capable of change.

After identifying these philosophical frameworks, the chapter explores the limits of prison literature. While there are notable distinctions between prison sociology and critiques of punishment, the two modes of prison scholarship share an attitude towards the state. In particular, they share an outlook in which the nation-state is an assumed concept at the background of prison analysis. Both strands of prison theory rely on the concept of the state: empirical scholars imagine more legitimate state institutions, while those who critique penality track the oppressive tendencies of state

[7] My analysis of contemporary criminology is confined to the Anglo-American context here not because it is the only one relevant to prison scholarship—indeed, I argue to the contrary throughout this book—but because the scholarly writing on imprisonment is heavily Anglo-American.

[8] Emile Durkheim, *Moral Education* (New York, NY: Free Press, 1961); Emile Durkheim, *The Division of Labour in Society*, 2nd edn (New York, NY: Free Press, 1964); Michel Foucault, *Discipline and Punish: The Birth of the Prison*, trans. Alan Sheridan (New York, NY: Vintage Books, 1977); Jürgen Habermas, *Legitimation Crisis*, trans. Thomas McCarthy (Boston, MA: Beacon Press, 1976); Max Weber, *Economy and Society: An Outline of Interpretive Sociology*, vols I and II, ed. Guenther Roth and Claus Wittich (Berkeley, CA: University of California Press, 1958); Max Weber, *The Theory of Social and Economic Organization*, ed. Talcott Parsons (New York, NY: Free Press, 1964).

power.[9] In each iteration of prison theory, the state is the key idea around which accounts of incarceration develop.

Yet neither branch of prison theory explains what it means to critique the state. Is the state synonymous with the nation? With state employees or penal policies? What exactly is the carceral state? The late modern state? The state in whose name penal institutions are run? These, it seems, are relatively unexplored questions at the ground level of prison theory. Moreover, they are questions that existing theories of imprisonment may not be able to answer. Given their theoretical origins and commitments, neither prison sociologies nor critiques of penal power are equipped, in their current form, to think outside the nation-state. Instead, both genres of prison scholarship tend to operate with a blind spot about the role that citizenship plays in penal regimes.[10]

Over the last decade, the sociology of punishment has grown into a broad and compelling subfield of socio-legal studies and, at least in England, the ethnography of the prison remains very much

[9] Alison Liebling uses the term 'interior life' and I borrow it from her. Liebling, *Prisons and Their Moral Performance*, p. 462. For other writing on this topic, see Cavadino and Dignan, *The Penal System*; Crewe, *The Prisoner Society*; and Sparks, Bottoms, and Hay, *Prisons and the Problem of Order.* For critiques of penality, see Alessandro Di Giorgi, *Re-thinking the Political Economy of Punishment: Perspectives on Post-Fordism and Penal Politics* (Aldershot: Ashgate Publishing, 2006); David Garland, *Punishment and Modern Society: A Study in Social Theory* (Chicago, IL: University of Chicago Press, 1990); and Wacquant, *Punishing the Poor.*

[10] Nancy Fraser uses the phrase 'blind spot' in her writing on globalization. Nancy Fraser, *Scales of Justice: Reimagining Political Space in a Globalizing World* (Cambridge: Polity Press, 2010), p. 85. My account builds not only on Fraser's framework, but also on the challenging, insightful body of writing on sovereignty and citizenship that legal scholars and criminologists such as Lucia Zedner, Katja Aas, and Judith Resnik have developed in the past several years. See, e.g., Aas, 'Analysing a World in Motion'; Judith Resnik, 'Gendered Borders and United States' Sovereignty', in Sarah Van Walsum and Thomas Spijkerboer, eds, *Women and Immigration Law: New Variations on Classical Feminist Themes* (Abingdon: Routledge-Cavendish Press, 2006), pp. 44–63; Lucia Zedner, 'Security, the State, and the Citizen: The Changing Architecture of Crime Control', *New Criminal Law Review* 13, no. 2 (Spring 2010): pp. 379–403; see also Mary Bosworth, 'Border Control and the Limits of the Sovereign State', *Social and Legal Studies* 17, no. 2 (June 2008): pp. 199–215; Juliet Stumpf, 'Doing Time: Crimmigration Law and the Perils of Haste', *UCLA Law Review* 58, no. 1705 (July 2011): pp. 1705–48.

alive.[11] Yet, as Ian Loader and Mary Bosworth have noted in their recent work, there remains the vague feeling that critical writing on prisons and punishment has reached a stagnant moment.[12] My sense is that this lull is related to the way we theorize the state, the way we approach globalization, and the way we understand the prison's relationship to both. My suggestion, in other words, is that scholars have not gone deep enough into the theoretical challenge that globalization poses to criminological thought. This chapter responds to that intuition.

Prison Sociology

Much academic writing about prisons takes the form of institutional sociology. This genre of prison scholarship tends to describe penal institutions in careful detail and to focus on the personal relationships and power structures behind bars. Scholars who write institutional sociologies of prisons are often motivated by the possibility of creating just systems of punishment—prisons that are less violent, more humane, and less prone to riots and disorder. The guiding question in this line of inquiry is whether and how incarceration can be legitimate.

Contemporary prison sociologies grew from the prison riots and reform movements of the 1970s. In academic circles, the discussion of prison legitimacy began to crystallize in 1974, when Thomas Mathieson published *The Politics of Abolition*.[13] Written

[11] See, e.g., Crewe, The Prisoner Society; Coretta Phillips, 'Ethnicity, Identity, and Community Cohesion in Prison', in Margaret Wetherell, Michelynn Lafleche, and Robert Berkeley, eds, *Identity, Ethnic Diversity, and Community Cohesion* (London: Sage Publications Ltd, 2007), pp. 75–86; Coretta Phillips, '"It Ain't Nothing like America with the Bloods and the Crips": Gang Narratives inside Two English Prisons', *Punishment and Society* 14, no. 1 (January 2012): pp. 51–68; Coretta Phillips and Rod Earle, 'Cultural Diversity, Ethnicity, and Race Relations in Prison', in Ben Crewe and Jamie Bennett, eds, *The Prisoner* (London: Routledge, 2011), pp. 117–30.

[12] Mary Bosworth, 'Reinventing Penal Parsimony: An Introduction', *Theoretical Criminology* 14, no. 3 (August 2010): pp. 251–6; Loader, 'For Penal Moderation'.

[13] Thomas Mathiesen, *The Politics of Abolition* (Oxford: Martin Robertson & Co. Ltd, 1974). For more on the role that Mathiesen's writing plays in the contemporary prison abolition movement, see Angela Davis and Dylan Rodriguez, 'History Is a Weapon. The Challenge of Prison Abolition: A Conversation', 15 April 2011, <http://www.historyisaweapon.com/defcon1/davisinterview.html>. While this chapter focuses on academic debates about imprisonment, it is

in response to the Attica prison riot in New York and other prison uprisings across Europe, Mathiesen's text advocated prison abolition on the grounds that incarceration is an inherently unjust exercise, or rather, a practice incompatible with the very idea of justice. As Mathiesen explained it, theories of abolitionism must 'compete with traditional paradigms of justice' because the 'prison . . . does not in a defence in justice'.[14]

In his now canonical treatise, Mathiesen invoked the limits of justice to advance a systematic critique of incarceration. This approach to the prison defined academic and activist writing during the 1970s and 1980s, when books like *Instead of Prison* dovetailed with wider social movements for gender and racial equality.[15] Like its feminist and black liberationist counterparts, the abolitionist movement of this period set existing social conditions against the promise of justice in an 'enlightened, free society'.[16] The 1980s also witnessed the publication of feminist ethnographies that examined women's particular experiences of incarceration.[17] This conversation took a turn towards political

crucial to recognize the influential body of work on prisons written by prisoners and other activists. See, e.g., Angela Davis, *Angela Davis: An Autobiography* (New York, NY: Random House, 1974); George Jackson, *Soledad Brother: The Prison Letters of George Jackson* (Chicago, IL: Lawrence Hill Books, 1994); Assata Shakur, *Assata: An Autobiography* (Chicago, IL: Lawrence Hill Books, 1987). For one compilation of prison writings from the United States, see Bruce Franklin, ed., *Prison Writings in Twentieth Century America* (New York, NY: Penguin Books, 1998). These activist writings informed and intersected with the abolitionist movement in academia.

[14] Thomas Mathiesen, *Prison on Trial: A Critical Assessment* (Thousand Oaks, CA: Sage Publications Ltd, 1990), p. 138; see also Russ Immarigeon, 'Abolitionism', in David Levinson, ed., *Encyclopedia of Crime and Punishment*, vol. 4 (Thousand Oaks, CA: Sage Publications Ltd, 2002), pp. 1–5.

[15] Fay Honey Knopp, Barbara Boward, Mary Jo Brach, Scott Christianson, Mary Ann Largen, Julie Lewin, Janet Lugo, Mark Morris, and Wendy Newton, *Instead of Prisons: A Handbook for Abolitionists* (Syracuse, NY: Prison Research Education Action Project, 1976).

[16] Davis and Rodriguez, 'History Is a Weapon'.

[17] See, e.g., Pat Carlen, *Women's Imprisonment: A Study in Social Control* (London: Routledge, 1983); Alexandra Mandaraka-Sheppard, *The Dynamics of Aggression in Women's Prisons in England* (Aldershot: Gower Publishing, 1986). For a short history of criminology's relationship to gender, see Mary Bosworth and Emma Kaufman, 'Gender and Punishment', in Jonathan Simon and Richard Sparks, eds, *The SAGE Handbook of Punishment and Society* (London: Sage Publications Ltd, 2012), pp. 186–204.

theory in the early 1990s, when British criminologists explicitly recast questions about justice around the concept of legitimacy.[18] As with the abolitionist critique, this body of writing developed in response to prison riots, specifically, a string of high-profile 'disturbances' that began with the twenty-five-day riot at Manchester (Strangeways) Prison in April 1990.

According to witnesses, the Strangeways riot and those that followed in its wake were 'the worst series of prison riots in the history of the British penal system'.[19] Prisoners at HMP Strangeways took control of the remand prison within that penal complex for nearly a month, climbing atop the roof to demand, among other things, time for exercise, better visiting facilities, and an end to 23-hour lockdown.[20] During the riot, the longest in British penal history, 147 prison officers and 47 prisoners were injured.[21] Over the next month, Strangeways sparked copycat riots—or solidarity uprisings, depending on one's perspective—at twenty-three prisons across the British penal estate. Prisoners in different facilities staged sit-downs, destroyed their cells, and flew banners that read 'Strangeways, we are with you'.[22]

This unprecedented wave of unrest prompted a formal inquiry into the causes and consequences of penal disorder.[23] In June

[18] Sparks, 'Can Prisons Be Legitimate?'; Richard Sparks and Anthony Bottoms, 'Legitimacy and Order in Prisons', The British Journal of Sociology 46, (March 1995): pp. 45–62; Sparks, Bottoms, and Hay, Prisons and the Problem of Order.

[19] Frances Simon, Prisoners' Work and Vocational Training (London: Routledge, 1999), p. 12.

[20] Remand prisons hold pre-trial detainees as opposed to sentenced prisoners. For a detailed account of the Strangeways riot, see Nicki Jameson and Eric Allison, *Strangeways: A Serious Disturbance* (London: Larkin Publications, 1995), pp. 40–1; see also Carrabine, *Power, Discourse, and Resistance*; Woolf and Tumim, *The Woolf Report*.

[21] Player and Jenkins, *Prisons after Woolf*, p. 2.

[22] Player and Jenkins, *Prisons after Woolf*, pp. 96–7.

[23] Calling the Strangeways uprising an instance of disorder is a political decision. Such language suggests that prison riots are the result of a breakdown in proper prison structure rather than evidence of prisoners' agency or attempts to communicate a legitimate message. Eamonn Carrabine has written several insightful pieces on the semantics of prison riots. See, e.g., Carrabine, *Power, Discourse, and Resistance*; Eamonn Carrabine, 'Prison Riots, Social Order, and the Problem of Legitimacy', *British Journal of Criminology* 45, no. 6 (November 2005): pp. 896–913.

1990, Lord Justice Harry Woolf, then the second-highest member of the British judiciary, joined with Judge Stephen Tumim, the Chief Inspector of Prisons, to launch a four-month study of the Strangeways riots. Lord Justice Woolf sent letters to every prisoner and prison officer in the penal estate. He received over 1,700 replies, and in February of the following year published *The Woolf Report*.[24] *The Woolf Report* explored both the breakdown at HMP Strangeways and broader questions about the origins of order in penal institutions. On the basis of his interviews, Lord Justice Woolf concluded that prison riots are related to prisoners' perceptions of their environment, and in particular, to their shared sense of injustice at the conditions of incarceration. Woolf argued that the Prison Service had 'a responsibility to act with justice' and warned that failing to do so would create 'serious difficulty in maintaining security and control in prisons'.[25]

The Woolf Report had significant effects on prison management and academic research. In the prison system, Lord Justice Woolf's recommendations led to a sweeping series of reforms, including the appointment of a Prison Ombudsman, revised grievance procedures, and improved sanitation.[26] At the time, commentators hailed these changes as the introduction of 'decency and justice into jails where conditions had become intolerable'.[27] For scholars, meanwhile, the potential of *The Woolf Report* lay in the suggestion that prison security is linked to prisoners' perceptions of justice. This claim prompted criminologists to focus on the relationship between order, justice, and collective belief. Motivated by Lord Woolf's conclusions, a collection of British criminologists began to argue that prison security is best understood through legitimacy, a paradigm from political theory.[28] These criminologists asserted that prisoners' compliance with authority—and hence, prison security—was a function of the legitimacy of a penal regime. They argued, in short, that order flows from legitimacy.

[24] Woolf and Tumim, *The Woolf Report*.

[25] Woolf and Tumim, *The Woolf Report*, p. 226.

[26] See Liebling, *Prisons and Their Moral Performance*, p. 10, for a fuller analysis of the effects of *The Woolf Report* within the prison system.

[27] Jameson and Allison, *Strangeways*, p. 138.

[28] See, e.g., Cavadino and Dignan, *The Penal System*; Sparks, 'Can Prisons Be Legitimate?'; Sparks and Bottoms, 'Legitimacy and Order in Prisons'.

Richard Sparks was a central voice in this discussion. In 'Can Prisons Be Legitimate?', now a classic text in the field, Sparks argued that the concept of legitimacy illuminates 'the problem of order' by identifying when obedience is 'moral' rather than merely superficial.[29] According to Sparks, 'only legitimate social arrangements generate commitments towards compliance on moral rather than just expedient grounds'.[30] In other words, legitimacy distinguishes authentic from coerced compliance. Sparks argued that the need for 'real' compliance 'constrains the actions of the powerful' because institutions structured on superficial obedience break down more easily than those based on a shared commitment to rules.[31] People in power, including prison officials, have a vested interest in the 'moral' compliance of their subjects. This interest checks their actions and produces orderly institutions. Sparks thus concluded that 'the presence or absence of legitimacy carries large consequences for all parties in a system of power relations'.[32]

Political scientists and sociologists will hear echoes of Max Weber in this account of prison regimes. Sparks's critique drew on Weber's political theory, and specifically, on his understanding of collective participation and belief.[33] In his writing on compliance and social order, Weber argued that 'the basis of every system of authority, and correspondingly every kind of willingness to obey, is a belief, a belief by which persons exercising authority are lent prestige'.[34] This claim transformed sociology by suggesting that the legitimacy of power structures originates in shared belief. Weber framed legitimacy as a crucial feature of stable social systems.[35]

Theorists debate how normative Weber's account of legitimacy is supposed to be. Political philosopher David Beetham argues that social scientists too often reduce the concept of legitimacy to a public opinion poll about whether people like or dislike their

[29] Sparks, 'Can Prisons Be Legitimate?', p. 15.

[30] Sparks, 'Can Prisons Be Legitimate?', p. 15.

[31] Sparks, 'Can Prisons Be Legitimate?', p. 15.

[32] Sparks, 'Can Prisons Be Legitimate?', p. 15.

[33] See Weber, *The Theory of Social and Economic Organization*; see also Weber, *Economy and Society*.

[34] Weber, *The Theory of Social and Economic Organization*, p. 382.

[35] See Fabienne Peter, 'Political Legitimacy', in *Stanford Encyclopedia of Philosophy* (April 2010), p. 3, <http://plato.stanford.edu/entries/legitimacy/>; see also Fabienne Peter, *Democratic Legitimacy* (New York, NY: Routledge, 2008).

government.[36] Beetham contends that legitimacy entails a rigorous interrogation of the sources of power; as he sees it, Weber's writing is not solely descriptive but is also a normative reflection on how power ought to work.[37] To emphasize this point, Beetham defines legitimacy as 'congruence between a given system of power and the beliefs, values, and expectations that provide it justification'.[38] Where belief is the basis for power, a regime can be called legitimate. Where it is not, the regime suffers from what Beetham calls a legitimacy deficit.[39] In this formulation, legitimacy becomes a way to judge whether a power regime is just.

Beetham's presentation of legitimacy inspired Richard Sparks's work on prisons. Emphasizing the foundations of power, Sparks argued that the prison faces a serious legitimacy dilemma as an intrinsically hierarchical and coercive institution.[40] For Sparks, the problem is definitional: prisons, by their very design, do not run on consent. While imprisonment involves some degree of agency, the prison is not premised on consent; it is not an institution in which power springs from the shared belief of its constituents.[41] Instead, the very nature of imprisonment creates a gap between the sources and justification of power. Prisons, precisely because they are prisons, are basically illegitimate institutions. As Alison Liebling puts it, 'prisoners are generally held against their will. In this sense, but also in others, prisons suffer from an inherent legitimacy deficit.'[42]

[36] David Beetham, *The Legitimation of Power* (London: Macmillan, 1991), p. 11.

[37] Beetham, *The Legitimation of Power*, p. 11. In emphasizing the normative dimensions of Weber's writing, Beetham echoed Jürgen Habermas's work on legitimacy. Habermas argues that legitimacy is both normative and contextual. In his view, while legitimacy captures how power ought to work in a normative sense, the concept also describes power relations within political systems that are historically contingent. See Habermas, *Legitimation Crisis*.

[38] Beetham, *The Legitimation of Power*, p. 11.

[39] Beetham, *The Legitimation of Power*, p. 20.

[40] Sparks, 'Can Prisons Be Legitimate?'; see also Sparks and Bottoms, 'Legitimacy and Order in Prisons'.

[41] For accounts of agency and consent inside prisons, see Mary Bosworth, *Engendering Resistance: Agency and Power in Women's Prisons* (London: Ashgate Publishing, 1999); and Carrabine, *Power, Discourse, and Resistance*.

[42] Liebling, *Prisons and Their Moral Performance*, p. 462. Tom Tyler has also written about the role that legitimacy plays in the production of order in social

Scholars have invoked the term 'legitimacy deficit' to advance both broad and narrow critiques of incarceration. In the early nineties, criminologists often cast legitimacy deficits as part of a systemic crisis in the operation of penal institutions.[43] Sparks, for instance, reread Thomas Mathiesen's abolitionism as a claim about the illegitimacy of prison regimes.[44] In the abolitionist account, the legitimacy gap inherent to the structure of the prison makes it impossible to achieve justice behind bars. Illegitimacy is a recurring and insurmountable feature of imprisonment.

The more reform-minded critique positioned legitimacy as a way to address inadequate prison conditions. While Sparks's writing can be read as a deep critique of incarceration, it also contained a subtle but definite impulse towards reform. The essay 'Can Prisons Be Legitimate?' was closely related to the findings in *The Woolf Report*, and through them, to Lord Justice Woolf's agenda.[45] Sparks explained:

> The concept of legitimacy carries an open and dialectical awareness of change, such that every time an attempt at legitimation...appears to promise a new settlement one can begin to discern within it the outlines of another emergent set of issues and possibilities and to reach towards them.[46]

Sparks suggested that legitimacy deficits can be isolated and ameliorated, leading to improved penal institutions. Within his broad critique, he presented legitimacy as a principle for identifying particular penal problems. This reading opened space for a more localized discussion of legitimacy in the prison system.

Scholars such as Alison Liebling have developed that space over the past decade.[47] Since 2004, Liebling has worked to situate legitimacy as a metric for prison reform. In *Prisons and Their Moral Performance*, Liebling argued that legitimacy can ground

institutions. See, e.g., Tom Tyler, *Why People Obey the Law: Procedural Justice, Legitimacy, and Compliance* (New Haven, CT: Yale University Press, 1990).

43 See, e.g., Sparks, 'Can Prisons Be Legitimate?'.

44 Sparks, 'Can Prisons Be Legitimate?', p. 17.

45 Sparks, 'Can Prisons Be Legitimate?'; Woolf and Tumim, *The Woolf Report*.

46 Sparks, 'Can Prisons Be Legitimate?', p. 26.

47 See Alison Liebling, *Deaths in Custody II: Caring for People at Risk* (London: Whiting and Birch, 1996); Alison Liebling, *Deaths of Offenders: The Hidden Side of Justice* (London: Waterside Press, 1998); Liebling, *Prisons and Their Moral Performance*.

a 'comparative moral evaluation of prisons', and in the process, can promote a better prison system.[48] Liebling is ambivalent about the term legitimacy—she repeatedly distances herself from Weber and Sparks and she asserts that criminologists need 'a slightly more complex and relational model of what matters in prison'.[49] Liebling also highlights the import of 'psychological well-being [and] the delivery of pain', two ideas she locates outside legitimacy's ambit.[50] In these moments, Liebling's writing is more aligned with sociological accounts of 'the pains of imprisonment' than with political theories of governance.[51]

Yet Liebling's aim originates in legitimacy theory. At the outset of *Prisons and Their Moral Performance*, Liebling describes her book as an 'operationalisation of legitimacy' that introduces 'moral concerns' into the conversation begun by Richard Sparks.[52] Specifically, Liebling wants to integrate moral questions, which she defines as 'questions about trust, respect, and well-being', into debates about order and authority in prisons.[53] To uncover these aspects of incarceration, Liebling develops a complex poll of prisoner and staff perceptions of the prison environment. She describes this poll as a way to measure 'the practice of values in prison'.[54]

Liebling's work bridges a divide between the academic and official discourses on incarceration. Since 1999, the British Prison Service has focused with increasing intensity on the use of 'key performance indicators' to measure a prison's success at, among other things, preparing prisoners for resettlement and reducing violence and drug use.[55] This focus on quantifiable success—and in particular, on the term performance—was the cornerstone of the New Labour approach to prison management.[56] Liebling's

[48] Liebling, *Prisons and Their Moral Performance*, pp. 261–340, 482.

[49] Liebling, *Prisons and Their Moral Performance*, p. 474.

[50] Liebling, *Prisons and Their Moral Performance*, p. 475.

[51] Gresham Sykes, *The Society of Captives: A Study in a Maximum Security Prison* (Princeton, NJ: Princeton University Press, 1958), p. 63.

[52] Liebling, *Prisons and Their Moral Performance*, p. 475.

[53] Liebling, *Prisons and Their Moral Performance*, p. xviii.

[54] Liebling, *Prisons and Their Moral Performance*, p. xviii.

[55] Liebling, *Prisons and Their Moral Performance*, p. 30.

[56] For a critical account of New Labour governance, see Lucia Zedner, 'Dangers of Dystopias in Penal Theory', *Oxford Journal of Legal Studies* 22, no. 2 (Summer 2002): pp. 341–66; and Zedner, 'Security, the State, and the Citizen'.

goal is to translate the critical discussion of legitimacy into a debate about specific prisons, one that asks questions about fairness and trust and frames their answers in a language familiar to the government. This approach has had notable traction within the Prison Service, which has adopted Liebling's model in its own internal evaluations.[57] Perhaps more than any other academic critique, Liebling's account of moral performance has succeeded in introducing ethical language into British prison practices.

From its origins in Weber's political theory and Mathiesen's abolitionism, the discussion of prison legitimacy has thus taken a pragmatic turn towards the government's own language for reform.[58] Concerns about the impossibility of just penal institutions have shifted towards debates about practical improvements in particular prisons. As a result, the scholarship on legitimacy looks more empirical, more local, and less abolitionist than the writing on prison justice during the 1970s and 1980s. Prison sociology has, it seems, changed with the times, from the holistic and radical critiques of the seventies towards the more flexible, managerial emphasis on 'what works' that took root under New Labour.[59] To be fair, Liebling does not embrace this managerialist project wholesale. Her work is in many respects a reminder that broad moral concerns matter to an otherwise 'value-free'

[57] The Prison Service uses Liebling's questionnaire to evaluate each prison every two years.

[58] To some degree, penology has always been a pragmatic project. Early prison reformers such as John Howard and Elizabeth Fry sought to ameliorate harsh prison conditions, as did later ethnographers like Donald Clemmer and Gresham Skyes. Donald Clemmer, *The Prison Community* (New York, NY: Holt, Rinehart and Winston, 1940); Elizabeth Fry, *Observations on the Visiting, Superintendence, and Government of Female Prisoners* (London: Hatchard & Son, 1827); John Howard, *The State of the Prisons in England and Wales: With Preliminary Observations, and an Account of Some Foreign Prisons* (London: William Eyres and T. Cadell, 1789); Sykes, *The Society of Captives*. My claim refers to a shift in the tone and goals of prison sociology over the last thirty years. For two accounts of the historical trend towards less holistic and less abolitionist penal theory, see Eugene McLaughlin, 'Critical Criminology: The Renewal of Theory, Politics, and Practice', in Mary Bosworth and Carolyn Hoyle, eds, *What Is Criminology?* (Oxford: Oxford University Press, 2011), pp. 49–59; and Zedner, 'Dangers of Dystopias in Penal Theory'.

[59] For an examination of the criminological implications of New Labour's emphasis on 'what works', see Zedner, 'Dangers of Dystopias in Penal Theory'.

discussion of imprisonment.[60] It is clear, however, that Liebling's writing on legitimacy marks a moment in prison sociology in which the implicitly achievable goal is to work within the state's framework to improve its penal institutions. This goal sets contemporary prison sociology apart from the body of scholarship that maps and critiques penal power.

Punishment and Society

Sociologists of punishment style their work in contrast to the official discourse on prisons. Rather than interrogating the legitimacy of penal regimes or attempting to improve specific facilities, theorists of penal power aim to locate the prison in a social world 'lacerated' by divisions of race, gender, and class.[61] Sociologists of punishment situate the prison in a legal system that systematically perpetuates inequality. They ask how and why the penal institution reproduces an unequal social order—how, in other words, penal power becomes an expression of state power.

In its current form, the sociology of punishment ranges from statistical accounts of felon disenfranchisement[62] to theoretical critiques of sex offender notification laws,[63] Foucauldian analysis of British

[60] Moral values play a significant role in much of Liebling's work. See Liebling, *Suicides in Prison*; Liebling, *Deaths of Offenders*; Alison Liebling and Shadd Maruna, *The Effects of Imprisonment* (Cullompton: Willan Publishing, 2005).

[61] Sim, *Punishment and Prisons*, p. 8. For more examples of this genre of academic writing, see Dana Britton, *At Work in the Iron Cage: The Prison as Gendered Organization* (New York, NY: New York University Press, 2003); Kathleen Daly, *Gender, Crime and Punishment* (New Haven, CT: Yale University Press, 1994); Garland, *The Culture of Control*; Marie Gottschalk, *The Prison and the Gallows: The Politics of Mass Incarceration in America* (Cambridge: Cambridge University Press, 2006); Howe, *Punish and Critique*; Joe Sim, 'Tougher than the Rest? Men in Prison', in Tim Newburn and Betsy Stanko, eds, *Just Boys Doing Business? Men, Masculinities and Crime* (London: Routledge, 1995), pp. 110–17; Wacquant, *Punishing the Poor*; and Bruce Western, *Punishment and Inequality in America* (New York, NY: Russell Sage Foundation, 2006).

[62] See, e.g., Jeff Manza and Christopher Uggen, *Locked Out: Felon Disenfranchisement and American Democracy* (Oxford: Oxford University Press, 2006).

[63] See, e.g., Jonathan Simon, 'Megan's Law: Crime and Democracy in Late Modern America', *Law and Social Enquiry* 25, (October 2000): pp. 1111–50.

crime control,[64] and historical analyses of the relationship between incarceration and the American civil rights movement.[65] There are perils to generalizing about this body of research. But there are also benefits to framing the sociology of punishment as a coherent collection of ideas. Examining this scholarship as its own genre clarifies the assumptions that motivate the dominant critical approach to prisons.

The sociology of punishment developed from post-structuralist critiques of the 1970s. Across academic disciplines, the seventies was a period of radical revision. Prompted by the same social movements that propelled prison abolitionism, academics of this era began to question the terms that defined their respective fields. In the humanities, Frederic Jameson contested classic formalist accounts of literature.[66] In the social sciences, Michel Foucault and Jean-François Lyotard questioned both the notion of universal truth and the scientific attempt to uncover it.[67] At the same time, feminist theorists pushed scholars to recognize how race, gender, and other aspects of identity inform subjectivity.[68]

Taken together, these critiques constituted a significant challenge to positivism, and hence, to the orthodoxy of criminological thought. Long tied to causal questions about crime—and in the United Kingdom, to the Home Office—criminology began to unmoor itself from the positivist project. In the late seventies, scholars started to explore how social responses to crime and

[64] See, e.g., Kevin Stenson, 'Sovereignty, Biopolitics, and the Local Government of Crime in Britain', *Theoretical Criminology* 9, no. 3 (August 2005): pp. 265–87.

[65] See, e.g., Western, *Punishment and Inequality in America*.

[66] Frederic Jameson, *The Prison-House of Language: A Critical Account of Structuralism and Russian Formalism* (Princeton, NJ: Princeton University Press, 1972).

[67] Michel Foucault, *The Order of Things: An Archaeology of the Human Sciences* (New York, NY: Random House, 1970); Jean-François Lyotard, *The Postmodern Condition: A Report on Knowledge*, trans. Geoff Bennington and Brian Massumi (Manchester: Manchester University Press, 1984).

[68] See Toni Cade-Bambara, *The Black Woman: An Anthology* (New York, NY: New American Library, 1970); Shulamith Firestone, *The Dialectic of Sex: The Case for Feminist Revolution* (London: Bantam Books, 1970); Sheila Rowbotham, *Woman's Consciousness: Man's World* (London: Penguin Books, 1973); Amrit Wilson, *Finding a Voice: Asian Women in Britain* (London: Virago Press, 1978). For a fuller history of this feminist scholarship as it relates to criminology, and to studies of imprisonment in particular, see Bosworth and Kaufman, 'Gender and Punishment'.

prison practices construct the concept of punishment.[69] In Britain, criminologists gathered at the National Deviancy Conference to call for a 'New Criminology', one equipped with a 'fully social' theory of deviance and a more explicit stance on the politics of crime control.[70]

The burgeoning movement for a more politicized account of criminal justice developed in several different directions. In the United Kingdom, the constructionist critiques of the seventies grew into critical criminology, a subfield focused on the reproduction of unequal social structures.[71] Following the American sociologist Howard Becker, who famously asked academics 'whose side' they were on, British criminologists voiced concerns about the political implications of their work.[72] These scholars noted a shift towards a less democratic, more authoritarian state and questioned where criminology sat in relation to political economic trends. This question prompted inquiries into the production of knowledge about crime. Writing 'against criminology', Stan Cohen demonstrated the academy's complicity in creating notions of deviance.[73] Stuart Hall and his contemporaries at the Birmingham Centre for Cultural Studies wrote *Policing the Crisis*, a powerful exploration of the way that the media creates crime 'crises' that, in turn, construct a class of deviants from young black men.[74]

Hall's work connected social responses to crime to the evolution of the authoritarian state.[75] Along with his co-authors, Hall located criminal justice institutions in a wider network of social control that systematically reifies disparities of race and class. This

[69] See, e.g., Stuart Hall, Chas Critcher, Tony Jefferson, John Clarke, and Brian Roberts, *Policing the Crisis: Mugging, The State and Law and Order* (London: Palgrave MacMillan, 1978); see also Foucault, *Discipline and Punish.*

[70] Ian Taylor, Paul Walton, and Jock Young, *The New Criminology: For a Social Theory of Deviance* (London: Routledge, 1973).

[71] For accounts of the history of Critical Criminology in Britain, see Kerry Carrington and Russell Hogg, *Critical Criminology: Issues, Debates, Challenges* (Cullompton: Willan Publishing, 2002); and McLaughlin, 'Critical Criminology'.

[72] Howard Becker, 'Whose Side are We On?', *Social Problems* 14, no. 3 (Winter 1967): pp. 239–47; see also Stan Cohen, *Against Criminology* (New Brunswick, NJ: Transaction Publishers, 1998); Taylor, Walton, and Young, *The New Criminology.*

[73] Cohen, *Against Criminology.*

[74] Hall, Critcher, Jefferson, Clarke, and Roberts, *Policing the Crisis.*

[75] McLaughlin, 'Critical Criminology', p. 50.

vision of state power became, as Eugene McLaughlin puts it, 'embedded in the neural wiring of Critical Criminology'.[76] Over the decades after it was published, *Policing the Crisis* set the agenda for critical accounts of law and order. After Hall, the 'primary task' was to identify and unravel the 'practices that emanated from and assisted the "authoritarian state" in its management of structural conditions'.[77] This project had clear roots in Marxist theory, and in particular, in the 'Marxist conceptualization of the state' as a more-or-less autonomous force for class inequity.[78] While not all critical criminology was explicitly Marxist, the subfield coalesced around the idea that scholars could link criminal justice practices to class structures through a critique of the state.

Studies of imprisonment reflected Hall's concerns.[79] Following Hall, legal theorists and criminologists of the 1980s routinely emphasized the prison's part in producing and 'warehousing' the dangerous classes, in stigmatizing minorities, and in entrenching poverty.[80]

[76] McLaughlin, 'Critical Criminology', p. 50.

[77] McLaughlin, 'Critical Criminology', p. 51.

[78] McLaughlin, 'Critical Criminology', p. 50. For more on the relationship between the state and class inequality in Marxist theory, see Robert Paul Resch, *Althusser and the Renewal of Marxist Social Theory* (Berkeley, CA: University of California Press, 1992); and Jutta Weldes, 'Marxism and Methodological Individualism', *Theory and Society* 18, no. 3 (January 1989): pp. 353–86. While the Marxist account of the state as a relatively coherent force and a unique object of critical analysis played a crucial role in the development of critical criminology, class is not the only site of analysis for Critical Criminologists. Critical scholars like Mary Bosworth, Jeanne Flavin, and Eamonn Carrabine have written extensively about how race and gender relate to imprisonment. See Mary Bosworth and Jeanne Flavin, eds, *Race, Gender, and Punishment: From Colonialism to the War on Terror* (London: Rutgers University Press, 2007); Eamonn Carrabine and Mary Bosworth, 'Reassessing Resistance: Race, Gender, and Sexuality in Prison', *Punishment and Society* 3, no. 4 (October 2001): 501–15.

[79] My claim is not that there was an abundance of critical prisons research in the United Kingdom during this period. To the contrary, access to British prisons became more difficult in the years immediately following the publication of *Psychological Survival*, which offered a sharp critique of imprisonment practices. See Stan Cohen and Laurie Taylor, *Psychological Survival: The Experience of Long-term Imprisonment* (New York, NY: Vintage Books, 1974). My limited claim is that theories of imprisonment, like theories of crime and deviance of the same period, took on a critical tone and a sceptical approach to state power during the late 1970s and 1980s.

[80] See, e.g., R. D. King and Rod Morgan, *The Future of the Prison System* (Surrey: Gower Publishing, 1980); Dario Melossi and Massimo Pavarini, *The Prison and The Factory: Origins of the Penitentiary System* (London: Macmillan,

Behind each of these trends, scholars identified an expanding state 'grounded in the interests' of the powerful.[81] These accounts situated the prison less as a site for legitimacy or justice than as the mechanism of an increasingly oppressive state. In this writing, the prison is one piece of a broadly unequal system and the academic works as a counter-hegemonic force.

The study of penal power took a slightly different form in the body of writing that emerged from the work of Michel Foucault. Like the neo-Marxist critical criminologists of the 1970s and 1980s, Foucault was interested in historical conditions and power relations. Foucault's seventh book, *Discipline and Punish*, traced the birth of the prison to the emergence of the modern state in the nineteenth century.[82] Foucault distinguished himself from more Marxist theorists, however, in his focus on the modes or 'technologies' through which state power gets expressed.[83] Foucault famously argued that the prison is a site for discipline, a form of social control that stakes its power on the minutia of daily life. Citing the exercise routines and architecture of imprisonment, he portrayed punishment as a practice that constructs and solidifies social norms. Foucault used the penal institution to advance a thesis about the nature of power, subjectivity, and social control in post-Enlightenment society.

David Garland points out that this approach to incarceration echoed the functionalist account of crime articulated nearly a century earlier by Emile Durkheim.[84] While Foucault differs from Durkheim in important and sometimes diametric ways, both thinkers were attuned to the sociological effects of criminal justice practices. For Durkheim, crime provided the deviant example

1981); Phil Scraton, *Law, Order, and the Authoritarian State: Readings in Critical Criminology* (London: Open University Press, 1987); see also Michael Ignatieff, *Just Measure of Pain: The Penitentiary in the Industrial Revolution, 1750–1850* (London: Penguin Books, 1995).

[81] McLaughlin, 'Critical Criminology', p. 51.

[82] Foucault, *Discipline and Punish*.

[83] Foucault, *Discipline and Punish*; see also Marianna Valverde, 'Specters of Foucault in Law and Society Scholarship', *Annual Review of Law and Social Science* 6, (December 2010): pp. 45–59.

[84] David Garland, 'Frameworks of Inquiry in the Sociology of Punishment', *The British Journal of Sociology* 41, no. 1 (March 1990): pp. 1–15; see also Durkheim, *Moral Education*; Durkheim, *The Division of Labor in Society*.

against which a common morality becomes clear.[85] Foucault was less explicitly functionalist and was certainly less optimistic about the role that punishment plays in society. He did, however, contend that punishment reproduces far-reaching social norms that establish the boundaries of human subjectivity. Foucault can be read as a neo-functionalist, the post-modern answer to Durkeim's classic sociology of crime.[86]

This new functionalism was immensely influential during the seventies and has been ever since.[87] Scholars concerned with imprisonment saw in Foucault's writing 'a more powerful set of tools for the analysis of state control'.[88] Garland explains that Foucault's work on the prison 'demonstrated . . . the far-reaching sociological significance of punishment and the kinds of insights which might be gained from a close examination of its practices'.[89] These insights fit well into the critical project of the time. Alongside *Policing the Crisis, Discipline and Punish* provided a model for moving beyond 'the workings of penal policy' to more philosophical questions about the relationship between penal practices and the constitution of the polity.[90] Foucault framed punishment as a fundamentally 'social phenomenon'.[91]

Criminologists have interpreted Foucault's writing in a variety of ways. Some scholars have adopted Foucault's ideas directly,

[85] See Durkheim, *Moral Education.*

[86] There are heated debates about whether it is appropriate to call Foucault a functionalist. Some scholars argue that calling Foucault a neo-functionalist suggests a determinism that his work does not endorse. See, e.g., Neil Brenner, 'Foucault's New Functionalism', *Theory and Society* 23 (October 1994): pp. 679–709. For more on Foucault's theoretical perspective, see Johann Graff, 'The Seductions of Determinism in Development Theory: Foucault's Functionalism', *Third-World Quarterly* 27, no. 8 (December 2006): 1387–1400. For a review of how these issues apply to criminology, see Garland, 'Frameworks of Inquiry in the Sociology of Punishment'; and Howe, *Punish and Critique.*

[87] For examples of scholarship that adopts a new functionalist approach to prisons, see Britton, *At Work in the Iron Cage*; Eamonn Carrabine, 'Discourse, Governmentality and Translation: Toward a Social Theory of Imprisonment', *Theoretical Criminology* 4, no. 3 (August 2000): pp. 309–31; Howe, *Punish and Critique*; Sim, *Punishment and Prisons*, Simon, *Governing Through Crime*; and Wacquant, *Punishing the Poor.*

[88] Garland, 'Frameworks of Inquiry in the Sociology of Punishment', p. 2.

[89] Garland, 'Frameworks of Inquiry in the Sociology of Punishment', p. 2.

[90] Garland, 'Frameworks of Inquiry in the Sociology of Punishment', pp. 1–2.

[91] Garland, 'Frameworks of Inquiry in the Sociology of Punishment', p. 2.

employing concepts like governmentality and biopower to critique criminal justice practices.[92] These terms are related attempts to understand how the state creates and regulates its subjects. Governmentality describes the wide-ranging set of techniques, from political campaigns to the production of medical knowledge, that the state uses to control its citizens, or more to the point, to encourage citizens to govern themselves.[93] Biopower, on the other hand, captures how techniques of governance operate on and through the 'docile' human body.[94] Inspired by these concepts, criminologists and legal scholars have developed governmentality into a theory of incarceration and have used biopolitics to explain everything from local prison policies to 'neoliberal discourses of crime control'.[95]

Other scholars have a less explicit relationship to Foucault's work. Criminologists including David Garland, Kelly Hannah-Moffat, Marianna Valverde, Adrian Howe, Jonathan Simon, Loïc Wacquant, and Joe Sim have all drawn on Foucauldian arguments to link punitive penal policies to the expansion of social control.[96] Not all of these scholars conceive of their work as Foucauldian—some bristle at the label, and others, including David Garland and Adrian Howe, purposefully distinguish their theories from Foucault's.[97] In prison studies and many other fields,

[92] See, e.g., Carrabine, 'Discourse, Governmentality and Translation'; David Garland, 'The Limits of the Sovereign State: Strategies of Crime Control in Contemporary Society', *British Journal of Criminology* 36 (Winter 1996): pp. 445–71; Stenson, 'Sovereignty, Biopolitics, and the Local Government of Crime in Britain'.

[93] Michel Foucault, 'Governmentality', in Graham Burchell, Colin Gordon, and Peter Miller, eds, *The Foucault Effects: Studies in Governmentality* (Chicago, IL: University of Chicago Press, 1991), pp. 27–104.

[94] Michel Foucault, *The History of Sexuality, Volume I: An Introduction*, trans. Richard Hurley (New York, NY: Vintage Books, 1978).

[95] See Carrabine, 'Discourse, Governmentality and Translation'; Torin Monohan, 'Identity Theft Vulnerability: Neoliberal Governance Through Crime Construction', *Theoretical Criminology* 13, no. 2 (May 2009): pp. 155–76; Stenson, 'Sovereignty, Biopolitics, and the Local Government of Crime in Britain'.

[96] Garland, *The Culture of Control*; Hannah-Moffat, *Punishment in Disguise?*; Howe, *Punish and Critique*; Sim, *Punishment and Prisons*; Simon, *Governing Through Crime*; Wacquant, *Punishing the Poor*.

[97] See Garland, 'Frameworks of Inquiry in the Sociology of Punishment'; Howe, *Punish and Critique*. Adrian Howe's account of penality also entails an explicit critique of Foucault.

citing Foucault has become a way to say that scholars are critical of the state and interested in power. This shorthand flattens both Foucault's contributions and the nuances of contemporary scholarship.

Yet, while the most famous writing on incarceration cannot be called Foucauldian without caveats, there is no doubt that books like *The Culture of Control, Governing through Crime*, and *Punishing the Poor* are shaped by Foucault's ideas.[98] *Discipline and Punish* introduced a new way of understanding the prison, one in which punishment is an independent and sociologically rich object of analysis. This approach encouraged scholars to think about prisons, and in particular mass imprisonment in the United States, as a defining feature of modernity.[99] For Foucault, punishment is a power-laden exchange between the disciplinary practices inside a prison and a much wider social space. Academics since Foucault have called this sociological exchange 'penality'.[100] These scholars have sought, as Foucault did, to think broadly about the relationship between penal institutions and the character of late modern governance. This perspective on the prison—as a lens into the nature of power and a metonym for modern society—defines much of today's writing on punishment.

Contemporary scholars have also embraced Foucault's descriptive vantage point. In his writing on prisons and other social institutions, Foucault advanced a contextual view of power by tracing expressions and variations of social control over time. Following Nietzsche, Foucault called this method genealogy.[101] Its main premise is that scholars can distance themselves from their object of study, and in doing so, can comment on the process by

[98] Garland, *The Culture of Control*; Simon, *Governing Through Crime*; Wacquant, *Punishing the Poor*.

[99] See, e.g., Garland, *Punishment and Modern Society*; Western, *Punishment and Inequality in America*; Michael Tonry, *Malign Neglect: Race, Crime and Punishment in America* (Oxford: Oxford University Press, 1996).

[100] Many scholars use the term 'penality'. For one example, see Pat Carlen, *Imaginary Penalities* (Cullompton: Willan Publishing, 2008).

[101] See Foucault, *The Order of Things*. For an incisive account of the Foucauldian method, see Nancy Fraser, *Unruly Practices: Power, Discourse, and Gender in Contemporary Social Theory* (Minneapolis, MN: University of Minnesota Press, 1989), p. 19. See also Friedrich Nietzsche, *On the Genealogy of Morals and Ecce Homo*, trans. Walter Kaufmann (New York, NY: Vintage Books, 1969).

which social norms are produced. This method has been key to the development of writing on punishment and society. Whether it be Critical Criminology or Foucauldian critique, scholarship in this field adopts a sceptical attitude towards state power, positioning the academic as a commentator on the machinations of the authoritarian state.[102] The goal in this line of thought is to trace the constitutive role that the prison plays in an unequal social system. Often, that goal gives rise to what Lucia Zedner calls 'grand narratives' of penality, sweeping accounts that describe imprisonment in critical and metaphorical terms.[103] Such accounts position the prison within a bigger story, one attuned primarily, though not only, to questions of power.

Academic writing on penality thus ends up looking different than contemporary prison sociology. Since the mid-nineties, and particularly since the publication of *Prisons and Their Moral Performance*, academic writing on prison life has veered towards policy-oriented empirical research.[104] This work coheres around the concept of legitimacy and culminates in an attempt to envision better prisons. It also tends towards what Zedner describes as 'the production of miniatures... accurately drawn and intentionally narrowly focused'.[105] In contrast, theoretical accounts of penal power frame imprisonment as a cultural practice and situate the academic as a social critic. In practice, the stylistic differences in prison research track deeper theoretical divisions in the field. Ultimately, we can discern two distinct ways of talking, thinking, and writing about the prison—one focused on the possibility of legitimate penal institutions, the other on the prison's part in a fundamentally stratified society.

[102] Eugene McLaughlin uses the term 'orthodox Critical Criminology'. McLaughlin, 'Critical Criminology', p. 56.

[103] Zedner, 'Dangers of Dystopias in Penal Theory', p. 341.

[104] Liebling, *Prisons and Their Moral Performance*; see also Megan Comfort, 'In the Tube at San Quentin: The "Secondary Prisonization" of Women Visiting Inmates', *Journal of Contemporary Ethnography* 32, no. 1 (February 2003): pp. 77–107; Crewe, *The Prisoner Society*, Pete Earley, *The Hot House: Life Inside Leavenworth Prison* (New York, NY: Bantam Books, 1995); Liebling and Maruna, *The Effects of Imprisonment*.

[105] Zedner, 'Dangers of Dystopias in Penal Theory', p. 347.

Blind Spots

Both of these approaches to prison theory tend to overlook the effects of globalization. Despite their many strengths, neither contemporary prison sociologies nor critical accounts of penality fully engage with the precariousness of national borders or the relationship between migration control and incarceration. Instead, the nation-state is an assumed frame of analysis in discussions of incarceration. Almost across the board, legal and sociological scholars invoke the state to advance arguments about the prison. Alison Liebling and Ben Crewe attempt to improve penal institutions in order to increase the state's overall legitimacy.[106] David Garland and Loïc Wacquant track the changing texture of state power in neo-liberal societies.[107] The state is an important term of art for all of these thinkers.

Yet, in both branches of prison studies, the state remains under-theorized. In Alison Liebling's work, the state is the geographical container for penal institutions that operate with greater and lesser degrees of 'morality'.[108] Liebling presents the state as a territorial idea; it is the setting for the British penal estate. She does not aim to problematize the nation-state, nor does she link prison practices to the production of national borders. Rather, as she makes clear at the outset of her book, her goal is an 'internal' and 'practical' model for prison reform.[109] The question is whether any model of reform can be practical if it fails to grapple with the consequences of mass mobility.

Some prison sociologies reach beyond the internal life of the prison. In his early work, Richard Sparks underscored the 'centrally important "external" issue' of the conditions under which prison sentences are appropriate.[110] There was a latent sociological focus to Sparks's inquiry and there is no question that Sparks was invested in a broad critique of imprisonment. But Sparks's work emphasized the justification for imprisonment rather than the prison's position in a wider social structure.[111] Sparks's critical

[106] Crewe, *The Prisoner Society*; Liebling, *Prisons and Their Moral Performance*.

[107] Garland, *The Culture of Control*; Wacquant, *Punishing the Poor*.

[108] Liebling, *Prisons and Their Moral Performance*.

[109] Liebling, *Prisons and Their Moral Performance*, p. xix.

[110] Sparks, 'Can Prisons Be Legitimate?', p. 10.

[111] Sparks, 'Can Prisons Be Legitimate?', p. 10.

question was when the state is using its power to incarcerate in an appropriate and just manner, not what the use of incarceration says about the changing nature of the state. Sparks interrogated the basis for state institutions. He did not take the state to be a malleable product of institutional practices.

This understanding of the state is characteristic of scholarship on compliance and order in prisons. Studies of prison legitimacy tend to be tied to the internal workings of state institutions and to a conception of the state as the origin of those institutions. For both Sparks and Liebling, legitimacy theory connects the internal life of the prison to sources of the power to incarcerate. Legitimacy links prison conditions to questions about how and whether the state's use of incarceration can be just, and for Liebling, moral. This conceptual shift makes sense in theory, but in practice the daily life of the prison extends well beyond the boundaries of the state. What becomes of legitimacy if prisons are connected not just to British society, but to a globalizing world?

Until about five years ago, this question did not get asked in prison studies. Despite the emergence of a body of criminological writing on borders and migration control, mainstream prison sociology remains more-or-less bound to the nation-state and to the philosophical assumptions that come with it.[112] Academic habit accounts for at least part of this trend. From its inception, prison sociology has been shaped by the spaces it explores. The prison is traditionally understood as a domestic institution, which, along with the police and the judiciary, constitutes a country's criminal justice system. Scholars have long approached these institutions as national in both purpose and scope. As a result, the study of legitimacy has been a state-centred project. The external world to which legitimacy scholarship refers has, at least implicitly, always been the nation-state.

[112] For recent writing on border control, see Aas, 'Analysing a World in Motion'; Bosworth, 'Border Control and the Limits of the Sovereign State'; Juliet Stumpf, 'The Crimmigration Crisis: Immigrants, Crime, and Sovereign Power', *American University Law Review* 56, no. 2 (2006): pp. 367–419; Leanne Weber and Benjamin Bowling, 'Policing Migration: A Framework for the Regulation of Global Mobility', *Policing and Society* 14, no. 3 (September 2004): pp. 195–212; Zedner, 'Security, the State, and the Citizen'.

Today's prisons, in contrast, are distinctly transnational institutions. A growing number of the people held in British prisons are non-citizens, and in the last two decades, the prison has become part of the government's migration policy.[113] The interior life of the twenty-first century prison flows well beyond national borders, into foreign policy, colonial history, and border control. This reality makes it impossible to conceptualize the link between justice and institutional order without reference to transnational trends and norms. The debate over prison legitimacy has to contend with global power dynamics.

It is not clear that legitimacy studies are up to this task. The concept of legitimacy derives from democratic theory, and like those theories, is connected to the classic conception of the state as a bordered, coherent, and territorially defined space.[114] Because it emerges from a particular vision of statehood, scholarship on the prison's legitimacy tends to stay within the confines of the nation-state rather than interrogating its limits. This genre of prison studies sidesteps questions about shifting borders, the emergence of new forms of social organization, and the transformation of late modern political membership. In this respect, prison sociology exemplifies what Nancy Fraser calls 'the Westphalian blindspot of public-sphere theory'.[115]

Fraser's term highlights the connection between the prison and the nation-state. In *Scales of Justice*, Fraser argues that legitimacy theories based in the work of Max Weber and Jürgen

[113] For assessments of the relationship between penal practices and migration policy in the United States, see Mary Bosworth and Emma Kaufman, 'Foreigners in a Carceral Age: Immigration and Imprisonment in the United States', *Stanford Law and Policy Review* 22, no. 1 (May 2011): pp. 429–54; and Jonathan Simon, 'Refugees in a Carceral Age: The Rebirth of Immigration Prisons in the United States', *Public Culture* 10, no. 3 (Spring 1998): pp. 577–607. For accounts of the same trends in the United Kingdom, see Bosworth and Guild, 'Governing through Migration Control'; Weber and Bowling, 'Policing Migration'.

[114] For further writing on the relationship between democratic theory and a territorial conception of the nation-state, see Benedict Anderson, *Imagined Communities: Reflections on the Origin and Spread of Nationalism* (New York, NY: Verso Books, 2006); Daniel Chernilo, 'The Critique of Methodological Nationalism: Theory and History', *Thesis Eleven* 106, no. 1 (August 2011): pp. 98–117; Fraser, *Scales of Justice*; Wendy Brown, *Walled States, Waning Sovereignty* (Cambridge, MA: Zone Books, 2010).

[115] Fraser, *Scales of Justice*, p. 85.

Habermas rest on 'a national subtext'.[116] These theories 'take for granted the Westphalian framing of political space' and 'fuse' the 'Westphalian territorial state' with 'the imagined community of the nation'.[117] Classic democratic theories of legitimacy assume that the world is organized into a series of bounded, discrete, and relatively autonomous territories called states, which correspond with the communities we call nations. This is an increasingly inaccurate assumption.

In the past thirty years, globalization has challenged the 'fused' nation-state.[118] Policing, banking, communication channels, and health and environmental regulations now operate across national borders. Immigration detention centres have sprung up at a rapid clip in the United Kingdom, the United States, and across Western Europe.[119] Governments have privatized prisons and placed the provision of public utilities in the hands of multinational corporations. As Fraser puts it, 'the problems debated are inherently transnational and can neither be located within Westphalian space nor resolved by a Westphalian state'.[120] Fraser's articulation of this claim is strong; she sees little room for national solutions to transnational dilemmas. Other scholars have argued that late modern social issues belong within the Westphalian framework.[121] In either version of the critique, the core claim is that many issues debated as national problems are not in fact bounded by national borders.

In the context of this critique, theories of prison legitimacy begin to look dependent on a political philosophy that is at odds with the current social world. Building from a 'Westphalian blind spot', many sociological accounts of prison life present the state as a static idea, the source rather than the effect of institutions like

[116] Fraser, *Scales of Justice*, p. 80.

[117] Fraser, *Scales of Justice*, p. 80. In making this claim, Fraser alludes to Benedict Anderson's famous assertion that nations are 'imagined communities'. See Anderson, *Imagined Communities*.

[118] Fraser, *Scales of Justice*, p. 80; see also Bauman, *Globalization*; Ulrich Beck and Edgar Grande, *Cosmopolitan Europe* (Cambridge: Polity Press, 2007); Judith Butler and Gayatri Spivak, *Who Sings the Nation-State? Language, Politics, Belonging* (Calcutta: Seagull Books, 2007).

[119] For one account of the spread of immigration detention centres, see Bosworth and Kaufman, 'Foreigners in a Carceral Age'.

[120] Fraser, *Scales of Justice*, pp. 85–6.

[121] See, e.g., Chernilo, 'The Critique of Methodological Nationalism', p. 99.

the prison. This presentation of the prison encourages what Fraser calls misframing, a situation in which 'actually transnational' questions about justice and punishment are presented as 'national matters'.[122] To extend Fraser's diction to the field of prison studies, it appears that the existing body of writing on the prison's legitimacy is largely misframed. This scholarship tends to reinforce an outmoded view of the world, and of the prison's place within it.

At first glance, theories of penality seem equipped to avoid and even to ameliorate these conceptual problems. From David Garland's writing on 'the culture of control' to Loïc Wacquant's account of 'the prison and the ghetto', theoretical work on punishment situates itself in an explicitly critical relationship to the state and the traditional institutions of criminal justice.[123] Sociologists of punishment adopt their own versions of what Paul Ricoeur called a hermeneutic of suspicion, tracking various incarnations of social control throughout history.[124] Such accounts place the academic at a remove from the state, in a position to comment on its shifting forms and, at least in theory, on its tenuous and politicized relationship to ideas about the nation.

Much of this critical distance comes from a purposeful rejection of legitimacy. In her early work, Nancy Fraser notes that Michel Foucault's unique contribution to political thought lay in his 'suspension of the problematic of legitimacy' as a paradigm for critical analysis.[125] Bracketing the concerns that shape modern liberal theory, in particular questions about 'the legitimate and illegitimate exercise of power', Foucault instead attempted to provide a descriptive account of power in the present.[126] Legal scholars

[122] Fraser, *Scales of Justice*, p. 6; see also Barbara Hudson, *Justice and the Risk Society* (London: Sage Publications Ltd, 2003).

[123] Barker, *The Politics of Imprisonment*; Garland, *The Culture of Control*; Loïc Wacquant, 'Deadly Symbiosis: When Ghetto and Prison Meet and Mesh', *Punishment and Society* 3, no. 1 (January 2001): pp. 95–133.

[124] Paul Ricoeur, *The Conflict of Interpretations: Essays in Hermeneutics* (Chicago, IL: Northwestern University Press, 1969). Jonathan Simon and Richard Sparks have compiled a comprehensive collection of essays on the sociology of punishment, while John Braithwaite and Lucia Zedner have both written important critiques of the field. See John Braithwaite, 'What's Wrong with the Sociology of Punishment?', *Theoretical Criminology* 7, no. 1 (February 2003): pp. 5–28; Simon and Sparks, *The SAGE Handbook of Punishment and Society*; Zedner, 'Dangers of Dystopias in Penal Theory'.

[125] Fraser, *Unruly Practices*, pp. 17–34.

[126] Foucault, *Discipline and Punish*; see also Fraser, *Unruly Practices*, p. 18.

and criminologists have continued this line of thought into the twenty-first century. With more and less fidelity to the Foucauldian method, sociologists of punishment have sought to reveal, expose, and describe where the state is at work.

This descriptive project seems like it would enable a critique of the nation-state. Theories of penality represent the state as a flexible social phenomenon. Over the past decade, scholars have turned with insight and increasing frequency to the study of transnational crimes and to the spread of concepts like risk and security.[127] Academics have also documented changes in the expression of state power. David Garland, for instance, situates the culture of control within a wider process of 'responsibilization' in which the state devolves criminal justice responsibilities to its citizens.[128] According to Garland, responsibilization spreads the burden of criminal justice across the polity, flattening the state while extending its reach.[129] In a similar vein, Jonathan Simon argues that the imagery of imprisonment allows American politicians to 'govern through crime', warping the practice of democracy.[130] This work is united by its creative approach to state power.

Yet, if critiques of punishment address transnational themes, they also tend to assume the nation-state's coherence. This assumption surfaces in two ways. First and foremost, the sociology of punishment often operates with its own blind spot about the construction of the nation-state. With notable exceptions, such as Bosworth and Guild's writing on border control and Ben Bowling's work on global policing, this scholarship does not distinguish between the state and the nation.[131] While sociologists

[127] See, e.g., Bowling, 'Transnational Policing'; David Garland, 'The Rise of Risk', in Richard V. Ericson and Aaron Doyle, eds, *Risk and Morality* (Toronto: University of Toronto Press, 2003); Hudson, *Justice and the Risk Society*; Lee, 'Human Trade and the Criminalization of "Irregular Migration"'; Ian Loader and Richard Sparks, 'Contemporary Landscapes of Crime, Order, and Control: Governance, Risk, and Globalization', in Mike Maguire, Rod Morgan, and Robert Reiner, eds, *The Oxford Handbook of Criminology*, 4th edn (Oxford: Oxford University Press, 2007), pp. 44–78.

[128] Garland, *The Culture of Control.*

[129] Garland, *The Culture of Control.*

[130] Simon, *Governing Through Crime.*

[131] Bosworth and Guild, 'Governing through Migration Control; Bowling, 'Transnational Policing'.

of punishment acknowledge that the state is a product of institutional practices, they rarely question the relationship between the state and beliefs about national belonging. Writing in this field tends to merge state with nation, or at least to ignore the fissures between the two.

Take scholarship on the 'punitive state', the 'carceral state', and the emergence of a 'neo-liberal state' keen to punish the poor.[132] While these accounts illuminate the creation of class and the articulation of power, they do not always identify the boundaries of their project. Do critiques of the carceral state apply only to domestic prison policies, or is the reach of 'the carceral' wider than that? When scholars write about the relationship between punishment and society, what—and who—is the society in question? Katja Aas presents this question in slightly different terms:

> We seldom seem to be aware of the fact that the objects of our research—often referred to as 'British society', 'American society', the EU, etc.—are the result of intense and strict social control and exclusion.[133]

According to Aas, penality theory tends to suppress the role that border controls play in shaping society.

A second, related problem is that theories of penality often overestimate the state's coherence. Critiques of punishment depict an expansive and increasingly authoritarian state behind crime control law and policy. Over and again, sociologists of punishment have demonstrated that practices like mass imprisonment and electronic tagging extend and consolidate state power.[134] The goal in these accounts is to find the state at work behind the scenes and to reveal and expose the state latent within penal practices. As

[132] Garland, *The Culture of Control*; Sim, *Punishment and Prisons*; Wacquant, *Punishing the Poor.*

[133] Aas, 'Analysing a World in Motion', p. 283. Aas's work on surveillance and mobility, Alessandro di Giorgi's writing on migration, and Mary Bosworth's account of border control provide noteworthy counter-examples to this claim. See Bosworth, 'Border Control and the Limits of the Sovereign State'; Alessandro di Giorgi, 'The U.S. Penal Experiment', in Salvatore Palidda, ed., *Racial Criminalization of Migrants in the 21st Century* (Surrey: Ashgate Publishing, 2011). On the whole, criminological writing on migration does not exhibit the same blind spot as other critical writing on punishment.

[134] See, e.g., Garland, *The Culture of Control*; O'Malley, 'Volatile and Contradictory Punishment'; Simon, *Governing Through Crime.*

Eugene McLaughlin puts it, 'Critical Criminology seeks to unmask the "authoritarian state" in all its guises—the "carceral state"; the "punitive state"; the "coercive state"; the "garrison state"; the "surveillance state"; the "national security state"; the "exceptional state"—etc.'[135] The aim, in sum, is to eke out the repressive workings of state power wherever they exist.[136] This goal has given rise to incisive accounts of crime control and has encouraged scholars to see parallels between practices, such as the use of CCTV and the creation of sex offender registries, that might otherwise seem distinct.[137] But it has also promoted a perhaps too tidy picture of the state. As a whole, the literature on penal power suggests that the state is a real and identifiable thing, the lurking force beneath justice policies and practices.

This book tells a different story. Drawing on observations and interviews in British prisons, the next six chapters depict a varied and deeply disjointed state, one in which penal policies contrast with prison practices and prisons differ from one another. The book also identifies tension between harsh penal policies and the flat, bureaucratic tenor of prison life. This account begs questions about the search for the state, and specifically, about what gets lost when criminologists and legal scholars seek to expose the authoritarian state rather than doing other kinds of intellectual work. Ultimately, I argue that a 'state-centred analysis' leaves too little room to explain the simultaneous banality and punitiveness of the contemporary prison.[138] The concern animating this study is that critical theories of penality and state power exaggerate the

[135] McLaughlin, 'Critical Criminology', p. 56.

[136] Mary Bosworth and Emma Kaufman, 'Gender and Punishment', in Jonathan Simon and Richard Sparks, eds, *The SAGE Handbook of Punishment and Society* (London: Sage Publications Ltd, 2012), p. 196.

[137] See, e.g., Jonathan Simon's account of the passage of Megan's Law and the creation of sex offender registries in the United States. Jonathan Simon, 'Megan's Law: Crime and Democracy in Late Modern America', *Law and Social Enquiry* 25, no. 4 (October 2000): pp. 1111–50. Ben Goold has written about implications of European surveillance strategies such as CCTV. Ben Goold, 'Technologies of Surveillance and the Erosion of Institutional Trust', in Katja Aas, ed., *Technologies of InSecurity: The Surveillance of Everyday Life* (Abingdon: Routledge-Cavendish Press, 2008). Both scholars depict an expanding apparatus for social control.

[138] McLaughlin, 'Critical Criminology', p. 56.

state at the expense of a more thoughtful analysis of its internal 'contradictions, dilemmas, and tensions'.[139]

As with the critique of legitimacy studies, this concern brings us back to basic questions about how theorists understand prisons. In the case of legitimacy theory, scholars appear too bound to penal institutions to advance a real critique of the state. In contrast, sociologists of punishment seem too committed to unveiling the state to acknowledge its incoherence. Critical criminologists of all stripes share this goal: neo-Marxists seek to 'expose the existence of the authoritarian state' that manages class conditions, while neo-Foucauldians compile the genealogy of a state that disciplines its citizens.[140] In both lines of thought, the state is the backdrop and final end of critical analysis. Theories of punishment conclude once the state is revealed, leaving unanswered questions about how the nation-state comes to be, fails in practice, yet continues to structure social inequality.

Conclusion

This chapter has characterized debates among prison scholars as an outgrowth of the tension between liberal and critical approaches to the state. It is also worth thinking about these problems in methodological terms. Particularly since the mid-nineties, prison sociology has become an empirical project. Criminologists such as Coretta Phillips, Ben Crewe, and Alison Liebling have produced comprehensive and detailed ethnographic accounts of life behind bars.[141] At the same time, the sociology of punishment has developed into a body of theoretical writing on neoliberalism, the 'rise of risk', and the 'culture of control'.[142] The philosophical

[139] McLaughlin, 'Critical Criminology', p. 56.

[140] McLaughlin, 'Critical Criminology', p. 56.

[141] See, e.g., Phillips, 'Ethnicity, Identity, and Community Cohesion in Prison'; Crewe, *The Prisoner Society*; Liebling, *Prisons and Their Moral Performance*; see also Comfort, 'In the Tube at San Quentin'; Rod Earle and Coretta Phillips, 'Con-viviality and Beyond: Identity Dynamics in a Young Men's Prison, in Margaret Wetherell, ed., *Identity in the 21st Century: New Trends in Changing Times* (Basingstoke: Palgrave MacMillan, 2009), pp. 120–38; Earley, *The Hot House*; Genders and Player, *Grendon*; Liebling and Maruna, *The Effects of Imprisonment*.

[142] Garland, *The Culture of Control*; Garland, 'The Rise of Risk'; see also Carlen, *Imaginary Penalities*; Gottschalk, *The Prison and the Gallows*; Sim, *Punishment and Prisons*; Western, *Punishment and Inequality in America*.

distinctions between prison theories have evolved into methodological divisions between different types of prison scholarship.

This is not the necessary trajectory of criminological thought. Legitimacy is not an inherently empirical idea, any more than punishment is essentially theoretical. Power was an empirical notion for both Marx and Foucault and legitimacy received highly theoretical treatment in Weber's work.[143] It was not until the mid-2000s that writing on prison legitimacy took a more empirical turn.[144] Prison scholarship did not have to develop as it did, but there is a clear lineage from particular theories of the state to distinct ways of doing prison research.

The influence of political theory is not the sole—nor even the primary—driver in this narrative. There are a number of reasons for the methodological division between empirical and theorietical work on prisons, many of which are entrenched in the structure of academia. The push to publish deters long-term empirical projects inside penal institutions. People's time and interests naturally segment the field into different academic agendas. Not everyone wants to go inside prisons and speak with prisoners, and not everyone who wants to go inside prisons can get into them.[145] The practical barriers to empirical prisons research are steep.

This chapter's concluding claim is thus limited and largely genealogical: there is an obvious gap between theory and practice in prison studies and it is worth thinking about how that gap relates to the field's origins in classic liberal theories of the state on one hand and neo-functionalist critical theories on the other. Scholars have pointed out that, in planning their research, social scientists tend to treat the nation-state 'as the natural and necessary representation of modern society'.[146] The question is whether

[143] See Foucault, *Discipline and Punish*, pp. 1–5. Foucault was deeply interested in the relationship between punishment and embodiment, and in this sense, was an empirical scholar of the prison. See also Sparks, 'Can Prisons Be Legitimate?'; Sparks and Bottoms, 'Legitimacy and Order in Prisons'; Weber, *Economy and Society*; Weldes, 'Marxism and Methodological Individualism'.

[144] Liebling, *Prisons and Their Moral Performance*.

[145] See Kelly Hannah-Moffat, 'Criminological Cliques: Narrowing Dialogues, Institutional Protectionism, and the Next Generation', in Mary Bosworth and Carolyn Hoyle, eds, *What is Criminology?* (Oxford: Oxford University Press, 2011): pp. 440–52; Loïc Wacquant, 'The Curious Eclipse of Prison Ethnography in the Age of Mass Incarceration', *Ethnography* 3, no. 4 (December 2002): p. 383.

[146] Chernilo, 'The Critique of Methodological Nationalism, p. 99; see also Craig Calhoun, 'Nationalism, Political Community and the Representation of

this tendency springs from an allegiance to particular methods. To apply the metaphor to prison studies, the concern is that criminology may be suffering from a widespread case of 'methodological nationalism', one that inhibits the development of transnational theories of punishment.[147] Chapter 2 explores whether the impasse in prison studies is at base a problem of method.

Society: Or, Why Feeling is Not a Substitute for Public Space, *European Journal of Social Theory* 2 (May 1999): pp. 217–31; Neil Smelser, *Problematics of Sociology* (Berkeley, CA: University of California Press, 1997); Peter Wagner, *A Sociology of Modernity: Liberty and Discipline* (London: Routledge, 1994).

[147] Chernilo, 'The Critique of Methodological Nationalism, p. 99. Chernilo argues that the problem of methodological nationalism, while real in social science, has also become a straw man for critical theorists in recent years. He notes that while many research studies assume a coherent nation-state, social scientists just as regularly lament methodological nationalism without exploring the potential benefits of thinking within a national frame.

2

Bearing Witness

The meaning of punishment depends on research methods. A strictly empirical perspective on penal institutions can suppress the politics of incarceration.[1] Tied to the boundaries of particular facilities, quantitative research on prisons can elide questions about who gets imprisoned, under what circumstances, and why. At the same time, a purely theoretical approach to punishment can obscure relevant features of the prison experience, such as its odd banality and intermittent humanity. Theories of punishment often grow grand in size and scope, concealing insights that arise from the people who live and work inside penal institutions.[2] To

[1] There is large body of research on race and punishment. For examples, see Asale Angel-Ajani, 'A Question of Dangerous Races?', *Punishment and Society* 5, no. 4 (October 2003): pp. 433–48; Mary Bosworth and Jeanne Flavin, eds, *Race, Gender, and Punishment: From Colonialism to the War on Terror* (London: Rutgers University Press, 2007); Mary Bosworth, Benjamin Bowling, and Maggy Lee, 'Globalization, Ethnicity and Racism: An Introduction', *Theoretical Criminology* 12, no. 3 (August 2008): pp. 263–73; Benjamin Bowling, *Violent Racism: Victimization, Policing and Social Context* (Oxford: Clarendon Press, 1998); Coretta Phillips and Rod Earle, 'Negotiating Identities: Ethnicity and Social Relations in a Young Offenders' Institution', *Theoretical Criminology* 12, no. 3 (August 2008): pp. 313–31; Julia Sudbury, 'Celling Black Bodies: Black Women in the Global Prison Industrial Complex', *Feminist Review* 70 (2002): pp. 57–74; Michael Tonry, *Malign Neglect: Race, Crime and Punishment in America* (Oxford: Oxford University Press, 1996); Loïc Wacquant, 'Deadly Symbiosis: When Ghetto and Prison Meet and Mesh', *Punishment and Society* 3, no. 1 (January 2001): pp. 95–133; and Bruce Western, *Punishment and Inequality in America* (New York, NY: Russell Sage Foundation, 2006). Chapter 5 examines the relationship between race and British penal policy.

[2] John Braithwaite, 'What's Wrong with the Sociology of Punishment?', *Theoretical Criminology* 7, no. 1 (February 2003): pp. 5–28; Lucia Zedner, 'Dangers of Dystopias in Penal Theory', *Oxford Journal of Legal Studies* 22, no. 2 (Summer 2002): pp. 341–66.

understand prisons, scholars need to think on simultaneous scales, with equal focus on power and daily life.

This chapter examines the exchange between theory and practice in the context of the British prison.[3] I begin with a discussion of ethnography, the dominant model for qualitative prison research.[4] Ethnography is a particularly difficult method to enact in prisons, which are by definition controlled and coercive spaces.[5] The first part of the chapter explores the methodological issues inherent to prison ethnography and considers how problems of method warp or magnify when documenting the experiences of non-citizens.[6]

The second part of the chapter addresses concerns about ethnography through the concept of witnessing. In the past decade, literary theorists have developed the term 'bearing witness' into a fresh and critical perspective on oral history.[7] Writing outside

[3] There is a long history of sociological scholarship on the relationship between theory and practice. See, e.g. Peter Bourdieu, *Outline of a Theory of Practice*, trans. Richard Nice (Cambridge: Cambridge University Press, 1977); Peter Bourdieu and Loïc Wacquant, *An Invitation to Reflexive Sociology* (Chicago, IL: University of Chicago Press, 1992); Pat Carlen, *Women's Imprisonment: A Study in Social Control* (London: Routledge, 1983); Mary Corcoran, *Out of Order: The Political Imprisonment of Women in Northern Ireland, 1972–1999* (Cullompton: Willan Publishing, 2006); Anthony Giddens, *The Constitution of Society: Outline of the Theory of Structuration* (Oakland, CA: University of California Press, 1986); Roger Matthews, 'Beyond "So What?" Criminology: Rediscovering Realism', *Theoretical Criminology* 13, no. 3 (August 2009): pp. 341–62; Ian Loader, 'For Penal Moderation: Notes toward a Public Philosophy of Punishment', *Theoretical Criminology* 14, no. 3 (August 2010): pp. 349–67.

[4] See, e.g. Ben Crewe, *The Prisoner Society: Power, Adaptation, and Social Life in an English Prison* (Oxford: Oxford University Press, 2009); Jeff Ferrell and Mark Hamm, *Ethnography at the Edge: Crime, Deviance, and Field Research* (Lebanon, NH: Northeastern University Press, 1998); Coretta Philips and Rob Earle, 'Reading Difference Differently? Identity, Epistemology and Prison Ethnography', *British Journal of Criminology* 50, no. 2 (March 2010): pp. 360–78.

[5] See Mary Bosworth, Debi Campbell, Bonita Demby, Seth Ferranti, Michael Santos, 'Doing Prison Research: Views from Inside', *Qualitative Inquiry* 11, no. 2 (April 2005): pp. 249–64; Jennifer Schlosser, 'Issues in Interviewing Inmates: Navigating the Methodological Landmines of Prison Research', *Qualitative Inquiry* 14, no. 8 (December 2008): pp. 1500–25.

[6] See Ferrell and Hamm, *Ethnography at the Edge*; Gayatri Spivak, 'Can the Subaltern Speak?', in Cary Nelson and Lawrence Grossberg, eds, *Marxism and the Interpretation of Culture* (Champaign, IL: University of Illinois Press, 1988), pp. 271–317.

[7] Aleida Assmann, 'History, Memory, and the Genre of Testimony', *Poetics Today* 27, no. 2 (2006): pp. 261–74; Marianne Hirsch and Leo Spitzer, *Ghosts of*

criminology and law, scholars such as Aleida Assmann and Annette Wieviorka have argued that witnessing is a distinct form of narrative, one that privileges subjective notions of the truth and helps to make sense of the divergent and non-linear ways in which people recollect traumatic personal experiences and contested political events.[8] Borrowing this term, the second half of the chapter frames prison ethnography as an act of witnessing, and in my own work, as an effort to witness the production of the nation-state. This formulation places the emphasis of ethnography on prisoners' testimonies and avoids some of the more troublesome ethical dilemmas that arise in classic prison research. Traditional prison ethnographies entail tenuous claims to objectivity and tend to efface, or at least obscure, the subjects of academic analysis.[9] Insisting on the humanity of our subjects, and on my own subjectivity, this chapter argues that witnessing is a productive and self-reflective way to conceptualize empirical work behind bars.

The last part of the chapter describes my own effort to witness imprisonment. This book developed from a year in and around five British prisons, where I interviewed foreign national prisoners and many other people involved in their incarceration. The chapter's final section describes why I chose to interview these prisoners, what I asked them, and how their responses shaped my understanding of twenty-first-century punishment. This section also recounts conversations with prison policymakers, prison reformers, and other people connected to the lives of incarcerated

Home: The Afterlife of Czernowitz in Jewish Memory (Berkeley, CA: University of California Press, 2010); Annette Wieviorka, *The Era of Witness* (Ithaca, NY: Cornell University Press, 2006).

8 Assmann, 'History, Memory, and the Genre of Testimony'; Wieviorka, *The Era of Witness*.

9 For examples of the traditional approach, see James Jacobs, *Stateville: The Penitentiary in Mass Society* (Chicago, IL: University of Chicago Press, 1977); and Gresham Sykes, *The Society of Captives: A Study in a Maximum Security Prison* (Princeton, NJ: Princeton University Press, 1958). For critiques of this approach, see Bosworth, Campbell, Demby, Ferranti, Santos, 'Doing Prison Research'; Maureen Cain, 'Realist Philosophy and Standpoint Epistemologies or Feminist Criminology as a Successor Science', in Loraine Gelsthorpe and Allison Morris, eds, *Feminist Perspectives in Criminology* (Milton Keynes: Open University Press, 1990), pp. 124–40; Phillips and Earle, 'Reading Difference Differently?'.

non-citizens. In sum, the chapter outlines the goals and challenges of twelve months of research and over 200 interviews.

Prison Ethnography

Punishment often looks incoherent on the ground. Despite uniform and centralized governing policies, prisons are radically different from one another. This variation frustrates streamlined claims about the purpose and social function of punishment. From inside prisons, it is clear that penal policy is neither easy to make nor to implement and that discussions of desert, retribution, racism, poverty, and power are far more complex than they seem from outside prison walls. The actual people in prisons also challenge prison theory. Line staff, teachers, librarians, volunteers, visiting family members, and prisoners themselves often fall into the footnotes of theoretical writing about incarceration. Yet these people constitute the prison, and each has her own story to tell.

The most compelling model for capturing the nuance inside prisons is ethnography. This method of social inquiry employs long-term observation, interviews, and participation to depict the interior life of institutions. Ethnography seeks to find knowledge about a particular place through first-hand experience and to describe that experience in terms that are neither categorical nor solely descriptive. An ethnography is grounded in the site being studied but is also aimed toward the wider world and interpreted from the perspective of a researcher coming from that 'other' world. As Clifford Geertz put it, ethnography aims 'to see another form of life in the categories of our own'.[10] The goal is to paint a picture of life—in this case, prison life—that is attuned both to complexity and to the shared assumptions that shape a social space. The account produced by ethnography is simultaneously personal and general. The account produced by ethnography is simultaneously personal and general. Ethnography emerges from the emerges from the researchers' own experience but extends beyond that experience into questions about the character of a culture.

This method of study is particularly hard to enact in prison. Traditional ethnographies enjoy deep and continued interaction

[10] Clifford Geertz, *The Interpretation of Cultures* (New York, NY: Basic Books, 1977), pp. 16–17.

between researcher and subject.[11] They also rely on standards of practice such as confidentiality, consent forms, audio recording, and transcription. Prison ethnography is less straightforward. Access to prisons can be prohibitively difficult to obtain. Kelly Hannah-Moffat's research in Canada suggests that barriers to entry are particularly high for critical criminologists, whose work is often deemed insufficiently practical or too political to warrant support from the government.[12] Even where research access is granted, the length of time it takes to gain access conflicts with professional pressures to find funding and publish results. The timelines of the academic and penal worlds are at odds with one another. The cumulative result of this reality is a general reluctance to pursue empirical prison research.

Additional issues reveal themselves as soon as an ethnographer steps inside prison gates. For one, the access granted by prison officials does not always allow the kind of sustained, confidential interaction a researcher might like. Access to prison wings is harder to obtain than entry into public spaces such as the chapel or the library. Security measures mean that researchers cannot always move freely or speak privately with prisoners and staff. There are also limits to which prisoners can be interviewed, when prisoners can be seen, and when, if it all, researchers can use recording equipment. In some prisons, I was not allowed to meet with 'vulnerable' prisoners, which typically means those charged with sex offences. No prison official permitted me to carry a digital recorder. These security provisions complicated an already transient research environment.

Despite their strictly controlled boundaries, prisons are in a constant state of transformation. Prisoners are regularly released, taken to court, or transferred between facilities, especially in remand institutions where prisoners await trial. The constant channels in and out of prison make it difficult to sustain contact with prisoners and to follow up with questions that arise after interviews. The movement in the prison system also creates

[11] Ferrell and Hamm, *Ethnography at the Edge*; Schlosser, 'Issues in Interviewing Inmates'.

[12] Kelly Hannah-Moffat, 'Criminological Cliques: Narrowing Dialogues, Institutional Protectionism, and the Next Generation', in Mary Bosworth and Carolyn Hoyle, eds, *What Is Criminology?* (Oxford: Oxford University Press, 2011), pp. 440–52.

basic complications when planning and attempting to complete a research project. Several times, I arrived at a particular prison to find that the prisoner I intended to interview had left the night before. Some prisoners were not available for the visits they had scheduled with me. In general, prisoner turnover meant that, for every twenty people who agreed to speak with me, I got to meet approximately four. At times, this situation stalled my research: I would agree to meet with someone on Friday and by Monday he was gone. In other cases, I ran into prisoners I had lost in one prison in another facility. These chance meetings expanded my vision of the penal estate and underscored the limitations of an ethnography confined to one prison's walls.

Prisons are also places where truth and trust, two tenets of ethnographic research, are deeply unstable. This problem springs from the coercive structure of the penal institution. Alison Liebling notes that prisoners 'are generally held against their will'.[13] Some prisoners are especially eager to have their stories heard, whether to recount painful experiences, lodge complaints, speak with a young female researcher, or simply leave their cells for an hour. Some prisoners are traumatized; some are mentally ill. Others appear to be high. No matter how faithfully a researcher explains consent, and no matter how closely a prisoner reads a consent form, prisons trouble the concept of free and voluntary participation. Ultimately, despite the fact that consent forms aim to ascribe agency to the subjects of research, the decision to conduct an interview falls to the researcher. This decision raises real ethical questions about the balance of power in prison research, about how—and indeed whether—ethnographies of imprisonment should be done.

One conclusion to draw from these critiques is that prison ethnography is inherently and insurmountably flawed.[14] This conclusion is based in valid concerns about exploitative research. Yet the same concerns also motivate ethnography, for the challenges of working in prisons are what make this academic practice worthwhile. The methodological limitations of the penal environment

[13] Alison Liebling, *Prisons and Their Moral Performance: A Study of Values, Quality, and Prison Life* (Oxford: Oxford University Press, 2004), p. 462.

[14] See Jonathan Spencer, 'Anthropology as a Kind of Writing', *Man* 24, no. 1 (1989): pp. 145–64; Spivak, 'Can the Subaltern Speak?'; Nicholas Thomas, 'Against Ethnography', *Cultural Anthropology* 6, no. 3 (August 1991): pp. 306–22.

tell us something important about the way the prison works, and more to the point, works precisely by being different than the rest of the world. Every security check, sudden prisoner transfer, and difficult conversation about consent demonstrates that prisons are purposefully styled in contrast to free society. The differences between the prison and 'the outside' would exist whether or not ethnographers documented them. But when we do, we create an opportunity to reconsider how societies express ideas about justice, punishment, and freedom.

Scholars have long used ethnography to engage in these debates. In one form or another, researchers have been going past prison walls and documenting daily prison life for more than a century. The British penal reformer Elizabeth Fry began visiting prisons, sometimes spending the night, and writing about her experiences as early as 1814.[15] In the United States, prison ethnography grew out of the culturalist sociology of the 1930s and 1940s, which sought to describe life in the aftermath of the Great Depression.[16] This strand of American prison ethnography emerged from a founding analogy between prisoners and immigrants.[17] In 1940, Donald Clemmer published *The Prison Community*, one of the first ethnographic depictions of life in an American prison.[18] Through comparison to the migrant experience in the United States, Clemmer described a process in which prisoners at an Illinois state prison conformed to the cultural norms of incarceration. He called this process 'prisonization'.[19]

Clemmer's account paved the way for works like Gresham Sykes's *The Society of Captives*, which explored prisoners' responses to maximum-security confinement and coined the term 'pains of imprisonment'.[20] These early ethnographies precipitated many others, including Erving Goffman's *Asylums*, John Irwin's *The*

[15] Elizabeth Fry, *Observations on the Visiting, Superintendence, and Government of Female Prisoners* (London: Hatchard & Son, 1827); see also June Rose, *Elizabeth Fry: A Biography* (London: Macmillan, 1980).

[16] Donald Clemmer, *The Prison Community* (New York, NY: Holt, Rinehart, and Winston, 1940); Sykes, *The Society of Captives*; see also Loïc Wacquant, 'The Curious Eclipse of Prison Ethnography in the Age of Mass Incarceration', *Ethnography* 3, no. 4 (December 2002): p. 383.

[17] Clemmer, *The Prison Community*.

[18] Clemmer, *The Prison Community*.

[19] Clemmer, *The Prison Community*, p. 299.

[20] Sykes, *The Society of Captives*, p. 63.

Felon, and James Jacobs's *Stateville*.[21] Loïc Wacquant argues that partisan politics and mass media have contributed to the eclipse of the American prison ethnography since the 1980s.[22] While ethnographies, particularly of men's prisons, have indeed dwindled in the past several decades, there remains a robust body of writing on women's imprisonment in the United States.[23] In Britain, scholars such as Alison Liebling, Ben Crewe, Coretta Phillips, and Mary Bosworth ensure that ethnographic work on imprisonment continues into the twenty-first century.[24]

These contemporary versions of prison ethnography look different than their predecessors. Many of the challenges of prisons research, such as barriers to audio recording or politicized ethics reviews, are relatively recent developments. Ethnographers have had to adapt to new technologies as they have arisen and their ethnographies have changed accordingly. Scholars also approach and describe prisons in a manner that would be foreign to their

[21] Erving Goffman, *Asylums: Essays on the Social Situation of Mental Patients and Other Inmates* (Garden City, NY: Anchor Books, 1961); James Irwin, *The Felon* (Berkeley, CA: University of California Press, 1970); Jacobs, *Stateville*.

[22] Wacquant, 'The Curious Eclipse of Prison Ethnography in the Age of Mass Incarceration', pp. 383–4.

[23] See, e.g. Lori Girshick, *No Safe Haven: Stories of Women in Prison* (Boston, MA: Northeastern University Press, 1999); Patricia O'Brien, *Making it in the 'Free World': Women in Transition from Prison* (Albany, NY: SUNY Press, 2001); Barbara Owen, *In the Mix: Struggle and Survival in a Women's Prison* (Albany, NY: SUNY Press, 1998); Nicole Hahn Rafter, *Partial Justice: Women in State Prisons, 1800–1935* (Boston, MA: Northeastern University Press, 1985); Luana Ross, *Inventing the Savage: The Social Construction of Native American Criminality* (Austin, TX: University of Texas Press, 1998); Ann Folwell Stanford, 'More than Just Words: Women's Poetry and Resistance at Cook County Jail', *Feminist Studies* 30, no. 2 (Summer 2004): pp. 277–301.

[24] Mary Bosworth, *Engendering Resistance: Agency and Power in Women's Prisons* (London: Ashgate Publishing, 1999); Mary Bosworth, 'Deporting Foreign National Prisoners in England and Wales', *Citizenship Studies* 15, no. 5 (August 2011): pp. 583–95; Crewe, *The Prisoner Society*; Liebling, *Prisons and Their Moral Performance;* Alison Liebling, *Suicides in Prison* (London: Routledge, 1992); Coretta Phillips, '"It Ain't Nothing like America with the Bloods and the Crips": Gang Narratives inside Two English Prisons', *Punishment and Society* 14, no. 1 (January 2012): pp. 51–68; Phillips and Earle, 'Reading Difference Differently?'.

forbears. On the whole, ethnography is a more self-reflexive project than it was for Fry, Clemmer, or Sykes.[25] Today's scholars are much more likely to speak in the first person and to incorporate reflections on method into the body of their research.

This stylistic shift is a response to critiques of ethnographic practice that began to develop in the 1970s.[26] During that period, scholars in many disciplines began to press for more self-conscious academic writing.[27] Following the Foucauldian line of thought described in Chapter 1, academics underscored the constructed nature of subjectivity and scholars' complicity in the production of knowledge.[28] These ideas prompted academics to challenge the claim, implicit in many prison ethnographies, that researchers can portray the prison based on objective observation.[29] In the context of post-structuralism, 'objective' studies of the prison seemed to minimize the researcher's interpretive role and to advance an ahistorical view of academic scholarship.[30]

[25] Clemmer, *The Prison Community*; Fry, *Observations on the Visiting, Superintendence, and Government of Female Prisoners*; Sykes, *The Society of Captives.*

[26] See Bosworth, Campbell, Demby, Ferranti, Santos, 'Doing Prison Research'; Ferrell and Hamm, *Ethnography at the Edge*; Susan A. Tilley, 'Conducting Respectful Research: A Critique of Practice', *Canadian Journal of Education* 23, no. 3 (Summer 1998): pp. 316–28.

[27] See, e.g. Hazel Carby, 'White Women Listen! Black Feminism and the Boundaries of Sisterhood', in The Centre for Contemporary Cultural Studies, ed., *The Empire Strikes Back: Race and Racism in 70s Britain* (London: Routledge, 1982) pp. 67–92; Angela Davis, 'Reflections on the Black Woman's Role in the Community of Slaves', *The Massachusetts Review* 13, no. 1/2 (Winter–Spring 1971): pp. 81–100; Shulamith Firestone, *The Dialectic of Sex: The Case for Feminist Revolution* (London: Bantam Books, 1970); Patricia Hill Collins, *Black Feminist Thought: Knowledge, Consciousness and the Politics of Empowerment* (New York, NY: Routledge, 1991).

[28] See Michel Foucault, *The Order of Things: An Archaeology of the Human Sciences* (New York, NY: Random House, 1970); Michel Foucault, *Discipline and Punish: The Birth of the Prison*, trans. Alan Sheridan (New York, NY: Vintage Books, 1977).

[29] Bosworth, Campbell, Demby, Ferranti, Santos, 'Doing Prison Research'; Ferrell and Hamm, *Ethnography at the Edge*; Schlosser, 'Issues in Interviewing Inmates'; see also Visweswaran, *Fictions of Feminist Ethnography.*

[30] Schlosser, 'Issues in Interviewing Inmates', p. 1501.

Race theorists and feminist criminologists were at the forefront of this critique.[31] Building from their foundational concern with the suppression of minority voices, critical race and feminist scholars argued that supposedly value-free ethnographies advance a paternalistic vision of prison.[32] In traditional prison ethnographies, researchers speak for prisoners and staff, translating individual claims into a general picture of imprisonment. But translation is never an objective act and speaking for others is an intrinsically precarious exercise.[33] Prison researchers always interpret and edit their observations; we are, in this sense, fundamentally creative writers. Objective ethnographies threaten to suppress this dimension of prison research. In doing so, they obscure both the voices of people in prison and the researcher's formative role in creating the truth of prison life. To borrow Gayatri Spivak's phrase, traditional ethnographies often cast the prisoner as an 'unfortunate marionette' 'in the service of the "truth"'.[34]

The result is a model of prison research that denies prisoners' agency, underemphasizes the very real agency of the ethnographer, and flattens the complexities of consent and resistance in coercive institutions. Rejecting this approach, feminist scholars insist on the multiplicity of truths and endorse a narrative, first-personal style of ethnographic writing.[35] In contrast to traditional ethnography, this narrative method foregrounds the researcher's authorship and incorporates direct testimony from prisoners and prison staff. It also highlights the particular and often political standpoint of the researcher and attempts to 'share the burden of storytelling' with research participants.[36]

[31] See Martin Bulmer and John Solomos, *Researching Race and Racism* (Basingstoke: Palgrave Press, 2004); Cain, 'Realist Philosophy and Standpoint Epistemologies or Feminist Criminology as a Successor Science'.

[32] Bosworth, Campbell, Demby, Ferranti, Santos, 'Doing Prison Research'; Bulmer and Solomos, *Researching Race and Racism*; Cain, 'Realist Philosophy and Standpoint Epistemologies or Feminist Criminology as a Successor Science'; Phillips and Earle, 'Reading Difference Differently?'; Richie, 'Feminist Ethnographies of Women in Prison'.

[33] See Spivak, 'Can the Subaltern Speak?'; Visweswaran, *Fictions of Feminist Ethnography*.

[34] Spivak, 'Can the Subaltern Speak?', p. 259.

[35] Bosworth, Campbell, Demby, Ferranti, Santos, 'Doing Prison Research'; Richie, 'Feminist Ethnographies of Women in Prison'; Phillips and Earle, 'Reading Difference Differently?'; Schlosser, 'Issues in Interviewing Inmates'.

[36] Schlosser, 'Issues in Interviewing Inmates', p. 1521.

This vision of ethnography has motivated a sea change in accounts of imprisonment. Given criminology's relatively widespread oversight of gender theory, it is counterproductive to exaggerate the impact of feminist and post-structuralist ideas.[37] But there has been a clear shift in empirical prison studies in recent years. While a bias toward positivist methodology still shapes research proposals and funding streams, the notion that researchers can or should be revealing the singular truth behind bars now looks 'antiquated and constraining' in the context of alternative qualitative methods.[38] Post-structuralist critiques have placed the assumptions of traditional ethnography into stark relief, demanding and encouraging new ways of studying punishment.

Ethnography as Witnessing

One promising avenue for qualitative research is to characterize ethnography as an act of witnessing. Over the last three decades, scholars including Gayatri Spivak, Donald Spence, Martha Minow, and Aleida Assmann have recast the relationship between narrative and truth.[39] These theorists have established that witnessing is a unique form of speech, one that privileges the subjectivity of the speaker. This argument can help criminologists theorize the ethical problems surrounding ethnographies of vulnerable and

[37] For more on the role that gender theory plays in criminology, see Mary Bosworth and Emma Kaufman, 'Gender and Punishment', in Jonathan Simon and Richard Sparks, eds, *The SAGE Handbook of Punishment and Society* (London: Sage Publications Ltd, 2012), pp. 186–204; see also Hannah-Moffat, 'Criminological Cliques'.

[38] Schlosser, 'Issues in Interviewing Inmates', p. 1501. For discussions of funding and research biases, see Mary Bosworth and Carolyn Hoyle, eds, *What Is Criminology?* (Oxford: Oxford University Press, 2011); Hannah-Moffat, 'Criminological Cliques'; Aiden Wilcox and Carolyn Hoyle, 'Are Randomised Controlled Trials Really the "Gold Standard" in Restorative Justice Research', *British Journal of Community Justice* 3, no. 2 (Spring 2005): pp. 39–49.

[39] Aleida Assmann, 'History, Memory, and the Genre of Testimony', *Poetics Today* 27, no. 2 (2006): pp. 261–74; Martha Minow, *Between Genocide and Forgiveness: Facing History after Genocide and Mass Violence* (Boston, MA: Beacon Press, 1998); Donald Spence, *Narrative Truth and Historical Truth: Meaning and Interpretation in Psychoanalysis* (New York, NY: Norton Publishing, 1984); Spivak, 'Can the Subaltern Speak?'.

marginalized populations. Theories of witnessing can also motivate a more transnational approach to prison ethnography.[40]

Scholarship on witnessing draws on two strands of literary theory. The first, which was famously developed by Gayatri Spivak, concerns the link between speech and subjectivity. In 'Can the Subaltern Speak?', a founding text of postcolonial theory, Spivak explained that silencing an individual's voice is one of the most powerful forms of oppression.[41] Spivak connected the capacity to speak with one's basic existence as a subject, or in literary terms, as a person capable of starting a sentence with the word 'I'.[42] She argued that imperial regimes deny colonial subjects the ability to speak, and hence, refuse to acknowledge their existence as subjects in the world. Colonial violence is in this sense 'epistemic violence'.[43] Spivak chided scholars for reproducing colonial patterns in their attempts to speak for historically oppressed groups.[44] Such accounts, which seek to give voice to those who cannot speak, homogenize and further marginalize a diverse group of individuals.

In the context of Spivak's critique, paternalistic ethnography starts to look like neocolonialism. Spivak's writing implicates ethnography in the politics of power and oppression by demonstrating that telling a story is a way to constitute the self. In 'Can the Subaltern Speak?' and other texts, Spivak linked the creation of narrative to structural disparities in power. She insisted that speaking for others is a violent denial of subjectivity and reminded academics that we are not exempt from the patterns of history. This vision of subjectivity, as a product of speech and a marker of power, is the first piece of witnessing.

The second proposition is that narratives operate according to their own kind of truth. Trauma theorist Donald Spence developed this claim in his writing on psychoanalysis and memory. According to Spence, there is a substantive distinction between 'narrative' and 'historical' notions of truth.[45] Historical truth aims

[40] Zsuzsa Gille and Seán Ó Riain, 'Global Ethnography', *Annual Review of Sociology* 28 (August 2002): pp. 271–95.

[41] Spivak, 'Can the Subaltern Speak?'.

[42] Spivak, 'Can the Subaltern Speak?'.

[43] Spivak, 'Can the Subaltern Speak?', 250.

[44] Spivak, 'Can the Subaltern Speak?'.

[45] Spence, *Narrative Truth and Historical Truth*.

at chronological and factual coherence, at an accurate and generalizable version of events. Narrative truth represents the meaning of an individual's experience. The narrative truth of a story is true for the person who tells it, and in that respect, reveals something important about the speaker. This type of truth is deeply personal; it expresses a subject's own vision of the world.

Literary theorists have invoked the distinction between narrative and historical truth to describe competing witness testimonies about the Holocaust and South African apartheid.[46] Scholars explain that telling one's story helps to empower survivors of mass violence. They also argue that narrative truth grounds a new kind of storytelling. Merging Spivak's insight into subjectivity with Spence's writing on memory, Aleida Assmann and others have begun to establish witnessing as a distinct genre of discourse.[47] Unlike other forms of speech, such as legal testimony or history, witnessing does not aspire to factual truth. Instead, this narrative form involves telling an individual story for its own sake.

This approach to narrative changes the purpose of academic writing. Assmann explains, 'the question to be asked is no longer merely what has happened, but also how was the event *experienced*, how is it *remembered* and *passed on*...?'.[48] This question shifts analysis from the 'true' story toward the person telling it. A witness recounts events as she experienced them, and in doing so, constitutes her own identity. Witnessing brings the witness into being; it is a self-creating act. In this respect, witness testimony not only empowers a speaker, but also reveals the stakes of individual identity. Witnessing is a way to think about how people come to conceive of themselves as agents in the world.

[46] See Assmann, 'History, Memory, and the Genre of Testimony'; Lawrence Douglas, *The Memory of Judgment: Making Law and History in the Trials of the Holocaust* (New Haven, CT: Yale University Press, 2001); Elizabeth Kiss, 'Moral Ambition within and beyond Political Constraints: Reflections on Restorative Justice', in Robert Rotberg and Dennis Thompson, eds, *Truth v. Justice: The Morality of Truth Commissions* (Princeton, NJ: Princeton University Press, 2000), pp. 141–57; Minow, *Between Genocide and Forgiveness*; Ruth Teitel, *Transitional Justice* (Oxford: Oxford University Press, 2000).

[47] Assmann, 'History, Memory, and the Genre of Testimony'; Wieviorka, *The Era of Witness*.

[48] Assmann, 'History, Memory, and the Genre of Testimony', p. 261. Emphasis added.

These theories of narrative can enrich prison studies. Eager to acknowledge the interior life of the prison but wary of speaking for its inhabitants, contemporary ethnographers could frame our project as an attempt to witness the penal institution. Criminologists could see and present ourselves as witnesses to the practice of late modern imprisonment and as writers bearing witness to the testimonies of prisoners and staff. This is not simply a semantic shift away from the terms of traditional ethnography. While it certainly involves describing the results of prison studies differently, the concept of witnessing also reconfigures the relationship between prison scholarship and truth. When ethnography is understood as witnessing, the burden to tell an authoritative version of events in the prison, or to explain why the picture we are depicting is not generalizable, diminishes significantly. Such an objective version of the truth is beside the point. Instead, the goal is to portray one version of events behind bars and to focus intellectual attention on the context and implications of that particular portrayal. If ethnography is witnessing, the relevant research question is not whether something is actually true, but why it becomes true and real for a person in a specific situation.

This question is revealing in prison. To take one example from the chapters that follow, I often witnessed prisoners' stories about racist and xenophobic treatment. Many of the foreign nationals I interviewed claimed to have experienced discrimination by staff, fellow prisoners, or both. These claims raise methodological questions about the nature of truth. It is certainly true, in an historical sense, that racism and xenophobia exist in the penal estate. It is also true, this time in a narrative sense, that prisoners invoke ideas about race and nationality to give force and meaning to their claims of injustice. The ambiguity of truth could catalyse a long inquiry into the veracity of particular prisoners' stories. An ethnographer could spend considerable time asking whether prisoners' accounts of racism were in fact true and whether it was ethical to include them in a prison study. Alternatively, and perhaps more fruitfully, prison scholars can ask how and why the concepts of race and nation become such potent metaphors in prisoners' narratives of their incarceration. Why does the treatment prisoners receive register to them as racism or xenophobia? How do ideas about race and nation shape prisoners' perceptions of themselves? Such questions emerge when scholars understand empirical data as witness testimony worth examining on and in its own terms.

These questions link prisoners' personal experiences to broader concerns about the role that race and nationality play in the operation of justice systems. By focusing on how prisoners choose to tell their stories rather than on whether those stories are representative samples, scholars can provide a fresh account of the relationship between punishment, political discourse, and social history. The content of a term like race, for instance, only becomes clear when scholars ask how that notion circulates in prison and why it divides prisoners in a way that other aspects of identity, such as hair colour or height, do not. In emphasizing narrative structure and diction, criminologists can shift attention from an unattainable objective truth toward the sociological context in which ideas about difference take root. Witnessing offers a new vantage point on old concerns about structural inequality.

Witnessing also better describes what ethnographers are actually doing behind bars. Given security measures and barriers to access, prison research almost never offers a full picture of the penal institution.[49] The practice of empirical research is neither so static nor so universal. Prison scholars gather testimonies from prisoners and staff members where and when we can; we record our critical observations as we see them; and we compile the two to present an account of prison life. That account is a subjective snapshot of imprisonment in a particular institution, not an insider's guide to the way the prison works. Every ethnographic account is shaped by its historical moment and by the researcher's own interests and goals, by what we care to notice within the penal institution and how we choose to recall it once we leave.

The presentation of prisons research ought to acknowledge this contextuality, which exists under even the best research circumstances. Thinking of ethnography as witnessing imprisonment rather than revealing the prison writ large is one way to achieve this goal. The witnessing framework foregrounds the constraints and the particularity of a research environment and highlights the researcher's creative role. An ethnographic witness does not claim to have an exhaustive understanding of all prisons; she has one experience worth retelling. The researcher is an editor of gathered

[49] Some researchers have offered a particularly vivid and in-depth picture of the penal institution. See, e.g. Phillips and Earle, 'Reading Difference Differently?'. Nonetheless, significant barriers to prison access remain, especially for critical criminologists.

testimonies, and crucially, is a witness to imprisonment herself. Witnessing encompasses the dual role that a researcher plays as an author and a witness to others' authorship.

The latter half of this equation is worth emphasizing. Prisons are, by their very nature, places where people are silenced and constrained. Prisoners are given identification numbers in place of their names; their visits with family members are controlled; they are moved without warning, and, at least in my experience, do not often get asked what they think. On the other side of the cell door, prison staff members are also small parts of a large system. 'Civilian' staff and line officers are regularly transferred between institutions and are rarely given a voice in the policies they enact. The prison structurally and often purposefully effaces the voices of its inhabitants. Framing ethnography as witnessing is an attempt to resist this trend.

Witnessing is also the basis for a more global approach to imprisonment. In recent years, social scientists in a range of disciplines have critiqued 'methodological nationalism', a problem introduced in the last lines of Chapter 1.[50] Scholars note that traditional ethnographies tend to overlook the transnational nature of twenty-first-century social relations. Critics of 'nationalist' methods call for 'global ethnographies' less bound to 'particular communities and places'.[51] Witnessing is a means to that end. When ethnography is recast as witnessing, the goal of critical scholarship is less to portray the prison than to present and contextualize testimonies produced by the experience of incarceration. Witnessing unmoors ethnographers from the confines of the prison, and more to the point, from the presuppositions that guide prison practices.

[50] Daniel Chernillo, 'The Critique of Methodological Nationalism: Theory and History', *Thesis Eleven* 106, no. 1 (August 2011): pp. 98–117; see also Martin Albrow, 'Traveling beyond Local Cultures: Socioscapes in a Global City', in John Eade, ed., *Living the Global: Globalization as a Local Process* (New York, NY: Routledge, 1997), pp. 20–36; Arjun Appadurai, 'The Production of Locality', in Richard Fardon, ed., *Counterworks: Managing the Diversity of Knowledge* (London: Routledge, 1995), pp. 204–25; Neil Brenner, 'Beyond State-Centrism? Space, Territoriality, and Geographical Scale in Globalization Studies', *Theory and Society* 28 (1999): pp. 39–78; George Marcus, *Ethnography through Thick and Thin* (Princeton, NJ: Princeton University Press, 1998).

[51] Gille and Ó Riain, 'Global Ethnography', p. 271.

Ultimately, emphasizing prisoners' testimonies challenges the prison's status as a domestic institution. Foreign national prisoners' narratives involve migration from Nigeria, Zimbabwe, and Sri Lanka, family members abroad, and the experience of race in a country with a long history of xenophobia. These testimonies extend well beyond Britain. In recording and reproducing such narratives, researchers can witness the British prison through the many stories that comprise it—stories that begin in China and Jamaica and refuse to stay within the nation's borders. By focusing on testimony, scholars can describe prisons without assuming a nationalist frame. We can also advance a critique of the nation-state grounded in its own institutions. This proved to be a productive and challenging way to think about my own research.

Witnessing Imprisonment

My fieldwork focused on men's prisons in northern, central, and south-eastern England. Over the course of twelve months, I interviewed prisoners and staff in five different penal institutions: HMP Woodhill, HMP Bullingdon, HMP Risley, HMP Canterbury, and HMP Manchester. These prisons capture some of the variety in the British penal estate.

Built in 1992, HMP Woodhill is one of eight Category A (high-security) facilities in England and Wales. Woodhill is located in Milton Keynes, in the centre of the country. The prison holds both male adults and juvenile prisoners and has a separate close supervision wing for prisoners deemed to be the most 'disruptive'. At any given time, Woodhill can incarcerate up to 819 prisoners, approximately 115 (14 per cent) of whom were foreign nationals at the time of my research. As Chapter 3 describes more fully, the British penal estate currently operates under a system in which certain prisons, known as hubs, are 'embedded' with full-time immigration staff.[52] The remaining prisons, which are called spokes, have less frequent contact with immigration personnel. HMP Woodhill is a spoke prison, which UK Border Agency representatives visited once a month during my fieldwork.

[52] Along with the term 'civilian' staff, this is an example of a militarized prison discourse that Chapters 3 and 7 examine in more detail.

HMP Risley is a hub prison, which means that immigration staff members work in the facility full-time to identify foreign nationals for deportation. Risley, which is in north-west England, opened in 1964 and today has an operating capacity of 1,085. The prison is designated as a Category C (low-security) training facility for men. It holds a number of 'vulnerable' prisoners, which typically means sex offenders, and is unusual in having mainly single-occupancy cells. Like Risley, HMP Bullingdon is a Category C prison, although it has an additional function as a Category B (medium-security) facility for prisoners on remand from local courts. Bullingdon is located in Oxfordshire and was built in 1992. It is a spoke prison that can hold up to 1,114 prisoners in its six housing units.[53]

The last two prisons I visited are the oldest and largest, respectively, in this study. Constructed in 1808 near Britain's south-east border, HMP Canterbury had an operating capacity of 304 when I visited it in 2010. In a twist that drove home the ephemerality of prison research, Canterbury closed for good in 2013 and became the grounds for a university a year later. At the time of my fieldwork, Canterbury was one of three 'dedicated foreign national only' prisons, which are part of Britain's experiment in 'all-foreign' penal institutions.[54] At least in theory, Canterbury held only prisoners who were serving less than five years 'with an expectation of removal' at or before the conclusion of their criminal sentences. When I was there, Canterbury was uniquely devoted to concerns about nationality and citizenship. Chapter 4 examines the culture of this peculiar institution.

HMP Manchester is also distinct, though less for its population than its famous history. Informally known as Strangeways, Manchester originally opened in 1868. More than a century later, in April 1990, it was the site of the largest prison riot in

[53] In HMP Bullingdon I conducted one-on-one interviews with prison officials but not with prisoners and in HMP Risley I interviewed the 'embedded' UKBA agents. In all other facilities, I spoke with both prisoners and staff one-on-one.

[54] When the hubs and spokes system was created in 2009, the only other 'dedicated foreign national prison' was HMP Bullwood Hall. See Ministry of Justice (MoJ) and UK Border Agency (UKBA), *Service Level Agreement to Support the Effective and Speedy Removal of Foreign National Prisoners* (London: MoJ and UKBA, 2009). In 2012, the Prison Service announced that HMP Huntercombe, a Category C men's prison, would be 'reroled' to become an all-foreign national facility.

British history.[55] The British government rebuilt and renamed Manchester after the riots. Today, it is a high-security prison with the capacity for 1,269 prisoners. At any one time, approximately 140 (11 per cent) of the prisoners held in Manchester are foreign nationals.[56]

The differences between these institutions shaped my research. I spent the first six months of my project in HMP Woodhill. Like Strangeways, Woodhill has a 'mixed' national population of both British citizens and foreign nationals. In prisons with such populations, my research typically began in foreign national 'surgeries', meetings in which immigration agents interview prisoners who staff have identified as non-citizens. These meetings occurred monthly at HMP Woodhill, twice a month at HMP Manchester, and less frequently at other prisons. I observed nine surgeries in HMP Woodhill and HMP Manchester over the course of a year.

During each of these surgeries, I joined a line-up of solicitors, border agents, and volunteers who were scheduled to speak to a room of prisoners. When my turn came, I introduced my project and asked for volunteers to participate in a study about the experience of incarceration. Based on prisoners' responses, I returned later for interviews. In sum, I spoke with 166 foreign national prisoners and 32 prison and immigration staff members. Of the 166 prisoner interviews, 81 were in-depth, one-on-one conversations. The others were more informal discussions held in the corner of the surgeries or other quiet spaces. I also interviewed two interpreters the Prison Service had hired to translate for Chinese prisoners.

[55] See Eamonn Carrabine, *Power, Discourse, and Resistance: A Genealogy of the Strangeways Prison Riot* (Aldershot: Ashgate Publishing, 2004); Lord Justice Harry Woolf and Judge Stephen Tumim, *Prison Disturbances April 1990: Report of an Enquiry by the Rt. Hon. Lord Justice Woolf (Part I and II) and His Honor Judge Stephen Tumim (Part III)* (London: Home Office, 1991).

[56] Prison staff told me these statistics on the number of foreign nationals in each prison's population. However, the prison population is extremely fluid and it has been some time since I completed my fieldwork. The number of foreign nationals in any given prison changes from day to day and it is quite possible that these percentages have changed significantly in the last few years. The purpose of including these numbers, given their potential inaccuracy, is to give some sense of how many foreign national prisoners were in each prison at the time of my research.

My research proceeded differently in HMP Canterbury, where all the prisoners were facing deportation. In that facility, I embarked on a relatively straightforward effort to gather individual prisoner and staff testimonies. I did not have to seek out foreign national prisoners in Canterbury, nor did I have to identify staff members who interacted with the non-citizen prisoner population. Instead, the entire prison was a case study in the imprisonment of foreign nationals and I interviewed any prisoners and staff who were interested in participating in my research. Over the course of several weeks, I observed the education, health care, and housing areas of the prison and held five focus groups with small groups of prisoners. I also interviewed prison managers, officers, and many prisoners one-on-one. This was the most condensed period of observation and interviewing in the course of my fieldwork.

My one-on-one interviews with foreign national prisoners were semi-structured. Each interview lasted between forty-five minutes and three hours. These conversations were open-ended—I was interested in what stories prisoners wanted to tell me and tended to let conversations develop on their own. However, each interview began with the same set of questions about prisoners' migration stories:

- Where were you born?
- When did you come to the UK?
- How long have you been in this prison?
- How long have you been incarcerated?
- When were you identified as a foreign national prisoner?
- When do you expect to be released?
- Where do you think you will go after release?

Conversation flowed from these questions. Some prisoners stopped after I asked where they were born and spoke at length about life in their home countries. Others answered my initial questions in quick succession, then focused on the conditions of incarceration, the circumstances of their criminal charges, or their concerns about deportation. Sometimes prisoners asked me if the introductory questions were an interrogation. One man told me, 'you sound like the UKBA'. In other interviews, prisoners seemed relieved to have an outlet for their feelings. No matter how the interviews developed, my last question was almost always, 'if you were writing a report about the experiences of foreign nationals, what would you say?'

Between that question and the start of the interview, I encountered a wide range of narratives. Some prisoners were engaged with the goals of my project and offered me advice. One man suggested that I write 'the life of a cell', a study that examined the stories of many prisoners who had passed through a single prison cell over time. Other prisoners were less interested in my research and more concerned with their cases. Amidst these variations, themes emerged. My interviews almost always covered the emotional experience of incarceration; race relations in the prison; attitudes toward immigration staff and the possibility of deportation; religion; coping mechanisms; family contact and social visits; the meaning of Englishness and Britishness; and the definition of home. Where prisoners did not raise these issues themselves, I asked questions to elicit them:

- Do you think you will be deported?
- What will you do if you are deported?
- How do you make friends within the prison?
- What is race?
- Does race matter inside the prison?
- Is race different here than outside prison?
- How do you cope with the stresses of incarceration?
- What is the biggest challenge to prison life?
- Who is the worst off behind bars?
- What is the difference between British and English?
- Where is home?

I chose these questions to prompt discussions about how conceptions of identity and foreignness shape the experience of incarceration.

Where it was relevant, my interviews with prisoners also included other topics: British colonialism; attitudes toward Islam, terrorism, and the 'War on Terror'; gangs, drug use within the prison; and gender, which surfaced both in terms of the relationships between male prisoners and female staff and in conversations about sex offenders' place in the prisoner hierarchy. The significance of these topics emerged over the course of my interviews rather than at the outset of my project. In one meeting, for example, a prisoner announced to me that being in handcuffs 'made him feel like a terrorist'. That claim prompted a discussion about terrorism and the stereotyping of foreign nationals. In another interview, a man told me that the biggest difference between foreign nationals and

British citizens was that foreigners have fewer connections to the outside community, and as a result, have a harder time finding drugs. We went on to discuss drug use in the prison. Slowly, I realized that these issues, which had not initially struck me as 'foreign national prisoner issues', were related in interesting and important ways to prisoners' perceptions of incarceration. So I began to ask more foreign nationals how they felt about Islam and war, colonialism, drugs, and gender. I took detailed notes during all of these interviews and I transcribed them, along with my personal reflections, as soon as possible after each meeting.

In most cases, my one-on-one interviews with prisoners took place in the small rooms set aside for confidential visits between prisoners and lawyers. In the Category A prisons where I conducted the bulk of my research, furniture was bolted to the floor and I had to press a red button to call prison guards when I finished interviews. The interview rooms usually had two chairs, a table, and windows on all four sides. Prison staff searched and fingerprinted me twice before I got to the rooms and escorted me on the way out. In the Category C prison, in contrast, I wore a personal alarm and wandered freely in the prison's open spaces. In that facility, I walked between art classes, computer courses, and the library interviewing any prisoners who were available to talk. I also observed education classes, toured the medical centre, and walked along the prison wings with a staff member.

The transparent, open qualities of Category A interview rooms—you can see into and out of them from all sides—affected my research experience in unexpected ways. Often, while talking with one prisoner, I saw border agents interviewing another in the next cubicle. Once, I saw a prisoner I had grown to know sign papers agreeing to return to Jamaica. That was the last time I saw him. At another point, I was speaking to a prisoner when I saw a man I had interviewed the week before out of the corner of my eye. He was waiting for his solicitor and had decided to lie on the interview table on his back while he passed the time. When he caught my eye, he had tilted his head back over the edge of the table and was watching me conduct my interview. He stayed like that, staring at me, upside down, for a full fifteen minutes. In moments like these, the experience of being in prison fails to translate onto the page.

Meetings in these security-conscious spaces contrasted with the interviews in places that were more familiar to me. In addition to interviewing prisoners, I spoke with prison staff members, border agents, and prison policymakers in prison governor's offices, Whitehall buildings, and Oxford libraries. In prisons, I met with staff members from both local and national immigration offices, as well as foreign national coordinators, the prison officials responsible for coordinating immigration surgeries. I also interviewed prison line staff, prison doctors, chaplains, librarians, art teachers, safer custody representatives, diversity managers, and volunteers. Those interviews focused on these people's interactions with foreign nationals and their perceptions of the management of the non-citizen prison population. When speaking to border agents, I asked about the new hubs and spokes system and other policies on foreign national prisoners. With doctors and diversity managers, I inquired about the aspects of prison life that were different for them when dealing with non-citizens.

I also met with policymakers from the UK Border Agency and the National Offender Management Service, the two agencies responsible for crafting the British policy on foreign nationals. Over the course of three separate interviews, I spoke with the senior managers who created the hubs and spokes system. I asked those policymakers why the new system had come about and how it had changed the institutions they managed. I also interviewed representatives from Her Majesty's Inspectorate of Prisons, the Independent Monitoring Board, the Prison Ombudsman, and several charities for immigration detainees. In sum, prisoners included, I interviewed 209 people.

Speaking with these people was often difficult. Though it is not consistently depressing or exciting, witnessing imprisonment is always an emotional project. At times, interviewing prisoners is sad; at others, it is frustrating, funny, mundane, or boring. Prisoners, particularly people held indefinitely as immigration detainees, told me harrowing stories, threatened suicide and self-harm, showed me their physical scars, and broke down in tears. One man showed me a suicide note he had given to an immigration agent. Another man, who was just eighteen, started crying as soon as I asked him how he was doing.

That moment illustrated just how odd prisons can be. For reasons that seem unclear in retrospect, I did not reach out and touch that prisoner or say that I was sorry. Perhaps the harshness of the interview room affected me. Perhaps my reaction to his emotions was about my identity as a young woman in a men's prison.

I might—or might not—have touched a crying female prisoner's shoulder. I might have reached toward the man had he looked up at me. Instead, I just sat there silently as he cried. In other interviews, people seemed intensely angry. Several prisoners stood up abruptly, paced around the room, and banged on the tables as they told their stories. Others brushed me off, yelled at me, or explicitly asked for help, which I almost always could not give.

The last of these situations was the most frustrating. It can be demoralizing to hear people's stories, to have them ask for something in return, and to realize that listening is your sole contribution. This was a particularly hard lesson during an interview with one man, who asked to remain anonymous. That man listened as I explained my consent form and then spoke with me for about an hour about his migration from Nigeria. Then, at the end of our interview, his tone changed. He pleaded with me to call his pastor in Nigeria and to make a case for his release. He told me that I was the only one who could help him and that I owed him this help because he had just helped me with my project. In response to the man's requests, I explained my role and its limitations in professional language that seemed sharply disjointed from his emotional plea. That interview ended with me telling the prisoner I could not do anything for him. Several months later, I encountered that same man in a different prison's immigration surgery. Still angry at me, he told the room full of people that I was really 'a spy for the UKBA'.

Witnessing imprisonment is difficult in other ways as well. In many of my interviews, I encountered serious language and cultural barriers and went home exhausted from trying to understand what I had heard. This sort of fieldwork can take a physical toll—I often returned from interviewing irritable or stunned into silence. I did, however, discover that my American accent endeared me to some prisoners as a fellow foreigner. Prisoners found my familiarity with the American prison system interesting and asked me about life in the United States. These moments of overlap helped me to connect. The counterpoint to that commonality was my rather obvious presence as a young white woman in a men's institution, and my perhaps less overt but at times equally significant Jewish surname, which became a topic of conversation and in some cases tension during conversations about religion.

All of these aspects of interviewing informed my research. Prisoners' behaviour toward me, my feelings about them, and the sheer intensity of doing work in this institutional space were important elements of this project. As empirical prison scholars well know, the emotional experience of being in prison becomes a substantive part of witnessing penal power. The affective dimension of incarceration remains the thing I remember most clearly about British prisons. In a sense, the next five chapters are a recollection of my own memories and feelings. While this book ultimately becomes a theoretical reflection on the purpose of late modern incarceration, it is also a personal testimony about the lives I saw, and the life I led, over the past several years.

Conclusion

Empirical scholars debate how much to discuss the affective aspects of our fieldwork.[57] Much empirical writing on the prison does not discuss emotion at all. The mores of academia, and particularly social scientific scholarship, do not include venting about the experience of doing research. Scholars in other disciplines do not typically describe what it is like to pore over archives or spend hours in a library. Perhaps it seems that the same should hold in criminology, that the emotional elements of fieldwork should remain beyond the scope of our reports.

The problem with this approach is that emotions are a window into the way punishment works. The texture of conducting interviews is one of the more 'hidden' aspects of prison ethnography.[58] Chapter 7 explores the implications of this hidden world. That chapter returns to the questions with which this one began—questions about the intersection of theory and practice and the possibility of better integrating the two—to argue that scholars should focus more fully on the affective nature of prison life. For the moment, my claim is simply that interviewing prisoners is an inescapably subjective exercise.

The chapters that follow arrange foreign national prisoners' narratives into distinct sections and coherent themes. In writing these chapters, I organized prisoners' stories and decided what about them was worth retelling. There are many things that prisoners

[57] See, e.g. Bosworth, Campbell, Demby, Ferranti, Santos, 'Doing Prison Research'; Phillips and Earle, 'Reading Difference Differently?': Schlosser, 'Issues in Interviewing Inmates'.

[58] Schlosser, 'Issues in Interviewing Inmates', p. 1500.

told me that I have left out for brevity, that I have chosen to omit, or that I did not comprehend. The last category is particularly troubling. Where I could not fit what prisoners were saying into my understanding of the world, or where I could not translate their language into my own, I left statements out of my account. This feels like an unfair editing practice, one in which my concerns and knowledge come to matter more than they should. It is worth emphasizing, then, that I am a witness, and that while I strive to quote the prisoners I interviewed, I am in the end reporting what made sense to me.

This does not make the story I tell any less true. Coretta Phillips and Rod Earle, two of the most thoughtful prison ethnographers, have argued that the truth of prison life includes those who write about incarceration.[59] According to Phillips and Earle, 'situating ourselves more explicitly within the co-construction of the prison world can provide an opportunity to disrupt the dehumanizing othering that is prison's principal social accomplishment'.[60] Phillips and Earle suggest that there is a politics to acknowledging the researcher's formative role in the creation of meaning in and around penal institutions.[61] This politics is worth echoing and making explicit, for it provides the connection between actual prisons and academic accounts of them. If scholars take the researcher's role in the production of knowledge seriously, there is a natural and necessary transition from what happens inside prisons to what we ask and aim to do in prison studies. The ultimately methodological bent of this book is a political move, a way to insist that scholarly accounts of the prison constitute its purpose and place in society.

Before turning to those politics, Chapter 3 examines why the British government has chosen to treat non-citizens differently than the rest of the prison population. The British approach to foreign national prisoners is the product of a recent prison policy and a century of ambivalence about colonialism. Chapter 3 dives into the fraught context in which foreigners end up behind British bars.

[59] Phillips and Earle, 'Reading Difference Differently?'.
[60] Phillips and Earle, 'Reading Difference Differently?', p. 375.
[61] Phillips and Earle, 'Reading Difference Differently?', p. 375.

3

Hubs and Spokes

The crisis began on 25 April 2006. That morning, Home Secretary Charles Clarke announced that in the preceding seven years more than one thousand foreign nationals had been released from prison without being considered for deportation.[1] Clarke's revelation prompted a media frenzy.[2] For weeks, headlines proclaimed a dangerous crisis: 'Home Office Blunders Left Foreign Rapists in the UK'; 'We May Never Find Foreign Murderers and Rapists'; 'Foreign Prisoners "On the Loose"'.[3] Across the board, news outlets broadcast an urgent national problem. One editorial asked why 'on-the-run convicts', such 'manifest undesirables', were in the country at all.[4] Even the relatively staid

[1] See 'How the Deportation Story Emerged', *BBC News*, 9 October 2006, <http://news.bbc.co.uk/1/hi/uk_ politics/4945922.stm>.

[2] See, e.g. 'Home Office Blunders Left Foreign Rapists in UK', *Daily Mail*, 26 April 2006, <http://www.dailymail.co.uk/news/article-384183/Home-Office-blunders-left-foreign-rapists-UK.html>; 'How the Deportation Story Emerged', *BBC News*; 'It's Not Only the Foreign Criminals Who've Vanished, but also Any Pretence that Britain Controls Its Borders or, Indeed, Its Very Destiny', *Daily Mail*, 26 April 2006, <http://www.dailymail.co.uk/debate/columnists/article-384284/Its-foreign-criminals-whove-vanished-pretence-Britain-controls-borders-destiny.html>; Phillip Johnston, 'We May Never Find Foreign Murderers, Says Home Office', *Telegraph*, 27 April 2006, <http://www.telegraph.co.uk/news/uknews/1516747/We-may-never-find-foreign-murderers-says-Home-Office.html>; Michael Lea, 'Clarke's Bungle Ends in Rape', *The Sun*, 3 August 2007, <http://www.thesun.co.uk/sol/homepage/news/46603/Clarke-bungle-ends-in-rape.html>.

[3] 'Home Office Blunders Left Foreign Rapists in UK', *Daily Mail*; 'It's Not Only the Foreign Criminals Who've Vanished, but also Any Pretence that Britain Controls Its Borders or, Indeed, Its Very Destiny', *Daily Mail*; Johnston, 'We May Never Find Foreign Murderers, Says Home Office', *Telegraph*.

[4] James Slack, 'Why Were on-the-Run Convicts Still Here? Deportation Row over Foreign Nationals Wrongly at Large', *Daily Mail*, 8 July 2009, <http://www.dailymail.co.uk/news/article-1198166/Why-run-convicts-Deportation-row-criminals-wrongly-large.html>.

BBC ran a series of stories describing how 'foreign criminals', notably 'murderers and rapists', had been 'allowed to walk free'.[5] Ten days later, Charles Clarke resigned.

The Home Secretary's dramatic departure provided a superficial conclusion to the crisis. Behind the scenes, however, the scandal continued long after the presses stopped. In the months following Clarke's dismissal, newly minted Home Secretary John Reid, promoted from his position as Defence Secretary, began to restructure both the Prison Service and the Immigration and Nationality Directorate. Vowing to do 'whatever it takes to make the public feel safe', Reid decided to integrate the two agencies involved in the incarceration of non-citizens.[6] His efforts culminated in a broad new policy on foreign national prisoners, which debuted in 2009. Dubbed hubs and spokes, the policy establishes special prisons for non-citizens and deputizes prison staff to act as quasi-immigration agents.[7] It also 'embeds' immigration officials in penal institutions and obliges prison managers to detain prisoners beyond the length of their criminal sentences as immigration detainees.

This chapter asks how such an expansive penal policy came to pass and what it says about the meaning of punishment. How did the hubs and spokes system develop from a short-lived political scandal? How do policies on non-citizens affect the purpose of the prison? These questions guide the chapter, which proceeds from an account of the scandal to an assessment of its aftermath in penal practice. Ultimately, the story of hubs and spokes illustrates the rocky relationship—at once codependent and conflicted—between criminal and immigration law. The new policy on non-citizen prisoners also highlights a growing gap between prisons and the concept of punishment.

In focusing on the minutia of the hubs and spokes policy, this chapter wrestles with a question about how to describe migration control. In recent years, criminologists and legal scholars have documented the criminalization of immigration, a trend that has

[5] 'Foreign Criminals "Not Deported"', *BBC News*, 25 April 2006, <http://news.bbc.co.uk/1/hi/uk_politics/4942886.stm>.

[6] 'Reid Vowing to Make Britain Safer', *BBC News*, 24 May 2006, <http://news.bbc.co.uk/2/hi/uk_news/politics/5010918.stm>.

[7] Ministry of Justice (MoJ) and UK Border Agency (UKBA), *Service Level Agreement to Support the Effective and Speedy Removal of Foreign National Prisoners* (London: MoJ and UKBA, 2009).

earned its own portmanteau, crimmigration.[8] Scholars invoke the term 'crimmigration' to explain not only the passage of laws that make undocumented migration a criminal offence—literal criminalization—but also the expansion of criminal justice methods and machinery beyond the realm of the criminal law.[9] Used in the latter sense, crimmigration is a common way to discuss the growth of immigration detention centres and, especially in the United States, the intensification of border policing.

This chapter explores the limits of the crimmigration framework, and in particular, the degree to which it fails to capture the prison's role in the dynamic it seeks to describe. In the last decade, the term 'crimmigration' has become a shorthand way to acknowledge the collusion of crime and border control. While useful, this shorthand can flatten and obscure the penal institution. Laws and policies on migration have not only exported the imagery of criminal justice out of courts, jails, and prisons. They have also imported a certain attitude towards citizenship into the prison, changing its basic purpose. This chapter examines that importation process. I argue that the crimmigration paradigm stalls inquiry into the legal, political, and social transformations taking place in late modern prisons.

[8] Juliet Stumpf, 'The Crimmigration Crisis: Immigrants, Crime, and Sovereign Power', *American University Law Review* 56, no. 2 (2006): pp. 367–419; see also Mary Bosworth and Emma Kaufman, 'Foreigners in a Carceral Age: Immigration and Imprisonment in the United States', *Stanford Law and Policy Review* 22, no. 1 (May 2011): pp. 429–54; Maggy Lee, 'Human Trade and the Criminalization of "Irregular Migration"', *International Journal of the Sociology of Law* 33, no. 1 (March 2005): pp. 1–15; Lucia Zedner, 'Security, the State, and the Citizen: The Changing Architecture of Crime Control', *New Criminal Law Review* 13, no. 2 (Spring 2010): pp. 379–403.

[9] See, e.g. Stumpf, 'The Crimmigration Crisis'; see also Mary Bosworth, 'Human Rights and Immigration Detention Within the United Kingdom', in Marie-Benedicte Dembour and Tobias Kelly, eds, *Are Human Rights for Migrants? Critical Reflections on the Status of Irregular Migrants in Europe and the United States* (Abingdon: Routledge Press, 2011), pp. 165–73; Arjen Leerkes and Dennis Broeders, 'A Case of Mixed Motives? Formal and Information Functions of Administrative Immigration Detention', *British Journal of Criminology* 50, no. 5 (Sept. 2010): pp. 830–50. On the issue of policing the United States border, see Wendy Brown, *Walled States, Waning Sovereignty* (Cambridge, MA: Zone Books, 2010).

The Crisis

The foreign national prisoner crisis was a half-decade ordeal. Nearly a year before it surfaced in tabloids, the scandal commenced relatively quietly in July 2005, when the National Audit Office (NAO), an independent government spending watchdog, published a sixty-page report on the return of failed asylum applicants.[10] The NAO's attention to this issue was not particularly notable at the time. Asylum, and especially so-called bogus refugees, had been a topic of intense debate in the United Kingdom since the early 1990s, when the collapse of the Soviet Union and European integration propelled a wave of migration from Eastern Europe.[11] By 2005, publishing a study critical of asylum policy did not make headlines.

A small section of the report, however, came as a surprise to some in the Home Office.[12] In a few paragraphs devoted to the disposition of criminal cases, the NAO noted that immigration authorities could not provide statistics on the number of foreign nationals who had been released from prison because 'removal could not be arranged'.[13] The report suggested, in other words, that some prisoners who could have been deported were instead released. This claim provoked a mild public reaction from Prime Minister Tony Blair, who announced an investment of £3 million in the management of failed asylum seekers.[14] The NAO report also caught

[10] National Audit Office (NAO), *Returning Failed Asylum Applicants* (London: NAO, 2005).

[11] See Matthew J. Gibney, 'Asylum and the Expansion of Deportation in the United Kingdom', *Government and Opposition* 43, no. 2 (Spring 2008): pp. 146–67.

[12] Those surprised by the NAO report included the Home Secretary. According to a BBC report from 2006, Charles Clarke 'admitted that his attention was first brought to the problem [of released foreign national prisoners] on publication of this report'. 'How the Deportation Story Emerged', *BBC News*.

[13] NAO, *Returning Failed Asylum Applicants*, p. 13.

[14] 'How the Deportation Story Emerged', *BBC News*. Blair's investment capitalized on the claim, oft articulated prior to his re-election, that deportation should be a cornerstone of New Labour migration policy. For accounts of this claim, see Nyta Mann, 'Blair's Asylum Gamble', *BBC News*, 7 February 2003, <http://newswww.bbc.net.uk/2/hi/uk_news/politics/2738065.stm>; Zedner, 'Security, the State, and the Citizen'. In this context, the NAO report provided an opportunity for Blair to fulfil a campaign promise.

the attention of Conservative MP Richard Bacon, representative for the constituency neighbouring Home Secretary Charles Clarke's Norwich South. Bacon, who was at the time running for re-election, caught wind of 'the foreign criminal issue' several months after the NAO published its study.[15] Five months before the local elections, he questioned the Home Secretary's leadership in a statement to the press.[16] Bacon then announced to the BBC that he had 'set in motion a whole set of procedures to change the way the Prison Service and the Nationality Directorate were working'.[17]

This effort gained steam and publicity a month later when Yusuf and Mustaf Jama, two brothers from Somalia, were charged with murdering Police Constable Sharon Beshenivsky during an armed robbery. Beshenivsky's murder generated an enormous amount of press coverage, fueling public debates over asylum and imprisonment.[18] Both of the Jama brothers had been granted asylum in the United Kingdom; one, Mustaf, had been released from prison six months prior to the robbery. Mustaf Jama escaped arrest by dressing in a niqab and using his sister's passport to fly to Somalia. He evaded arrest for nearly two years before the British government arranged his capture in Somalia and brought him to the United Kingdom.[19] This dramatic turn of events—the murder of a female

[15] Public Accounts Committee (PAC), *Hearing of Commons Committee of Public Accounts, Thirty-Fourth Report of Session 2005–6, HC 620* (London: PAC, 2006).

[16] 'How the Deportation Story Emerged', *BBC News*.

[17] 'How the Deportation Story Emerged', *BBC News*.

[18] See Sam Greenhill, Michael Seamark, and Paul Sims, 'The Killer Asylum Seekers', *Daily Mail*, 19 December 2006, <http://www.dailymail.co.uk/news/article-423813/The-killer-asylum-seekers.html>; Phillip Johnston, 'Veil Escape "Exposes Chaos in Border Controls"', *Telegraph*, 21 December 2006, <http://www.telegraph.co.uk/news/uknews/1537514/Veil-escape-exposes-chaos-in-border-controls.html>.

[19] Mustaf Jama's capture was a coordinated effort between the Home Office, the Foreign and Commonwealth Office, a Somali militia, and the West Yorkshire police. The militia stopped Jama in Somalia; he was then flown to Dubai, where members of the West Yorkshire police met him. The cost of the operation was shared between the Home Office and Foreign Office, which paid for the Somali operation, and the West Yorkshire police, who bought his Virgin flight to London. 'Sharon Beshenivsky Suspect Is Captured in Somalia and Flown to Britain', *The Somaliland Times*, 7 November 2007, <http://somalilandtimes.net/sl/2007/302/40.shtml>; see also Michael Black, 'Killer Snatched in Desert', *Telegraph & Argus*, 22 July 2009, <http://www.thetelegraphandargus.co.uk/news/4507490.Killer_snatched_in_desert/>. Jama was convicted of Beshenivsky's murder after being captured. He

police officer, followed by an escape involving cross-dressing in a religious veil and a secret paramilitary operation—raises questions about British attitudes towards race, gender, religion, and international policing. During the spring of 2006, the Jama case also bolstered Richard Bacon's campaign.

In the midst of the public search for Mustaf Jama, referred to in the press as 'Britain's Most Wanted Man' and the 'the killer asylum seeker', Bacon repeatedly pressed the Home Office for information on the release of foreign national prisoners.[20] His efforts landed him re-election, and ultimately, the title 'Backbencher of the Year'.[21] They also precipitated the Home Secretary's announcement to the press, which pre-empted the next day's parliamentary hearing on the issue. Nine days after that announcement, and just one day after Labour's poor showing in the local elections, the Prime Minister dismissed Charles Clarke. In tendering his resignation, the Home Secretary presented the failure to consider foreign national prisoners for deportation as a problem of dysfunctional bureaucracy. 'The issue is not people going free', Clarke explained, but rather 'getting the various aspects of our operation functioning properly'.[22]

The media saw it differently. In contrast to Clarke, many headlines framed the release of the foreign nationals as an urgent threat to public safety.[23] Most accounts of the scandal, including the one

is serving a life sentence in England. Andrew Norfolk, 'Beshenivsky Killer Mustaf Jama Captured in Secret Somalia Operation', *The Times*, 23 July 2009, <http://www.thetimes.co.uk/tto/news/uk/crime/article1876768.ece>.

[20] Greenhill, Seamark, and Sims, 'The Killer Asylum Seekers'; Norfolk, 'Beshenivsky Killer Mustaf Jama Captured in Secret Somalia Operation'.

[21] 'Bacon Named as Backbencher of the Year', *Richard Bacon MP*, 19 July 2006, <http://www.richardbacon.org. uk/parl/backbencher_060719.html>.

[22] 'In Quotes: Clarke and Deportation', *BBC News*, 26 April 2006, <http://news.bbc.co.uk/1/hi/uk_politics/4945736.stm >.

[23] See 'Foreign Criminals "Not Deported"', *BBC News*; 'Home Office Blunders Left Foreign Rapists in UK', *Daily Mail*; Johnston, 'Veil Escape "Exposes Chaos in Border Controls"'; Slack, 'Why Were on-the-Run Convicts Still Here?'. The distinction between Clarke's articulation of the issue and its presentation in the media reflects a persistent tension between populist visions of crime control and what Ian Loader calls platonic guardianship, a notion of governance in which crime is managed by expert bureaucrats. Ian Loader, 'Fall of the "Platonic Guardians": Liberalism, Criminology and Political Reponses to Crime in England and Wales', *British Journal of Criminology* 46, no. 4 (Oct. 2005): pp. 561–86.

penned by the Home Office, adopted the choice term 'foreign criminal' to describe the released prisoners.[24] As Hindpal Bhui notes, this language 'conjure[s] up over-dramatic and frightening "underworld" images' to distinguish a largely unexceptional group in the prison population.[25] The Home Office's own statistics suggest that rates of recidivism and violent offences among foreign nationals are either comparable to or lower than those of British nationals.[26] Of the 1,023 foreign nationals that were released under Charles Clarke's watch, only 36 had committed offences classified as 'most serious'.[27] Moreover, when they are released into Britain, foreign nationals are subject to the same probation and other supervision arrangements as British citizens. Nevertheless, the coverage of Clarke's dismissal proclaimed—or as Stuart Hall would remind us, created—a widespread crisis of governance.[28]

This crisis overshadowed Clarke's resignation and laid the groundwork for an aggressive response from a New Labour government keen to assert its seriousness about both crime and border control. In the wake of the scandal, the British government made a series of public overtures. First, it petitioned the European Court of Human Rights to reconsider the absolute ban on deporting people to countries where they could face torture or death.[29] The Blair

[24] See Home Office, *A Review of the Failure of the Immigration & Nationality Directorate to Consider some Foreign National Prisoners for Deportation* (London: HMSO, 2007).

[25] Hindpal Bhui, 'Alien Experience: Foreign National Prisoners after the Deportation Crisis', *Probation Journal* 54, no. 4 (December 2007): p. 379.

[26] See, e.g. Ministry of Justice (MoJ), *Offender Management Caseload Statistics 2009* (London: Ministry of Justice, 2010).

[27] In the Prison Service lexicon, 'most serious' offenders are people convicted of murder, manslaughter, rape, and child sex offences. See John Vine, *Thematic Inspection of How the UK Border Agency Manages Foreign National Prisoners: February–May 2011* (London: HMSO, 2012): p. 7.

[28] See Stuart Hall, Chas Critcher, Tony Jefferson, John N. Clark, and Brian Roberts, *Policing the Crisis: Mugging, the State, and Law and Order* (London: Palgrave MacMillan, 1978).

[29] 'UK Seeks Human Rights Law Review', *BBC News*, 20 May 2006, <http://news.bbc.co.uk/2/hi/uk_news/politics/5000238.stm>. The European Court of Human Rights' ban on deportation to countries that condone torture became UK law in the 1998 Human Rights Act. As Lucia Zedner notes, that ban was 'portrayed in the media as a charter for foreign criminals and terrorists' throughout the foreign prisoner scandal. Zedner, 'Security, the State, and the Citizen', p. 383. The government sought to have the ban lifted in late May of 2006, just two weeks after Clarke's dismissal.

administration then invested more money in the 'problem' of failed asylum seekers and Parliament passed legislation expanding the use of deportation for foreign national prisoners.[30] The government also initiated a transformation of the British bureaucratic machinery.

The internal response to the foreign national prisoner scandal extended the 'crisis' far beyond its origins in an East Anglian election. In the weeks after Clarke left office, new Home Secretary John Reid introduced a number of changes to the Prison Service and the Immigration and Nationality Directorate. Reid began by formally separating the two agencies, placing prisons under the Ministry of Justice and immigration under the Home Office.[31] He then released an 'eight point plan of action' encouraging the newly distinct arms of government to prioritize the management of non-citizens.[32] Among other things, Reid's plan instructed agencies to 'make it an obligation for suspects and criminals to declare their nationality'.[33] The plan also ordered all government officials

[30] For a description of the response from the Blair administration, see 'How the Deportation Story Emerged', *BBC News*. For relevant legislation, see the UK Borders Act 2007. Under this Act, all non-citizen prisoners are automatically considered for deportation, while non-European nationals sentenced to at least one year and European Economic Area (EEA) nationals sentenced to at least two years face mandatory deportation. These sentence lengths—one year for non-European nationals and two years for EEA nationals—are both cumulative and retroactive. This means, for instance, that a non-European foreign national with a prior record of nine months in prison would face 'removal' based on a three-month sentence, regardless of when the original nine months was served. In addition to establishing these criteria for deportation, the Borders Act also provides immigration officers with police powers of detention, search, and seizure and introduces compulsory biometric residence permits for non-EU immigrants. For further accounts of this legislation, see Mary Bosworth and Mhairi Guild, 'Governing through Migration Control: Security and Citizenship in Britain', *British Journal of Criminology* 48, no. 6 (Fall 2008): p. 715; Gibney, 'Asylum and the Expansion of Deportation in the United Kingdom'; see also Elinor Harper and Steve Symonds, *Borders, Citizenship and Immigration Act 2009: Ministerial Statements, Prepared for the Immigration Law Practitioners' Association* (London: ILPA, 2009).

[31] Reid's reformulation also placed probation services under the Ministry of Justice and policing under the Home Office.

[32] Her Majesty's Prison Service (HMPS), *Prison Service Instruction 21/2007: Immigration and Foreign Nationals in Prison (Amended Version)* (London: MoJ, 2007); see also 'Immigration System Unfit—Reid', *BBC News*, 23 May 2006, <http://news.bbc.co.uk/1/hi/uk_politics/5007148.stm>.

[33] 'Immigration System Unfit—Reid', *BBC News*.

to 'audit-trail' any policy related to deportation and to facilitate the early return of incarcerated foreign nationals.

Reid's directive led to a trio of new prison policies on non-citizens. The most notable was Prison Service Order (PSO) 4630, the first British prison regulation to engage with immigration in explicit terms.[34] PSO 4630 defined the term 'foreign national' and outlined an expanded relationship, based largely on data collection and information sharing, between the Prison Service and the Nationality Directorate. In formalizing communication between prison and immigration staff, the policy officially introduced the demands of migration control into the prison estate. It also reversed the Prison Service's stance on foreign national prisoners. Prior to the 2006 scandal, the Prison Service maintained that there was no need for formal guidance on foreign national prisoners, whose treatment fell under existing policies on race relations. Despite public calls for such guidance, including a 2004 report in which Her Majesty's Inspectorate of Prisons noted 'an institutional blind spot for foreign nationals within the Prison Service', prison officials insisted that concerns about the treatment of foreigners were coextensive with concerns about race.[35] The Prison Service changed course with the publication of PSO 4630.

The Home Secretary's emphasis on 'foreign offenders' also prompted broad shifts inside the Nationality Directorate. In the months following Reid's appointment, the Immigration and Nationality Directorate officially became the Border and

[34] Her Majesty's Prison Service (HMPS), *Prison Service Order 4630: Immigration and Foreign Nationals in Prison* (London: MoJ, 2006). Other policies addressing 'performance indicators' related to nationality accompanied PSO 4630. See, e.g. Her Majesty's Prison Service (HMPS), *Prison Service Order 7100: Key Performance Indicators, Key Performance Targets and Additional Measures* (London: MoJ, 2007). PSO 4630 was amended several times after its release in 2006, and in November 2011 was replaced with a new Prison Service Instruction (PSI) with similar aims. See Her Majesty's Prison Service (HMPS), *Prison Service Instruction 52/2011: Immigration, Repatriation, and Removal Services* (London: MoJ, 2011).

[35] HMIP, *Annual Report of HM Chief Inspector of Prisons for England and Wales 2002–2003* (London: HMIP, 2004); see also Hindpal Singh Bhui, *Going the Distance: Developing Effective Policy and Practice with Foreign National Prisoners* (London: Prison Reform Trust, 2004). Bhui describes the Prison Service's resistance to publication of a stand-alone policy on nationality prior to the 2006 scandal. My interviews with Prison Service officials confirmed the account in Bhui's report.

Immigration Agency (BIA), a title that would last a year before it changed again, to the UK Border Agency (UKBA).[36] The newly named BIA then introduced the Facilitated Returns Scheme (FRS), a programme intended to increase deportation rates. Debuted in tandem with a target number of annual 'removals', FRS incentivizes deportation by providing cash and grants to non-European prisoners who 'volunteer' to leave the country.[37] This scheme accounted for one third of the total deportations in 2009 and almost half of the deportations in 2010. Each year, it saves the Prison Service £18 million and costs the Border Agency £7–10 million.[38] As of 2011, FRS opened up an average of 500 new prison beds each month.[39] The creation of FRS aimed to relieve what one high-ranking Border Agency official called the 'huge political pressure around the numbers of foreign national prisoners'.

That pressure contributed to the Border Agency's budget. In the aftermath of John Reid's appointment as Home Secretary, the BIA began to redirect resources to its Criminal Casework Directorate (CCD), the division responsible for managing prisoners with open immigration cases. By 2008, two years after the scandal, CCD's

[36] Throughout this book, I refer to the Border Agency using whatever name it had at the time. In 2013, the government split the UKBA in two and renamed it, yet again. However, reports suggest that the agency continues to operate in largely the same manner under Theresa May. See, e.g. 'U. K. Border Agency to Be Abolished, Theresa May Announces', *The Guardian*, 26 March 2013, <http://www.theguardian.com/uk/2013/mar/26/uk-border-agency-broken-up?guni=Article:in%20body%20link>.

[37] See HMPS, *Prison Service Instruction 21/2007*. The Facilitated Returns Scheme is only available to foreign national prisoners who are not citizens of nation-states within the European Economic Area. Both the *Vine Report* and my interviews with policymakers reveal that the scheme has changed slightly since its debut in 2007. See the *Vine Report*, pp. 11–12. As of 1 October 2010, the grants offered to foreign nationals who agree to their own 'removal' have gotten smaller. Originally, prisoners were offered £5,000 to return to their 'home' countries, with a small portion as cash up front and the rest upon arrival. That number shifted to £1,500 for serving prisoners and £750 for those who have completed their criminal sentences.

[38] According to the *Vine Report*, the Facilitated Returns Scheme (FRS) accounted for 49 per cent of the total 5,235 deportations in 2010 and 30 per cent of the total 5,530 deportations in 2009. That report also states that FRS cost the Border Agency £7.1 million (including £2.3 million of EU funding) in the 2009–2010 fiscal year and cost a projected £9.7 million (including £2.7 million of EU finding) in the 2010–2011 fiscal year. *Vine Report*, pp. 11–12.

[39] *Vine Report*, p. 3.

budget had increased by £40 million.[40] This 'very significant injection of resources from elsewhere in the organization' propelled a bureaucratic inflation: in the wake of the scandal, CCD grew to thirty-five times its original size.[41] The problem of foreign prisoners thus created its own solution in the form of a dramatically expanded state apparatus for finding and deporting non-citizens. As one Border Agency official put it, 'this organization grew out of crisis'.

The crisis also catalysed a new relationship between once-estranged state agencies. In response to Reid's eight-point plan, the Prison Service and the Border Agency not only recalibrated their own internal operations. The two agencies also entered into a long—and by all accounts tense—series of negotiations about how to work together to handle the 'problem' of non-citizen prisoners. Over the course of three years, from 2006 to 2009, Border Agency officials met with their counterparts at the National Offender Management Service, the umbrella agency that includes prisons and probation. The meetings led to a joint operating agreement, which took effect in June of 2009 and leaked to the press shortly thereafter.[42] Referred to as hubs and spokes, the agreement set out the terms for enhanced communication between prison and immigration officials. It also reorganized the penal estate around the concept of foreignness.

At least in theory, the hubs and spokes agreement creates a panoptic model for the management of incarcerated foreign nationals. Under the new policy, non-citizens, who make up around 14 per cent of the total prison population, are concentrated in particular prisons known as hubs.[43] Hub prisons are geographically

[40] Ministry of Justice (MoJ), *Letter from Maria Eagle, MP, to Mr John Shine, Chair of the Independent Monitoring Board*, 20 September 2007, p. 2.

[41] MoJ and UKBA, *Service Level Agreement*; MoJ, *Letter from Maria Eagle, MP.*

[42] MoJ and UKBA, *Service Level Agreement.*

[43] See MoJ and UKBA, *Service Level Agreement.* For statistics, see MoJ, *Offender Management Caseload Statistics 2009*; see also Bhui, *Going the Distance*; Bhui, 'Alien Experience'; *Vine Report.* When the hubs and spokes agreement was drafted, the hub prisons were: HMP Risley; HMP Hewell; HMP Morton Hall; HMP The Mount; HMP The Verne; HMP Wandsworth; and HMP Wormwood Scrubs. Morton Hall, which became a prison for women in 1996, was reroled in May 2011 as a men's immigration detention centre. It is now jointly operated by the Prison Service and the UK Border Agency. For a full list of the

distributed across England and Wale and each is 'embedded' with full-time immigration staff members, who communicate with caseworkers in the UKBA's Criminal Casework Directorate.[44] The remaining prisons, which are known as spokes, hold fewer non-citizens and receive fewer visits from immigration officials. The hubs and spokes agreement also created two 'dedicated foreign national-only prisons', which are supposed to hold prisoners facing deportation who are within five years of the end of their criminal sentences.[45] As a whole, the new policy redistributed the prison population according to nationality. This redistribution involved hundreds of prisoner transfers, many of which took place overnight the day after the policy took effect.[46]

In addition to shuffling the penal population, the hubs and spokes policy laid out detailed guidelines for the relationship between prison and immigration employees. Among those guidelines is a mandate: in prisons not staffed with immigration officials, prison guards are obliged to identify and refer all foreign nationals to the UKBA. The Border Agency builds from those referrals to determine which foreign nationals will face deportation.[47] The hubs and spokes policy thus inaugurated an inter-agency effort to identify the non-citizens in British prisons. The new policy also

original hub, spoke, and non-spoke prisons, see the Service Level Agreement between UKBA and NOMS. MoJ and UKBA, *Service Level Agreement.*

[44] MoJ and UKBA, *Service Level Agreement*, p. 9.

[45] At the time of the hubs and spokes agreement, the two 'dedicated foreign national only prisons' were HMP Canterbury and HMP Bullwood Hall. See MoJ and UKBA, *Service Level Agreement.* HMP Huntercombe has since become a dedicated foreign national prison, while HMP Canterbury has closed.

[46] These transfers were challenged under the Race Relations Act of 1976, but were ultimately upheld in court. See *R (On the Application of the Equality and Human Rights Commission) v. Secretary of State for Justice* [2010] EWHC 147, [2010] All ER (D) 198.

[47] In determining whether a prisoner will be deported, UK Border Agency caseworkers follow the guidelines of the 2007 UK Borders Act. These guidelines determine which prisoners will face deportation, but they do not dictate which prisoners will ultimately be deported. Often, prisoners identified for deportation under these guidelines are released into the United Kingdom at the conclusion of their sentences, either because they qualify for temporary leave to remain or because they cannot be deported due to human rights restrictions or a failure to procure travel documents from the country of origin.

required prisons to 'maximize' the detention estate by holding some ex-prisoners as immigration detainees.[48]

This last requirement is the most contentious one among prison staff, and at least in terms of legal trends, is one of the most notable aspects of hubs and spokes. According to the new policy, the Prison Service is expected to hold time-served immigration detainees—that is, prisoners facing deportation whose criminal sentences have expired—until they are released, transferred to one of the UKBA's detention centres, or 'removed' from the United Kingdom.[49] Ex-prisoners are held in prisons under civil rather than criminal powers and their detention is indefinite so long as there is a 'reasonable prospect' of their removal.[50] This ambiguous legal standard has enabled detention 'pending deportation' for upward of five years.[51] Unlike countries such as the United States, Britain has no time period after which detention becomes presumptively unreasonable.[52] In this respect, Britain sits at the harsh end of immigration law.

[48] *Vine Report*, p. 9. Prisons have long been used to detain people both pre- and post-sentence. The Service Level Agreement between the UKBA and NOMS does not inaugurate this practice, but rather condones it in explicit terms.

[49] MoJ and UKBA, *Service Level Agreement*, p. 9.

[50] Specifically, time-served prisoners are detained in prisons under what are known as IS 91 Detention Holds. The authority to hold deportees under such orders stems from the 1971 Immigration Act, Schedule 3, Para 2(3) (UK).

[51] In theory, the UKBA has the power to detain foreign national prisoners indefinitely in Immigration Removal Centres or prisons 'for the purpose of removing them from the UK'. *Vine Report*, p. 19. While this power to detain is not limited to a specific timescale, detention is only lawful where there is a 'reasonable prospect' of removal within a 'reasonable timescale'. *R v. Governor of Durham Prison, Ex parte, Hardial Singh* [1983] Imm AR 198, [1984] 1 All ER 983; see also the *Vine Report*, p. 19. Several prisoners have challenged their post-sentence detention within the prison, arguing that it constitutes a form of false imprisonment. See, e.g. *Lumba (WL) (Congo) v. Secretary of State for the Home Department* [2011] UKSC 12, [2011] All ER (D) 262; *AP (Trinidad and Tobago) v. Secretary of State for the Home Department* [2011] EWCA Civ 551, [2011] All ER (D) 108; *RU (Bangladesh) v. Secretary of State for the Home Department* [2011] EWCA Civ 651, [2011] All ER (D) 38.

[52] See the cases cited in note 51 for examples of the British context, where courts have upheld indefinite detention for periods of up to six years. After a landmark decision by the American Supreme Court, the presumptive limit on indefinite detention in the United States is six months. See *Zadvydas v. Davis*, 533 U.S. 678 (2001).

The number of detainees held in British prisons is notoriously difficult to find. Despite publishing a slew of other statistics, neither the Prison Service nor the UKBA reports how many detainees are held in penal institutions. The hubs and spokes agreement, which was penned between 2006 and 2009, set the target number for 'time-served prisoners' at 200.[53] As of March 2011, the actual number of detainees in prisons was, according to one prison official, 'over 600'. In early 2012, the UKBA published a report that placed the number of imprisoned detainees at 760, and in 2013, reports listed the figure as 1,500.[54] If these figures are accurate, roughly half of all ex-prisoners who become immigration detainees are held in prisons rather than detention centres.[55] This statistic

[53] MoJ and UKBA, *Service Level Agreement*, p. 5.

[54] The *Vine Report, Thematic Inspection of How the UK Border Agency Manages Foreign National Prisoners*, p. 19; see also Matt Chorley, 'Revealed: British Prisons Holding 1,500 Foreign Offenders Beyond the End of their Sentence because They Can't Be Sent Home', *Daily Mail*, 15 January 2013, <http://www.dailymail.co.uk/news/article-2262791/Revealed-British-prisons-holding-1-500-foreign-offenders-end-sentence-sent-home.html>. The *Vine Report*, which was published in 2012 by the Chief Inspector of the UK Border Agency, is the first official document in some time to state the number of ex-prisoners held under immigration powers in British prisons. The fact that this number is well above the agreed-upon performance target of 200 ex-prisoners in the penal estate raises a series of questions. It is unclear whether that performance target still holds weight within the Prison Service and the UKBA, or indeed if it ever did. Moreover, it is not clear from interviews or published documents whether the detention of ex-prisoners within prisons is a growing trend or if the numbers have always been well above 200. Border Agency and Prison Service representatives were reticent to discuss this statistic, which suggests that they acknowledged, at least in part, the legal and political problems surrounding the indefinite detention of ex-prisoners in British prisons.

[55] To be clear, this statistic refers only to the number of *ex-prisoners* who are detained under immigration powers, not to the total number of immigration detainees in the United Kingdom. In January 2011, at the time of my fieldwork, the UK Border Agency was detaining 1,667 ex-prisoner foreign nationals. Of those 1,667 detained ex-prisoners, 907 (54 per cent) were detained in immigration removal centres (IRCs) and 760 were detained in prisons. At that time the total number of detainees, many of whom do not have criminal records, was close to 3,000. *Vine Report*, p. 19. The most recent statistics on this prison population come from a National Audit Office report, which stated in October 2014 that '[a]bout 1,400 [ex-prisoners] are detained in prison or an immigration removal centre. ...' National Audit Office (NAO), *Managing and Removing Foreign National Offenders* (London: NAO, 2014), p. 35. The report does not clarify how many of those 1,400 people are held in prisons as opposed to detention centres.

hints at how central the penal estate is to the project of immigration detention.

The indefinite detention of hundreds of ex-prisoners in British prisons raises concerns about the scope of the criminal law and the erosion of due process rights. This practice also compels a critical examination of the government's reaction to the foreign national prisoner scandal. According to the people that drafted it, the hubs and spokes policy was created to facilitate deportation of foreign national prisoners. The agreement puts this goal in official terms: its stated purpose is to formalize 'the traditional informal working practices between parts of the NOMS and UKBA', which were 'no longer appropriate' after 2006.[56] The agreement also cites 'significantly improved' 'joint data . . . and risk management' as a rationale for hubs and spokes.[57] This bureaucratic language echoes Charles Clarke's proclamation that the challenge of the scandal was 'to [get] . . . our operation functioning properly'.[58] On a deeper level, the hubs and spokes agreement evinces an actuarial understanding of crime control that prioritizes the classification and expulsion of a risk posed to the state. In this case, the risk was 'the foreign criminal' and the aim was to identify and expel him from the United Kingdom in accordance with carefully calculated performance targets.

At first glance, this actuarial vision of penal policy appears to contrast with the heated populism that fueled the prisoner scandal. Headlines warning of foreign criminals and rapists 'on the loose' seem at odds with the muted managerialism of programmes like the Facilitated Returns Scheme, which present the foreign prisoner as a number to be crunched. Yet the difference between these approaches is largely a question of tone. In practice, actuarial offender management strategies often converge with strands of popular punitivism to legitimate new forms of state power.[59] In the

[56] MoJ and UKBA, *Service Level Agreement*, p. 5.

[57] MoJ and UKBA, *Service Level Agreement*, p. 5.

[58] 'In Quotes: Clarke and Deportation', *BBC News*.

[59] See Malcolm Feeley and Jonathan Simon, 'The New Penology: Notes on the Emerging Strategy of Corrections and Its Implications', *Criminology* 30, no. 4 (Nov. 1992): pp. 449–74; Malcolm Feeley and Jonathan Simon, 'Actuarial Justice: The Emerging New Criminal Law', in David Nelkin, ed., *The Futures of Criminology* (London: Sage Publications Ltd, 1994): pp. 173–201; Pat O'Malley, 'Volatile and Contradictory Punishment', *Theoretical Criminology* 3, no. 2 (May 1999): pp. 175–96; Lucia Zedner, 'Terrorism, the Ticking Bomb, and Criminal

spring of 2006, the foreign national prisoner crisis propelled a drastic expansion of the government's capacity to monitor and control migration. Specifically, the hubs and spokes policy deployed the power of the prison towards the state's efforts to police its borders. One senior civil servant in the UKBA described this shift in the border agency's mission: 'crisis points create opportunities. Call it responsive; call it exploiting. If you set up a project, it gets going and people get on board.'

The pressing critical question is precisely what opportunity the crisis created. The answer, it seems, is a new vision of the prison's place in migration control. Under hubs and spokes, the prison becomes a practical site for the implementation of immigration law and a piece of the UKBA's wider deportation strategy. The policy positions the prison—its prisoners, prison staff, and the notion of imprisonment itself—as part of the government's attempt to police the contours of political membership. Hubs and spokes implicates the prison in what Matthew Gibney calls 'the deportation turn', an historical moment in which the 'problem' of migration is increasingly understood through the solution of incarceration.[60] Born from scandal, the policy has introduced a new organizing principle—expulsion—into the operation of prisons. This development challenges basic intuitions about the purpose of a prison system.

Immigration Postmen

The hubs and spokes policy alters the balance of power between the Prison Service and the Border Agency by enlisting prison staff in migration control. To some extent, this policy supplants punishment with identification and expulsion. Yet, in practice, the implementation of hubs and spokes is piecemeal and personalized. Prison staff reinterpret and resist border control measures as they apply them to the carceral setting. On the ground, hubs and spokes illustrates both the reach and the limits of the effort to merge migration control with punishment.

There is no question that hubs and spokes has made citizenship status more relevant to prison life. It is simplifying only slightly to

Justice Values', *Criminal Justice Matters* 73, no. 1 (Jan. 2008): pp. 18–19; Zedner, 'Security, the State, and the Citizen'.

[60] Gibney, 'Asylum and the Expansion of Deportation in the United Kingdom'.

say that the policy has recast Prison Service staff as quasi-immigration officers. From day to day, prison line staff collect prisoners' travel documents, transport prisoners to immigration hearings, and search prisoners' cells for passports and other forms of identification. While they cannot legally provide immigration advice, prison staff serve legal notices on behalf of the UKBA,[61] and the hubs and spokes agreement requires every prison governor to appoint a 'Foreign National Coordinator'. These staff members take on a substantive role in prisoners' immigration cases, calling foreign embassies and mediating between prisoners and immigration agents. Often, Foreign National Coordinators become well versed in migration policy and practice, from the United Kingdom's legal obligations under the Vienna Conventions to the Border Agency's thirteen-point list of questions to help 'establish nationality more accurately in cases where there is some uncertainty'.[62]

In these and other senses, prison staff sit in 'structured subordination' to the Border Agency.[63] Pursuant to PSO 4630, prison employees deliver information, promote the Facilitated Returns Scheme, and enable the administrative detention of ex-prisoners. This entire endeavour is shaped not only by the UKBA's mission, but also by its method. In one revision of PSO 4630, for instance, the Border Agency provides detailed instructions on how prison staff should serve immigration documents to foreign national prisoners. 'If you are asked to date a notice, please do so', the order reads:

> At worst a failure to date the notice can lead to serious problems at the appeal; at best, it gives the appellant's legal representatives an easy way of casting doubt on Home Office competence.[64]

This directive frames officers in the Prison Service, a division of the Ministry of Justice, as ambassadors and defenders of the Home

[61] See HMPS, *Prison Service Order 4630*.

[62] HMPS, *Prison Service Order 4630*, pp. 1, 52. Not all the Foreign National Coordinators I met were familiar with migration policies. Some seemed to know very little about the hubs and spokes system, while others avoided their role in border control altogether.

[63] Stuart Hall used the term 'structured subordination' to describe the relationship between politicians and the press. Hall, Critcher, Jefferson, Clark, and Roberts, *Policing the Crisis*. Hall argues that the media is structurally dependent upon politicians and, in reporting on politics, reproduces and bolsters their power.

[64] HMPS, *Prison Service Order 4630*, p. 31.

Office's legitimacy. As that section of the order rather bluntly concludes, 'You are, essentially, the postman.'[65]

In casting Prison Service staff as UKBA postmen, new prison policies extend the practical reach of migration control deep into the penal estate. These policies also situate the prison as a symbolic representation of the border. In the hubs and spokes system, prison officials identify, segregate, and incarcerate foreign nationals in prisons until the UKBA approves their release. Since the 2006 scandal, the UKBA has spent an increasing proportion of its time and budget on the management of the criminal population. In this framework, release from prison becomes a certification of legal residency and finding 'foreign criminals' becomes a guiding and self-fulfilling goal for the Border Agency. The hubs and spokes policy figures the prison as a kind of immigration net, an integral site at and through which migration is policed.[66]

The counterpoint to this symbolic process is that prisons are actual physical sites for holding non-citizens. At the time of my fieldwork, the 139 prisons in England and Wales held somewhere between 11,000 and 13,000 foreign nationals, many of whom were facing deportation.[67] In housing these prisoners, particularly those who had completed their criminal sentences, prisons extend the immigration detention estate. This new role was made explicit,

[65] HMPS, *Prison Service Order 4630*, p. 31.

[66] The prison is one of many such sites. Migration control also unfolds in airports, embassies, and police stations. Under hubs and spokes, the penal institution joins these spaces as a potent symbol of the British border.

[67] See MoJ, *Offender Management Caseload Statistics 2009*. The number of foreign national prisoners varies depending on the size of the remand and time-served populations, while the number actually 'removed' from the United Kingdom is even more difficult to track. Ministry of Justice statistics from year end 2010 place the foreign national population at 10,866. That number does not include the 1,794 prisoners listed as 'nationality not recorded', nor the close to 800–1,500 ex-prisoners detained in British prisons under immigration powers. *Vine Report*. Hindpal Singh Bhui notes that many prisoners with unrecorded nationalities are in fact foreign nationals. Bhui, 'Alien Experience'. If one were to combine the recorded, unrecorded, and time-served statistics, the number of foreign nationals in the British penal estate would have been 13,260 in 2010. That number represents a drop from the nearly 14,000 foreign nationals imprisoned at the time of Bhui's 2007 report. The explanation for this drop is not entirely clear—it may stem from an increase in deportation rates, a decrease in the number of imprisoned foreign national women, or an increase in the numbers of foreign nationals transferred into the immigration detention estate.

and more or less permanent, when the UKBA and NOMS negotiated an acceptable target for the number of time-served detainees in prisons. In a subsection titled 'What UKBA Expects of NOMS', the hubs and spokes agreement straightforwardly states that the Prison Service should 'allow UKBA to maximize the immigration removal estate'.[68]

This expectation makes the boundary between prisons and detention centres porous. Despite official claims that ex-prisoners are assigned to prisons or detention centres based on a risk assessment, the transfer policy for time-served prisoners is unclear. In practice, transfers between penal institutions and detention centres appear to depend as much on facility capacity and concerns about order as they do on risk. In some cases, the prisoners I interviewed were transferred to detention centres for persistently 'causing problems' in the prison or to prisons from detention centres for 'inciting misbehaviour' there. The overlap between prisons and detention centres is also complicated by the increasing criminalization of immigration offences, which can lead to prison sentences for crimes such as possession of false documents and assisting illegal entry.[69]

In addition to holding detainees—literally serving as detention centres—prisons also provide a controlled space for interaction between alleged non-citizens and immigration authorities. PSO 4630 requires all prisons to permit border agents to interview prisoners in meetings called immigration 'surgeries'.[70] During these interviews, border agents fingerprint and photograph prisoners. UKBA staff also use what one official called 'assertive interviewing

[68] MoJ and UKBA, *Service Level Agreement*, p. 7.

[69] The *Vine Report* offers a small but illuminating view of the effects that the criminalization of immigration offences has had on the prison population. Based on a sample of 132 case files, that report found that 27 per cent of foreign national prisoners were incarcerated for fraud and forgery, the typical charges levied against those who possess false identification documents. *Vine Report*, p. 8. That offence ranks highest in the breakdown of offences for which foreign nationals are incarcerated. The next is drug charges, which account for 23 per cent of the foreign national prisoner population, and then violent offences, which account for 22 per cent. The list drops off significantly after violent offences. While based on only a limited sample, these numbers suggest that criminalizing the possession of false documents has contributed in significant ways to the make-up of the prison population.

[70] HMPS, *Prison Service Order 4630*. The frequency of these meetings depends on whether a prison is categorized as a hub or spoke.

practices' and 'police techniques' to determine prisoners' nationalities. In one immigration surgery I attended, a border agent told a 'non-compliant' foreign national prisoner—that is, a man who would not agree to his own deportation—that unless he acquiesced to 'removal' proceedings, immigration could 'hold him in prison as long as we want'. The hubs and spokes policy positions the prison as a bargaining chip for the UKBA, which employs the threat of imprisonment to achieve its aims.

Yet, if it enables expulsion, the hubs and spokes policy also frustrates UKBA goals. In practice, the implementation of hubs and spokes is localized and controversial. While the formal agreement between NOMS and UKBA established specific 'hub' and 'spoke' facilities, many prisons diverge from this script. Some of the spoke prisons I visited employed full-time immigration staff, who were technically meant to be 'embedded' in hub prisons. Other spoke prisons, which are supposed to hold mainly British citizens, incarcerated a significant number of foreign nationals. The role that immigration personnel played in the prison differed in each institution, and in a few prisons, staff members assigned to manage non-citizens had never heard of hubs and spokes.

The relationship between prison and immigration staff also varied by institution. This bureaucratic dynamic was one of the main targets of the hubs and spokes agreement, which made plain that the foreign national prisoner scandal was caused, at least in part, by poor communication between state agencies.[71] In most of the prisons I visited, UKBA and Prison Service staff members communicated according to the formal dictates of that agreement and were cooperative and cordial with one another when doing so. In individual interviews, however, conflicts between these groups emerged. Both prison staff and border agents expressed concerns that their missions were too different for the hubs and spokes system to work.

Prison staff complained that they had little control over prisoners' immigration cases, a situation that they found especially frustrating when dealing with the 'difficult' and 'volatile' detainees who remain in prisons after the end of their criminal sentences.[72]

[71] See MoJ and UKBA, *Service Level Agreement*, pp. 1–2.

[72] Time-served prisoners—that is, those who have completed their criminal sentences and are detained in prisons under immigration powers—are especially volatile. In my experience, these prisoners tend to be more vocally angry, resistant, and frustrated than prisoners who know their date of release. Chapter 7

Prison officials also worried about how the UKBA's priorities affected the division of labour in the prison. One Foreign National Coordinator recounted the problems that arise when border agents introduce immigration casework into the prison system and leave prison staff to handle the maintenance of order. 'If you're coming with bad news, I'm giving it to [the prisoners]', she said. 'You're not coming into my prison and giving my prisoners bad news.'

Articulating a complex blend of protectiveness, defensiveness, and ownership over the prison and its prisoners, this Foreign National Coordinator suggested that the hubs and spokes policy disrupts the daily organization and hierarchies of prison life. More senior Prison Service officials reiterated this argument on a grander scale, noting that the hubs and spokes system transposes the demands of migration control onto a penal estate already arranged by security classification and pinched by overcrowding. As one Prison Service policymaker put it, the hubs and spokes policy necessitates prisoner transfers and particular prison assignments when 'we are already bursting at the seams'.

These criticisms hint at the discord underlying hubs and spokes. They also clarify the Prison Service's perception of its purpose. Prison officials' complaints about hubs and spokes reflect an interest in maintaining their own authority, both in penal institutions and in the broader government bureaucracy. Inside prisons, this goal takes the form of debates about the UKBA's power and the conflict between deportation and the need to maintain order. Prison officials often asserted the primacy of the need for order, and with it, the import of the Prison Service's existing classification system. These claims suggest that the Prison Service understands itself through the lens of order, and at least in some cases, sees that paradigm as incompatible with the notion of 'removal'.

Prison staff also expressed concerns about the treatment of foreign national prisoners. One officer predicted that the hubs and spokes policy would ultimately fail because the two agencies implementing it had fundamentally different approaches to prisoners. 'The difference between the Prison Service and the UKBA is that

explores the experience of indefinite detention in more detail. For a psychological account of the pressures of indefinite detention as they relate to tendencies towards self-harm, see Jo Borrill and Donna A. Taylor, 'Suicides by Foreign National Prisoners in England and Wales 2007: Mental and Cultural Issues', *Forensic Psychiatry and Psychology* 20, no. 6 (Nov. 2009): pp. 886–905.

we see them as people and they see them as numbers', he explained. This is a biased perspective, but it captures the values at play in the implementation of penal policy. According to one official familiar with hubs and spokes, debates over core institutional values were part of the reason the inter-agency agreement took three years to negotiate. That official said that hubs and spokes was created 'for UKBA convenience' and that during negotiations the Prison Service had voiced fears about its capacity to uphold a 'decency agenda' while indefinitely detaining deportees.[73] The UKBA, on the other hand, was singularly focused on the effort to 'detain and deport'.

The two agencies selected to manage the foreign prisoner crisis thus had distinct and conflicting aims in creating hubs and spokes. The Prime Minister's Delivery Unit (PMDU) report commissioned in response to the crisis acknowledged this conflict. In its report, the PMDU found that 'NOMS and UKBA are ultimately working towards different objectives in managing F[oreign] N[ational] P[risoners].'[74] According to its mission statement, the National Offender Management Service (NOMS) exists both 'to protect the public' and 'to reduce re-offending rates'.[75] The Prison Service is not explicit about how it intends to reach these goals and reformers have questioned the depth of its commitment to resettlement.[76] Nonetheless, the Prison Service's emphasis on reducing reoffending by helping prisoners lead 'law-abiding and useful lives in custody and after release' suggests a conceptual investment in the

[73] Prison Service Director General Martin Narey introduced the 'Decency Agenda' in 1999. While there is no consensus on what this agenda entails, Alison Liebling argues that it is an explicit move away from notions of justice and liberality and towards concepts like 'fairness, minimum standards, security, order, the challenging of offender behavior, and a reduction in the availability and use of drugs'. Alison Liebling, *Prisons and Their Moral Performance: A Study of Values, Quality, and Prison Life* (Oxford: Oxford University Press, 2005), p. 478. Despite the conceptual ambiguity of the Decency Agenda, prison officials and prison staff regularly cite it when asked to explain the purpose of the prison.

[74] MoJ and UKBA, *Service Level Agreement*, p. 3.

[75] 'About HM Prison Service', *Ministry of Justice*, <http://www.justice.gov.uk/about/hmps/>.

[76] See, e.g. Kimmett Edgar, Andreas Aresti, and Neil Cornish, *Out for Good: Taking Responsibility for Resettlement* (London: Prison Reform Trust, 2011); NACRO Policy Team, *Developing Proposals for Sentencing and Achieving a Rehabilitative Revolution* (London: NACRO, 2010).

connection between offenders and the British polity. The UKBA, in contrast, aims to expel.[77]

The clash between these goals plays out in a subtle but constant tension between immigration and prison staff. That tension is more than bureaucratic boundary drawing. It is a window into the conceptual problems that arise when, in the name of efficiency, governments merge migration control and punishment. Policies like hubs and spokes seem to blend border control with imprisonment, and in doing so, to police both migration and crime. Behind prison walls, however, these policies prompt serious debate about transfers and prisoner treatment—debates that are, at their base, about the purpose of the prison and the legitimacy of the UKBA's presence behind bars. Accordingly, one official advised me to 'hesitate when talking about any "integration" of the UKBA and the Prison Service'. Instead, criminologists need to dig deeper into the relationship between borders and punishment.

The Criminalization of Immigration

This chapter has painted a slightly schizophrenic portrait of the prison system. I have argued that the hubs and spokes policy turns prisons into borders and, at the same time, that the new policy is fraught and incomplete. This could simply be a case of policy in practice. No Prison Service order—no regulation of any kind—looks the same on its face as it does in action. Hubs and spokes is typical of bureaucratic administration in this respect. Yet, if it raises classic questions about bureaucracy, this policy also

[77] The UKBA's emphasis on deportation is evident in its response to foreign national prisoners who appeal deportation orders on human rights grounds. Between March and December 2010, the Border Agency's decisions to deport were overturned by the courts in 425 cases, 'the overwhelming majority on human rights grounds'. *Vine Report*, p. 15. That number compares with only 151 prisoners the UKBA granted permission to remain on human rights grounds during the same period. The Border Agency thus had a particularly limited interpretation of whether a foreign national should be entitled to remain in the United Kingdom. As the *Vine Report* notes, this legal record is both costly—the 425 appeals in 2010 cost the government around £480,000—and ineffective. *Vine Report*, p. 15. The *Vine Report* calls on the Border Agency to bring its deportation decisions more in line with the view expressed by the courts. *Vine Report*, p. 3. The UKBA's record on appeal suggests a fundamental disagreement between the Border Agency and the courts about the meaning and relevance of human rights.

highlights novel concerns about the way criminologists and legal scholars conceive of punishment. The tension pervading hubs and spokes suggests that scholars have a distorted view of the relationship between immigration and imprisonment.

Academics often present policies like hubs and spokes as examples of the criminalization of immigration, or as Juliet Stumpf calls it, 'crimmigration'.[78] This is a helpful way to describe legal trends. Laws such as the 2007 UK Borders Act and the Borders, Citizenship and Immigration Act of 2009 treat undocumented migration as an ongoing crime rather than a regulatory violation. This approach to immigration transposes the language of criminality onto migration policy, effectively criminalizing foreign nationals for their mere presence in a foreign nation. The term 'crimmigration' captures this development and connects the creation of new offences and sanctions—formal criminalization—to broader shifts in legal culture.

The crimmigration critique has produced compelling scholarship. Under this rubric, academics have documented the birth of a vast network of detention centres and the passage of laws that prioritize border security over other social values.[79] Legal scholars have invoked crimmigration to comment on the decline of national sovereignty, the obfuscation of due process rights, and

[78] Stumpf, 'The Crimmigration Crisis'; Juliet Stumpf, 'Doing Time: Crimmigration Law and the Perils of Haste', *UCLA Law Review* 58, no. 1705 (July 2011): pp. 1705–48; see also Bosworth and Guild, 'Governing through Migration Control'; David Cole, *Enemy Aliens: Double Standards and Constitutional Freedoms in the War on Terrorism* (New York, NY: The New Press, 2003); Sang Hea Kil and Cecilia Menjivar, 'The War on the Border: Criminalizing Immigrants and Militarizing the U.S.–Mexico Border', in Ramiro Martinez, Jr and Abel Valenzuela, Jr, eds, *Immigration and Crime: Race, Ethnicity and Violence* (New York, NY: New York University Press, 2006), pp. 164–88; Maggy Lee, 'Human Trade and the Criminalization of "Irregular Migration"', *International Journal of the Sociology of Law* 33, no. 1 (March 2005): pp. 1–15; Pamela Preston and Michael Perez, 'The Criminalization of Aliens: Regulating Foreigners', *Critical Criminology* 14, no. 1 (March 2006): pp. 43–66; Irum Sheikh, 'Racializing, Criminalizing, and Silencing 9/11 Deportees', in David Brotherton and Phillip Kretsedemas, eds, *Keeping Out the Other: A Critical Introduction to Immigration Enforcement Today* (New York, NY: Columbia University Press, 2008), pp. 81–107.

[79] See, e.g. Stumpf, 'The Crimmigration Crisis'; Zedner, 'Security, the State, and the Citizen'.

the practice of local forms of resistance to migration control.[80] In criminology and anthropology, scholars have explored how the criminalization of immigration reiterates racism in new forms. Alessandro di Giorgi, Asale Angel-Ajani, Salvatore Palidda, and others have demonstrated that national stereotypes collude with assumptions about race to further marginalize migrant communities.[81]

The crimmigration paradigm has also provided solid ground to challenge the conflation of migration, criminality, and terrorism.[82] Particularly since 9/11, though also before, politicians and members of the press have described undocumented migration as a terrorist threat and a phenomenon that necessitates incarceration.[83] Such language characterized media reports of the foreign prisoner crisis—recall that the scandal began with Mustaf Jama's escape

[80] On declining sovereignty, see Brown, *Walled States, Waning Sovereignty.* For an account of the role that local politics play in regulation migration into the United States, see Christina Rodriguez, 'The Significance of the Local in Immigration Regulation', *Michigan Law Review* 106 (Jan. 2008), pp. 567–643. For one discussion of local and other sub-national resistance to border control, see Jessica Bulman-Pozen and Heather K. Gerken, 'Uncooperative Federalism', *Yale Law Journal* 118 (2009), pp. 1256–1310. For a discussion of due process protections in the realm of immigration law, see Ingrid Eagly, 'Prosecuting Immigration', *Northwestern University Law Review* 104 (2010), p. 1281; and Allegra McLeod, 'The US Criminal–Immigration Convergence and its Possible Undoing', *American Criminal Law Review* 49 (2012), p. 105. For an earlier example of the due process debate, see Cole, *Enemy Aliens*. Cole's book precedes Stumpf's article, which coined the term 'crimmigration', but his work tackles many of the same questions about the collusion of immigration and criminal law. The claim in this chapter is not that the term 'crimmigration' inaugurated a new line of thought, but rather, that it captured a set of concerns about migration control that had been percolating in Anglo-American criminology and legal scholarship since the mid-1990s.

[81] Asale Angel-Ajani, 'A Question of Dangerous Races?', *Punishment and Society* 5, no. 4 (October 2003): pp. 433–48; Alessandro di Giorgi, 'The U.S. Penal Experiment', in Salvatore Palidda, ed., *Racial Criminalization of Migrants in the 21st Century* (Surrey: Ashgate Publishing, 2011), pp. 133–46; Salvatore Palidda, ed., *Racial Criminalization of Migrants in the 21st Century* (Surrey: Ashgate Publishing, 2011).

[82] See Cole, *Enemy Aliens*; Jef Huysmans, *The Politics of Insecurity: Fear, Migration, and Asylum in the EU* (Abingdon: Routledge Press, 2006); Zedner, 'Security, the State, and the Citizen'.

[83] While this claim refers to the British press, this account of post-9/11 political rhetoric rings true in other countries, most notably the United States. On American migration rhetoric, see Cole, *Enemy Aliens*; Sheikh 2008.

to Somalia in a niqab and culminated in frenzied declarations that foreign criminals, once released, would 'never be found'.[84] Criminologists have been quick to note that this presentation of migration enables imprisonment.[85] In their analysis of British immigration laws, Mary Bosworth and Mhairi Guild indict a 'legislative framework that identifies the most vulnerable migrants as potential terrorists'.[86] Bosworth and Guild argue that 'fear of the shadowy figure of the terrorist suspect has . . . rendered the majority of migrants a priori suspect' and has propelled the expansion of imprisonment in the United Kingdom.[87]

The hubs and spokes policy is laced with fear-filled language about national security. The formal agreement between the Prison Service and the Border Agency adopts the language of war—and pits the penal institution as a battleground—when it 'embeds' immigration staff in the prison system.[88] The agreement also calls forth 'the shadowy figure of the terrorist suspect' when it defines the term foreign national prisoner 'in its broadest sense', as 'a remand, sentenced or time-served detained prisoner . . . *known or believed to be a foreign national*'.[89] PSO 4630 codifies this murky definition and mandates that prison staff report to the UKBA 'when there is reason to suspect that the prisoner is a foreign national'.[90] This expansive, almost McCarthyist description hints at the Border Agency's deeper interest in using hubs and spokes to police terrorism. In interviews, UKBA officials were open about this goal. One Border Agency policymaker called the process of determining a prisoner's citizenship status 'intelligence-gathering' and explained that migration control is important because 'to a terrorist, a document is a weapon'.

[84] See, e.g. 'Home Office Blunders Left Foreign Rapists in UK', *Daily Mail*; Johnston, 'We May Never Find Foreign Murderers, Says Home Office'.

[85] See, e.g. Bosworth and Guild, 'Governing through Migration Control'; Frederico Rahola, 'The Detention Regime', in Palidda, ed., *Racial Criminalization of Migrants in the 21st Century*, pp. 95–106; Leanne Weber, 'The Shifting Frontiers of Migration Control', in Sharon Pickering and Leanne Weber, eds, *Borders, Mobility, and Technologies of Control* (Dordrecht: Springer, 2006).

[86] Bosworth and Guild, 'Governing through Migration Control', p. 711.

[87] Bosworth and Guild, 'Governing through Migration Control', p. 711.

[88] See MoJ and UKBA, *Service Level Agreement*, pp. 5, 9.

[89] Bosworth and Guild, 'Governing through Migration Control', p. 711; MoJ and UKBA, *Service Level Agreement*, p. 5. Emphasis added.

[90] HMPS, *Prison Service Order 4630*, p. 7.

The crimmigration framework contextualizes this policymaker's vision of hubs and spokes. Literature on crimmigration is sensitive to the power of rhetoric and to the legally dubious practices that flow from the conflation of foreignness and crime. This literature offers a useful way to understand how a policy like hubs and spokes could emerge from a scandal and develop into a tool to manage crime, migration, and terrorism all at once. Yet this paradigm also threatens to obscure notable features of the British government's approach to foreign national prisoners. As it has become a metaphor for legal developments, crimmigration has encouraged several assumptions about the relationship between punishment and border control.

Most obviously, this framework emphasizes criminalization, which is only one of several emergent trends in immigration law and policy. Crimmigration scholarship foregrounds the expansion of criminal law, the use of criminal imagery to describe migrants, and the development of policing practices along national borders. These criminalizing processes are important to understanding the treatment of migrants in the twenty-first century, but they are also accompanied by a series of non-criminal trends, such as the growth of administrative detention and the curtailment of due process for non-citizens. In many ways, contemporary migration control practices depend less on a connection between immigration and crime than on the particularly non-criminal nature of foreignness.

Bosworth and Guild explore this point in their work on immigration detention in the United Kingdom. They argue that migrants are 'in a substantially different, and far more vulnerable position [than] ... domestic UK criminal[s]'.[91] In virtue of their legal status, criminal defendants have more fully articulated, if not fully realized, due process rights.[92] Some of the most serious concerns about the treatment of migrants stem from non-citizens' distance from the criminal code. The due process protections afforded

[91] Bosworth and Guild, 'Governing through Migration Control', p. 712.

[92] For literature on the due process debate, see Ingrid Eagly, 'Prosecuting Immigration', p. 1281; and Allegra McLeod, 'The US Criminal–Immigration Convergence and its Possible Undoing', p. 105. These American scholars point out that, as an empirical matter, criminal defendants' due process rights are rarely realized. This fact puts relative claims about the legal protections afforded criminal defendants and immigrants into relief.

non-citizens, even those who have lived in the country for years, are thinner and less stable than those linked to the criminal law. Restrictive migration policies are more connected to fears of foreignness, and less dependent on criminality, than terms like 'crimmigration' suggest.

A second, less well-documented drawback of the crimmigration paradigm is its tendency to overemphasize the exportation of crime control models. In much of the crimmigration scholarship, the dominant concern is that criminal justice imagery is applied where it does not belong. Take discussions of border policing and accounts of immigration detention. The standard critique of these practices is that governments are borrowing from the vocabulary of criminal justice in objectionable ways—ways that merge and ultimately eliminate the difference between punishment and border control. Scholarship on immigration detention, for instance, describes the incarceration of non-citizens under prison-like circumstances.[93] In the United States, Australia, and the United Kingdom, academics have charted the emergence of detention regimes that look nearly indistinguishable from criminal imprisonment.[94] This is a vivid picture, but it tends to suppress distinctions between prisons and detention regimes.

In the United Kingdom, prisons and detention centres are contructed along the same architectural blueprint. Many British detention centres are built to the model of Category B (medium-security)

[93] See, e.g. Asale Angel-Ajani, 'A Question of Dangerous Races?'; Bosworth 2007; Bosworth and Kaufman, 'Foreigners in a Carceral Age'; Michael Grewcock, 'Punishment, Deportation and Parole: The Detention and Removal of Former Prisoners under Section 501 Migration Act 1958', *Australia and New Zealand Journal of Criminology* 44, no. 1 (April 2011): pp. 56–73; Leerkes and Broeders, 'A Case of Mixed Motives?'; Jonathan Simon, 'Refugees in a Carceral Age: The Rebirth of Immigration Prisons in the United States', *Public Culture* 10, no. 3 (Spring 1998): pp. 577–607; Jacqueline Stevens, *States without Nations: Citizenship for Mortals* (New York, NY: Columbia University Press, 2009); Weber, 'The Shifting Frontiers of Migration Control'; Zedner, 'Security, the State, and the Citizen'.

[94] See, e.g. Stevens, *States without Nations*; Jacqueline Stevens, 'America's Secret ICE Castles', *The Nation*, 4 January 2010, <http://www.thenation.com/article/americas-secret-ice-castles>. For an account of the conceptual and practical parity between the immigration detention and prison systems in the United States, see Bosworth and Kaufman, 'Foreigners in a Carceral Age'; see also Bosworth, 'Deporting Foreign National Prisoners in England and Wales'; Weber, 'The Shifting Frontiers of Migration Control'.

prisons, a choice immigration officials described as a 'flexible solution' should the prisoner population grow or detainee population shrink. Under the hubs and spokes policy, detention centres and prisons hold many of the same prisoners. These custodial spaces share performance targets and policymakers, and with immigration officials 'embedded' in prisons, they share staff as well. On both conceptual and practical levels, prisons and detention centres are involved in the same project. These institutions are two arms of the government's effort to 'shore up' national borders and reinforce a waning sense of sovereignty.[95] From this perspective, prisons and detention centres are part of a particular and shared late modern moment.

In a different and important sense, however, prisons are not a part of the immigration estate, nor are they completely consistent with the project of migration control. In the law and the minds of many prison staff, prisons remain distinct institutions. Prison officials I interviewed chafed at the idea that prisons were de facto detention centres. Line staff explained that they did everything they could to downplay the idea of deportation and to limit the number of detainees held in prisons, a practice that made them 'uncomfortable'. Staff often described small acts of resistance to migration control, from lobbying immigration officials to take detainees out of prisons to advocating for more frequent visits from the UKBA, which would in theory accelerate prisoners' immigration casework and reduce the number of time-served prisoners. For many prison employees, the introduction of border agents into the prison system made it more necessary for prisons to reflect the criminal law. A policy created to merge punishment and expulsion has thus had the curious effect of clarifying and hardening the distinctions between the two.

The difference between prison and detention also mattered to the UKBA. One Border Agency official I interviewed, a high-ranking policymaker involved in the creation of hubs and spokes, appreciated the prison's uniqueness as a carceral institution. She explained that prisons are unusual sites for border control: 'You can look at their property, their phone calls, their visitors', she

[95] Bosworth and Guild, 'Governing through Migration Control', p. 712; Brown, *Walled States, Waning Sovereignty*; see also Leanne Weber and Benjamin Bowling, 'Policing Migration: A Framework for the Regulation of Global Mobility', *Policing and Society* 14, no. 3 (2004): pp. 195–212.

said. 'In a prison regime', information about a prisoner's nationality 'is easier to get. Removal centres are a different regime.' This official did not distinguish between remand, sentenced, and post-sentence prisoners. Technically, time-served prisoners have the same legal status as detainees in 'removal' centres and are treated as pre-sentence prisoners when held in prisons.[96] In legal terms, the prison is not a separate sphere from the detention centre and information about prisoners' nationalities should not be much 'easier to get' in prisons. Yet this policymaker presented the prison as an especially controlled, and hence desirable, environment for Border Agency practices.

This articulation of border control illustrates the prison's conceptual role in the UKBA lexicon. Whether prisoners are actually subject to different enforcement practices in prisons and detention centres is not entirely clear. The UKBA official I interviewed seemed to suggest they were; the formal policy on foreign national prisoners indicates otherwise. What is clear, however, is that the prison occupies an important position in the Border Agency's understanding of itself.[97] Prisons are institutions that look a certain way, where practices such as keeping people behind bars and searching their cells become normal. These practices, and the very idea of the penal institution, hold a particular place in the UKBA imagination. The prison is the paradigm against which the Border Agency compares its activities and makes sense of its mission.

The distinction between prisons and detention centres is then both salient and substantive. While there is no question that the prison is a practical site for migration control and that prisons increasingly function as 'removal' centres, the prison also serves as a conceptual foil to the detention centre and as an aspirational model of incarceration for the Border Agency. The prison and the detention centre are related by analogy, and for that matter, through an imperfect analogy that preserves key features of the penal institution. No matter how similar these spaces look, there remains a legal and conceptual gap between prisons and detention centres—a gap that justifies the existence of both incarceration regimes. There would be no argument for detention centres

[96] HMPS, *Prison Service Order 4630.*
[97] HMPS, *Prison Service Order 4630.*

if imprisonment and expulsion were as fully merged in the law as they are in practice. Policies like hubs and spokes depend upon the prison's character as an institution, namely, one defined by the totality of its control over its inhabitants and bounded, at least in theory, by the criminal law.[98]

The narrow definition of punishment legitimates immigration detention. Confining the concept of punishment also enables increasingly harsh penal regimes. Again, this phenomenon is clearest in practice. In one interview, a prison staff member described the challenges she experienced with time-served prisoners, who became increasingly angry and irritated as their detention persisted. Recounting her efforts to calm a particular prisoner and to 'trade' him for another detainee, that officer told me that she was frustrated by detainees' continued presence in the prison system. Shaking her head, she said, 'this is just an immigration capacity issue'.

This prison officer is technically correct. Under the hubs and spokes policy, it is the UKBA and not the Prison Service that decides when, if ever, a foreign national prisoner gets released.[99] That policy allows the UKBA to detain more people and, to the extent that the most 'difficult' prisoners remain in prisons, to avoid the problems created by its own policies. However, if it divorces the Border Agency from the consequences of its work, the UKBA's control over detainee casework also lets prison staff and officials defer responsibility for those in their charge. Insisting that the problems of foreign nationals are 'just immigration issues' places time-served prisoners who threaten suicide and foreign nationals who resist 'removal' outside the scope of the prison. Yet these

[98] For the classic account of the prison as a total institution, see Michel Foucault, *Discipline and Punish: The Birth of the Prison*, trans. Alan Sheridan (New York, NY: Vintage Books, 1977). For an analysis of the relationship between punishment and criminal law, see R. A. Duff, 'A Criminal Law for Citizens', *Theoretical Criminology* 14, no. 3 (Aug. 2010): pp. 293–309.

[99] The broad power to determine a detainee's date of release is checked by the judiciary, which can order an ex-prisoner's release. The High Court has, for the most part, upheld detention 'pending deportation' under the 1971 Immigration Act. See, e.g. *Lumba (WL) (Congo) v. Secretary of State for the Home Department* [2011] UKSC 12, [2011] All ER (D) 262; *AP (Trinidad and Tobago) v. Secretary of State for the Home Department* [2011] EWCA Civ 551, [2011] All ER (D) 108; *RU (Bangladesh) v. Secretary of State for the Home Department* [2011] EWCA Civ 651, [2011] All ER (D) 38.

people remain within the prison and their concerns become a part of prison life. The sense of the prison as a unique and bounded institution—one where only particular people are held and only particular problems are handled—allows those who manage prisons to ignore what is actually happening in the penal institution, and how that institution has changed.

Over the past five years, the British government has built border control into the structure of the penal estate. Under the hubs and spokes policy, foreign national prisoners are distinguished from British citizens from the moment they enter the prison and prison managers are guided, at least in part, by the demands of migration control. These developments have made finding non-citizens 'known or believed to be foreign nationals' a constitutive part of the criminal justice system.[100] They have also introduced the legal and ethical dilemmas of detention into prison life. The interaction between crime control and immigration policy has reverberated back into the core institution of punishment, shifting its character. If the goal is to understand how globalization affects penal institutions, it would be a mistake to overlook this fact.

The crimmigration paradigm encourages such mistakes. While the concept of crimmigration is illuminating, scholarship in this field tends to be outward looking. In an effort to critique legal developments, academics have underscored the blurring of criminal and migration policy and the slippage between different bodies of law. Yet policies like hubs and spokes operate as much through the hardening of legal boundaries as they do through their dissolution. Practices cited as evidence of crimmigration—the birth of detention centres, the creation and professionalization of a border police force—are concerning, no question. These trends are also met with resistance and complicated by what looks like a decriminalization of the prison's day to day character. In the face of globalization, the prison serves as a site for migration control and, at the same time, represents a narrow notion of criminal punishment. Under policies like hubs and spokes, there is a real and growing gap between conceptions of the prison and the institution's actual use.

[100] MoJ and UKBA, *Service Level Agreement*, p. 5.

Conclusion

Almost forty years ago, Stuart Hall transformed criminology with his insight into the relationship between political crises and national cultures. In *Policing the Crisis*, Hall described how a moral panic over crime, in that case mugging, positioned an entire class of young black men as deviants and outcasts.[101] Hall and his contemporaries were concerned with the ways in which decolonization and migration become 'problems' of crime. His writing demonstrated that national crises are moments when a society is coming to grips with its values, and with itself.

Decades on, Hall's account holds true. In 2006, a short-lived prisoner scandal did more than prompt a Home Secretary to resign. As it rippled through the government bureaucracy, the foreign national prisoner crisis signalled and enabled a reconstruction of the prison's basic purpose. The scandal gave rise to a new kind of prison, one less tied to punishment and to the terms of the criminal law.

British citizens still make up the vast majority of the prison population. For many people, concerns about citizenship, nationality, and expulsion may never enter into prison life. Yet, for a significant group of prisoners, penal institutions now serve as detention centres, staff are basically border agents, and the end of the criminal sentence is 'removal' from the United Kingdom. In an era of migration and deportation, it is not clear that prisons are institutions for incapacitating, rehabilitating, or deterring criminals before their eventual return to the polity. With the advent of policies like hubs and spokes, the classic conception of the prison looks increasingly alien.

[101] Hall, Critcher, Jefferson, Clark, and Roberts, *Policing the Crisis*.

4

Making Citizens

Inside a stout brick prison, seven men sit in a classroom. Each is facing deportation in the coming months, but for the moment, they are learning English as a second language. Their teacher, a woman of roughly fifty, refers to the reading assignment from the previous class: 'Tell me which words you found difficult.' After several long beats, one man raises his hand. 'Coronation', he says. 'Coronation. Alright, coronation', she responds. 'Coronation is the ceremony of putting the crown on the queen. Any other questions?'

Another prisoner raises his hand: 'heritage'. 'History, man', his classmate interjects. 'Heritage is your history.' Their teacher expounds, 'It's to do with the history of your people. Our heritage is Dover Castle and the NHS. Part of your heritage, even if you don't like it, is that a lot of your people speak French because the French came to your country. Do you understand?' The man nods. He understands. A third prisoner joins in, 'what about "anxious"?' 'Anxious?' his teacher replies. 'Anxious is like, oh no, they're sending me to prison, what's it going to be like?'

Classes like these take place in prisons every day. They are one of the many ways that the British government teaches prisoners about British culture. Together with citizenship courses and nationality questionnaires, these classes shape prisoners' experiences of incarceration. Over time, they construct and confirm a particular notion of Britishness, one that extends beyond prison walls and involves more than immigration status. This chapter examines the process by which ideas about British national belonging are built into incarceration. Drawing on interviews and observations, I document how prisons become sites for the production of British citizens, and moreover, for a vision of citizenship as a privilege to be earned.

In the past decade, scholars have voiced concern about the development of what Lucia Zedner calls contingent citizenship, a rhetorical frame in which civic membership is a 'status granted only to those able to...accord with preset norms'.[1] Zedner's critique is aimed at a series of legislative and policy developments that have transformed the meaning of British citizenship, most notably the Borders, Citizenship, and Immigration Act of 2009. This chapter provides an empirical perspective on Zedner's claims. The narratives told by prisoners and prison officers demonstrate that citizenship is often a barometer for 'British values'.[2] When identifying the non-citizens in the prison population, prison staff exercise wide discretion about who looks and sounds 'foreign enough' to warrant a referral to immigration authorities. Prisoners who fail to pass this test enter a separate system in which transfers, treatment, and release dates are determined by nationality. Today, penal institutions are places where citizens are made.

Finding Foreigners

Chapter 3 excavated the hubs and spokes policy, which debuted in 2009 as part of an effort to integrate the Prison Service with the UK Border Agency. Under that policy, prison staff members must identify any non-British citizen in the prison population to immigration authorities.[3] This mandate makes citizenship an immediate concern for both prisoners and staff. Within a day or so of their incarceration, all prisoners are given a questionnaire that asks, among many other things, where prisoners were born. The answer to that question has lasting and in some cases unintended consequences on prison life.

Asking prisoners where they were born is an explicit attempt to identify people who do not or do not want to conceive of themselves as foreign. Both penal policymakers and prison staff explained that the question 'where were your born?' is a 'more effective' way

[1] Lucia Zedner, 'Security, the State, and the Citizen: The Changing Architecture of Crime Control', *New Criminal Law Review* 13, no. 2 (Spring 2010): p. 383; see also Mary Bosworth and Mhairi Guild, 'Governing through Migration Control: Security and Citizenship in Britain', *British Journal of Criminology* 48, no. 6 (Fall 2008): p. 715; David Cole, *Enemy Aliens: Double Standards and Constitutional Freedoms in the War on Terrorism* (New York, NY: The New Press, 2003).

[2] Zedner, 'Security, the State, and the Citizen', p. 387.

[3] Ministry of Justice (MoJ) and United Kingdom Border Agency (UKBA), *Service Level Agreement to Support the Effective and Speedy Removal of Foreign National Prisoners* (London: MoJ and UKBA, 2009).

to identify foreign nationals than asking other questions, such as 'where are you from?' or 'what is your nationality?' The point of the chosen question, in other words, is to catch prisoners who think they are British or want to be British, but who are not legally citizens of the United Kingdom.

This approach can be misleading, most obviously because the conflation of birthplace and nationality often conflicts with prisoners' own senses of national identity. Many prisoners who were raised but not born in the United Kingdom conceive of themselves as British. Some are the only non-British citizens in their families. Others did not know their citizenship status until they were arrested. These stories raise philosophical and ethical questions about what it means to be a citizen, and specifically, whether a person can be British without being a legal citizen of the United Kindgom. There are also more technical cases in which birthplace and nationality do not align. Many British citizens acquire citizenship after their birth, and hence, are citizens of the United Kindgom despite being foreign-born. People born in the United Kingdom or in former British colonies can also give up or lose their citizenship, making them British-born but not legal British citizens.[4]

For these and other reasons, asking prisoners where they were born leads to the over-identification of foreign nationals, many of whom are in fact British citizens. While neither the Prison Service nor the Border Agency publishes statistics on the number of prisoners misidentified as foreigners, thirteen months of observation in prisons suggests that misidentification is widespread. In one of the immigration meetings I observed, nearly half of the forty prisoners in the room were British nationals. This held true, though not always in such high numbers, in nearly every meeting I attended. In other instances, the prisoners selected to meet with immigration authorities had indefinite leave to remain in the country, had lived in the United Kingdom for decades, had British national families, or had migrated to the United Kingdom in their infancy. Circumstances such as family ties and prior leave to remain preclude neither prisoners' deportations nor their formal designation as foreign nationals. But these prisoners' presence in immigration

[4] Chapter 6 examines the particular case of foreign nationals born in former British colonies.

surgeries does highlight a contrast between colloquial and legal notions of national belonging.

In theory, or at least in the theory espoused by the Prison Service and the UKBA, over-inclusiveness is not a problem. According to Prison Service and Border Agency policymakers, prison staff ought to refer anyone who is foreign-born to the UKBA in order to avoid 'mistakes', for any prisoner who is not referred is assumed to be a British citizen. Under pressure to help the UKBA meet its annual 'removal targets', the Prison Service has thus adopted and propagated a purposefully blunt measure of citizenship. This approach bothered many prisoners, particularly those who did not identify as foreigners or who were themselves xenophobic. Exemplifying the latter group, one prisoner complained that he 'didn't know why they dragged me down here like an illegal'.

Another prisoner, Patrick, felt that the nationality identification process sent misleading messages to the public.[5] 'They have you believe that foreign nationals... are fresh, just through the tunnel', he told me. 'But it's not true.' Patrick immigrated to the United Kingdom during his infancy but was not a legal British resident or citizen when we spoke. He resisted identifying as foreign, instead referring to foreign national prisoners in the third person. 'Most of them have lived here all their life', he explained. 'They speak proper English. Even people who came to England as a one month old baby.' A prisoner named Gus agreed. He wondered aloud why the Prison Service needed to distinguish foreigners at all. 'I always put myself down as human', he said. 'Why is there no human box on the form?'

For Gus and Patrick, prison questionnaires imposed a foreign identity. Other prisoners had the inverse experience. Testifying to the complexity of national belonging, several British citizens I met had self-identified in ways that led them to be categorized as foreign nationals. One man had drunkenly told the police that he was born in St. Vincent when he had in reality never left the United Kingdom. Another prisoner, Leon, was born in the United States and held dual nationality with the United Kingdom. Despite his citizenship status, and despite never having visited Jamaica, Leon chose to identify himself as Jamaican on the reception questionnaire. He

[5] As in other chapters, all of the names referenced here are pseudonyms chosen by the prisoners. Where they are not named, quoted prisoners asked to remain anonymous.

'felt Jamaican', he explained, because he had grown up in a largely Jamaican immigrant community in London. 'I would say I'm half British, half Jamaican', Leon told me. 'Although', he added, 'America is number one because that's my birthplace.' Robert, another prisoner waiting to meet with UKBA authorities, had a similar response to questions about his nationality. He had explicitly chosen not to identify as British despite holding citizenship in the United Kingdom. 'I know I'm British', Robert told me. 'But I've always been proud of my roots. So I said I was Dominican because I class myself that way.'

These personal narratives of national belonging conflict with rudimentary penal practices that aim to cast the widest possible immigration net. Prisoners' stories also defy a one-dimensional account of agency in the citizen-making process. Identifying foreigners is an imbalanced process in which power tilts toward the Prison Service and the Border Agency. Yet that effort is also a 'negotiated settlement' between prisoners and prison staff, one in which prisoners' political and multiple articulations of their own identities matter a good deal.[6] The settlement achieved through the exchange between prisoners and staff does not depend on a prisoner's cooperation; prison staff will refer any prisoner whose nationality is in question. But the texture of that exchange—the length of time it takes to determine someone's nationality, the tone of prisoners' interactions with prison and immigration staff—varies based on a prisoner's initial and continued representations of himself. A prisoner's own conception of his nationality plays an important part, often a role of resistance, in the push to find foreigners.

Legal conceptions of citizenship also fail to align with perceptions of foreignness in prison. At least initially, a prisoner's citizenship status is distinct from whether he will be 'tagged foreign', as one prisoner called the practice. Instead, citizenship is a vague concept that connects the operations of the Prison Service with the goals of the UK Border Agency. Prison and immigration policies require anyone identified as a foreign national to attend mandatory immigration meetings, to manage simultaneous immigration and criminal cases,

[6] Phillip Goodman uses the term 'negotiated settlement' to describe race in California prisons. See Philip Goodman, 'It's Just Black, White, or Hispanic: An Observational Study of Racializing Moves in California's Segregated Prison Reception Centers', *Law and Society Review* 42, no. 4 (December 2008): pp. 735–70.

and to provide documented proof of their nationalities. These requirements are especially difficult for 'undocumented' prisoners and certain groups of migrants, such as Palestinians, Roma, and prisoners from the Western Sahara. Noishime, whose birth certificate had been destroyed in the Rwandan genocide, explained the conundrum: 'I'm Rwandan, I always tell them that. But I don't have any proof. They keep asking me for stuff. But it was all lost. I have to prove I'm destitute, but they know how I'm living. It's just terrible.' The obligation to provide identity documents also proves problematic for prisoners who faced basic logistical difficulties when asked to produce their passports from behind prison walls. Scott, a Polish national, had surrendered his passport to his landlord when he failed to pay rent. Augustus's passport was with his ex-wife, with whom he was on poor terms. Many prisoners had neither family, friends, nor lawyers to retrieve their identity documents.

This situation casts routine aspects of incarceration, such as dealing with legal counsel, in a new light. Upon seeing a solicitor in one of the immigration meetings I attended, one prisoner whispered, 'she's like gold dust'. Another prisoner explained that imprisonment and immigration casework are fundamentally incompatible:

> There's fifty foreign national prisoners here. How come there's only one coordinator? The facility ain't here to figure out immigration cases... You're just sitting... sitting like a duck. You need fax machines, access to solicitors, paperwork. It ain't here. It's harder to do everything here.

Conflicts between the structural realities of incarceration and the demands of immigration casework shifted many prisoners' attention to deportation. 'It adds stress', Patrick explained, 'imagining being dumped at an airport not knowing where I was going to go'. Another prisoner told me that being foreign was harder than being a 'normal' prisoner:

> I believe you do the crime, you do the time. What I don't like is this immigration stuff. I could do my time fine. But I can't focus properly with all this in my mind. My stress is about the rules, not being in prison.

For this prisoner, getting 'flagged foreign' meant that the real challenge of incarceration lay beyond the prison's gates.

For other prisoners, the struggles of citizenship inhered in the prison system. Almost every prisoner told me that he was treated differently once he was identified as a foreign national, whether or not he was in fact a non-British citizen. Prisoners debated whether the main source of discrimination was fellow prisoners or prison staff, but they almost universally agreed that xenophobia and anti-immigrant feeling circulated in prisons. Vernon, a forty-one-year resident of the United Kingdom, told me that prison staff stereotyped and mistreated him as soon as they identified his birthplace. 'From the minute you say you were born in a foreign country, it's like "well, well, well"... but I can't deny where I was born.' Damien concurred: 'Once the English prisoners know you aren't from here, they say you are going to get deported... treat you differently... don't care.'

A prisoner named Alvin said he was surprised at the categorical treatment of those classified as non-citizens. Born in Jamaica, Alvin was a British citizen who prison staff had misidentified as a foreign national. When I met him, Alvin had lived in England for thirty-seven years. In a thick British accent, he told me about his children and grandchildren, all of whom were British citizens. 'I think of myself as British. I have never been back to Jamaica' since leaving at fourteen, he said. Yet once staff identified him as a foreign national, Alvin felt that his immigration status became irrelevant. As he put it, 'if you're a foreigner, it doesn't matter if you have a British passport'.

Prisoners who came to the United Kingdom more recently than Alvin and Vernon said they faced discrimination specific to new migrants.[7] That discrimination centred on the competing claims that foreigners steal British jobs and come to Britain for its welfare system. One prisoner, who asked to remain nameless, recounted his experience:

> There's lots of racism, bigotry, stupidity, shouting insults and abuse, especially if you're a foreigner who doesn't understand the language or is weak in body. They got the wrong perception that foreigners come to this country to suck benefits.

[7] For an insightful analysis of the concept of new migration, a term used to describe the wave of migration from Eastern Europe after the fall of the Soviet Union, see Leanne Weber and Benjamin Bowling, 'Policing Migration: A Framework for the Regulation of Global Mobility', *Policing and Society* 14, no. 3 (September 2004): pp. 195–212.

Another man, an Albanian prisoner, offered a similar account. He too had been charged by other prisoners with migrating to 'steal their benefits':

> I spent twelve years in England. In their eyes they are racist...think you are here for benefits. English prisoners are the worst. Outside, you work with them, they stay like that for a year or two. In prison you get bullied a lot. No one ever asked me where I came from, how hard I worked, did I get benefits. They never bother asking you. You end up getting bullied.

A third prisoner, Charles, described discrimination as an economic problem. Charles was born in Nigeria and immigrated to London at the age of twenty-three. He contested the notion that migration is motivated by the lure of benefits, arguing that the desire for jobs pulls migrants toward the United Kingdom:

> The world globally is not evenly distributed. The wealth. It's obvious...A lot of us from Africa came to better our lives, to do jobs you'd pay for your children not to do...No one wakes up and says, 'God, let me be a cleaner'. But you just take what comes your way when you're trying to keep your head above water.

In Charles's account, migration unfolds on a global scale and has less to do with welfare than with work. Yet Charles said 'citizen' prisoners regularly told him to 'return to where I came from'. Scott, a Polish national, heard the same refrain. He told me that 'English people be racist to Lithuanian, Polish...they call me names, spit on you. Inside prison, "Polish bastard, go back to your country!"'

These accounts suggest that prisoners are subject to the same anti-immigrant sentiment that migrants face outside the penal estate.[8] Like other foreign nationals, non-citizen prisoners are charged with stealing jobs, depleting the welfare system, and making 'bogus' asylum claims to avoid deportation. Inside prisons, moreover, some immigration and prison staff rely on specific

[8] For empirical accounts of anti-immigrant and anti-asylum seeker sentiment in Britain, see Nick Lynn and Susan Lea, '"A Phantom Menace and the New Apartheid": The Social Construction of Asylum-Seekers in the United Kingdom', *Discourse and Society* 14, no. 4 (July 2003): pp. 425–52; Margaret Malloch and Elizabeth Stanley, 'The Detention of Asylum Seekers in the UK: Representing Risk, Managing the Dangerous', *Punishment and Society* 7, no. 1 (January 2005): pp. 53–71; Rosemary Sales, 'The Deserving and the Undeserving? Refugees, Asylum Seekers and Welfare in Britain', *Critical Social Policy* 22, no. 3 (August 2002): pp. 456–78; Weber and Bowling, 'Policing Migration'.

stereotypes of 'foreign criminality'. Immigration agents offered me detailed typologies of prisoner behaviour based on nationality: the Jamaicans are 'loud and aggressive'; Eastern Europeans are 'alcohol-related violent offences'; Nigerians 'are all document offences'; Vietnamese prisoners are 'marijuana dealers'. One border agent who worked in a prison with a high percentage of foreign nationals told me that 'the Vietnamese are especially compliant'. He explained that '80 to 90 per cent take FRS', a programme that provides cash and grants to prisoners who agree to deportation.[9] As he put it, 'they are like a conveyor belt'.

These generalizations surfaced in each of the five prisons I visited. While I heard nationality stereotypes most frequently from immigration officials, prisoners reported that prison staff, and particularly line officers, relied on the same tropes. Robert, a misidentified British citizen, said that prison officers, 'treat foreign nationals differently...They say ching-chong to the Chinese...and to the Jamaicans, the guards can't understand, so they say "what the fuck is he talking about?" They be mugging everyone off.' Robert attended British schools and grew up with friends who were British citizens. So did Damien, who told me that his education changed the way he viewed officers' treatment of foreign nationals:

> The officers treat you differently because you're a foreign national. I've grown up in school with them, so I know. You can tell when an English person is trying to get...like the way you see them talk with the Congolese. Just because they don't know doesn't mean I don't know. They don't give them solicitor phone calls...they're not allowed to come out and make phone calls.

Damien's identification with British culture clashed with his immigration status, prompting him to describe the treatment of foreigners as both a participant and an observer. The Prison Service's loose definition of foreignness encouraged this kind of double perception.[10] Under the hubs and spokes system, prisoners who

[9] Chapter 3 describes the origins and funding of the Facilitated Returns Scheme, a Border Agency programme designed to incentivize migrants' return to their birth countries.

[10] The service level agreement between UKBA and NOMS, which gave rise to the hubs and spokes policy, defines the term foreign national prisoner 'in its broadest sense' as 'a remand, sentenced or time-served detained prisoner...known or believed to be a foreign national'. MoJ and UKBA, *Service Level Agreement*, p. 5. Prison Service Order 4630 mandates that prison staff report to the UKBA

conceived of themselves as British prior to incarceration came to see xenophobia in a new light, both as a distant phenomenon that applies to 'real foreigners' and as a form of discrimination that affected them. In this respect, the process of finding foreigners enabled empathy as well as mistreatment.

The identification process also complicated discrimination. While some of the prisoners I interviewed reported explicit instances of stereotyping, like when a guard told me that 'the Pakis smell', many prisoners described a more subtle experience of favouritism. One prisoner, who requested anonymity, told me that officers 'do English prisoners more favours' and 'they talk with them. They don't do that with us.' Other prisoners said that foreign nationals were overlooked for jobs and delayed with requests, particularly for access to the mosque and the imam.[11] In general, prisoners seemed to feel that xenophobia existed, but could not explain precisely why. Rus said that officers looked at him differently:

> They only have x-ray vision eyes for me. It's like, this is our country, this is our prison, so we only look after our own.

Another prisoner felt the term 'foreign national' enabled abuse:

> The reason they call us foreign nationals is to abuse us. They wouldn't treat the English boys the way they treat us. The place would be burning.

In this man's testimony, citizenship picks out those who will and will not—or can and cannot—resist mistreatment. This

'when there is reason to suspect that the prisoner is a foreign national', HM Prison Service, *Prison Service Order 4630: Immigration and Foreign Nationals in Prison* (London: MoJ, 2008), p. 7. Chapter 3 discusses the implications of this definition of foreign nationality.

[11] Hindpal Bhui has written about inequity in job assignments between foreign and British nationals. See Hindpal Singh Bhui, 'Foreign National Prisoners: Issues and Debates', in Hindpal Singh Bhui, ed., *Race and Criminal Justice* (London: Sage, 2009), pp. 154–69; Hindpal Singh Bhui, *Going the Distance: Developing Effective Policy and Practice with Foreign National Prisoners* (London: Prison Reform Trust, 2004). Bhui has also documented the treatment of Muslim inmates, many but not all of whom are foreign nationals. See Her Majesty's Inspectorate of Prisons, *Muslim Prisoners' Experiences: A Thematic Review* (London: HMIP, 2010). Discrimination against Muslim prisoners is a complex phenomenon. It intersects with questions about foreignness—particularly where fears of foreignness and terrorism are conflated—but also raises distinct concerns about religion, ethnicity, and race in prisons. Chapter 5 considers these issues.

description is notably disconnected from a legal status or the likelihood of deportation. Rather than classifying prisoners who face expulsion, the term 'foreign national' identifies the most vulnerable members of the prison population and distinguishes them from the 'English boys'. Foreignness is about a prisoner's place in the penal hierarchy.

This account raises questions about the consequences of penal policy. Like many of the people I met, this prisoner presented citizenship as an interpretive frame for the entire experience of imprisonment. In several interviews, prisoners described having to wait for the bathroom or disliking their cell assignments as instances of discrimination against foreign nationals. These claims present an epistemological puzzle about whether and how discriminatory practices can be distinguished from other harsh realities of incarceration. [12] One approach to these testimonies is to ask when poor treatment is in fact discrimination. Another, better option is to ask why prisoners articulate the pressures of prison life through the idea of foreignness—why, in other words, concepts of citizenship and nationality have such currency as prisoners share their lives.

In answering that question, it is important to acknowledge that I explicitly asked prisoners about the hubs and spokes system. My emphasis on the new penal policy could have affected prisoners'

[12] Scholars have spent considerable time exploring the nature of discrimination in prisons. See, e.g. Ted Candle, *Community Cohesion: A Report of the Independent Review Team* (London: Home Office, 2001); Leonidas Cheliotas and Alison Liebling, 'Race Matters in British Prisoners: Towards a Research Agenda', *British Journal of Criminology* 46, no. 2 (March 2006): pp. 286–317; Commission for Racial Equality, *Stereotyping and Racism: Findings from Two Attitude Surveys* (London: CRE, 1998); Commission for Racial Equality, *A Formal Investigation by the Commission for Racial Equality into HM Prison Service of England and Wales—Part 1: The Murder of Zahid Mubarek* (London: CRE, 2003); Commission for Racial Equality, *A Formal Investigation by the Commission for Racial Equality into HM Prison Service of England and Wales—Part 2: Racial Equality in Prisons* (London: CRE, 2003); Elaine Genders and Elaine Player, *Race Relations in Prison* (Oxford: Clarendon Press, 1989); Her Majesty's Inspectorate of Prisons, *Parallel Worlds: A Thematic Review of Race Relations in Prisons* (London: HMIP, 2005); Derek McGhee, 'Moving to "Our" Common Ground: A Critical Examination of Community Cohesion Discourse in Twenty-First Century Britain', *The Sociological Review* 51, no. 3 (August 2003): pp. 376–404; Coretta Phillips, 'Ethnicity, Identity, and Community Cohesion in Prison', in Margaret Wetherell, Michelynn Lafleche, and Robert Berkeley, eds, *Identity, Ethnic Diversity, and Community Cohesion* (London: Sage Publications Ltd, 2007), pp. 75–86.

claims about its effects. Nonetheless, prisoners' testimonies suggest that the policy on foreign nationals has amplified the role that citizenship plays in the experience of incarceration. According to Patrick, nationality mattered more than it used to for prisoners and staff:

> This all started in 2006. I've been to prison before. I never used to hear about these things. I was in prison from 2000 to 2001 for twelve months and I had no problems with immigration then. It's since John Reid, he started all these things.

Prison researchers voiced concerns about the treatment of foreign nationals before John Reid, the British Home Secretary, introduced the hubs and spokes policy.[13] For many prisoners, however, that policy felt like a turning point. Gus had lived in the United Kingdom for more than four decades and had been incarcerated twice. He had a different experience of incarceration the second time around. 'I was in prison in 1997', Gus said. 'Nationality wasn't an issue then.' Rather, nationality has become 'an issue' as the prison has become a site for migration control. Nowhere is this development clearer than in the prisons selected to hold only people facing deportation.

Second-Class Service

The 'foreign-only' prison is an unusual place. The all-foreign national facility I visited, HMP Canterbury, was 'reroled' for this purpose in 2007, a year after the prisoner scandal described in Chapter 3. Canterbury was a particularly anachronistic building for the turn toward border control. The prison was originally designed in 1808 as a county gaol and still bears the inscription 'House of Corrections' over its stone gate. In the last 200 years, Canterbury has served as a Home Office archive, a Naval Detention Centre, and a prison for men. When I visited, it was a newly minted site for migration control. Canterbury has since closed its doors. The prison shut for good, or at least for now, in March 2014. Rather unexpectedly, my fieldwork has become a snapshot of the government's fledgling effort to organize prisons by nationality.

Canterbury was by most standards small and safe.[14] The prison held just over 300 prisoners at maximum capacity and was

[13] See, e.g. Bhui, *Going the Distance.*

[14] See Her Majesty's Inspectorate of Prisons, *Report on An Unannounced Short Follow-Up Inspection of HMP Canterbury* (London: HMIP, 2010).

officially designated a Category C facility, the lowest security classification before the Category D open prison. As a foreign national facility, the prison was supposed to hold non-citizens who were within five years of the end of their criminal sentences and had an 'expectation of removal' from the United Kingdom.[15] In practice, Canterbury housed a wider group of prisoners. There as elsewhere, some of the prisoners identified as foreign nationals were actually British citizens and many of the non-British citizens were not facing 'imminent removal'.[16] One prisoner from the Congo, who had been incarcerated 'pending deportation' for years, explained:

> They keep telling me 'you will be removed imminently'. They've been saying that for four years.

After a prolonged period of post-sentence detention, that Congolese prisoner was ultimately released into Britain.

In interviews, prison staff estimated that fewer than 20 per cent of the prisoners in Canterbury were deported directly from prison. The remaining prisoners were either released into the United Kingdom or transferred to immigration detention centres, where again many ex-prisoners—one official told me 'about 60 per cent'—were released. Wary in the wake of the prisoner scandal, neither the Prison Service nor the UKBA publishes the number of non-citizen prisoners who are released rather than 'removed'. One Home Office report found that in 2010 a total of 5,235 foreign national prisoners were deported, while 1,211 ex-prisoners were released into Britain.[17] Given that finding, it is unclear whether

[15] See 'Sold: Former HMP Canterbury', *Ministry of Justice*, <http://www.moj-prisondisposals.co.uk/south-east/canterbury.aspx>.

[16] The courts disagree with this claim and opt for a wider interpretation of the term 'imminent removal'. To date, British courts have upheld foreign national prisoners' detention, including post-sentence detention, for as long as six years. See, for example, the following cases challenging the post-sentence detention of foreign national prisoners: *Lumba (WL) (Congo) v. Secretary of State for the Home Department* [2011] UKSC 12, [2011] All ER (D) 262; *AP (Trinidad and Tobago) v. Secretary of State for the Home Department* [2011] EWCA Civ 551, [2011] All ER (D) 108; *RU (Bangladesh) v. Secretary of State for the Home Department* [2011] EWCA Civ 651, [2011] All ER (D) 38.

[17] John Vine, *Thematic Inspection of How the UK Border Agency Manages Foreign National Prisoners: February–May 2011* (London: HMSO, 2012), pp. 11, 22. The *Vine Report* suggests that the vast majority of prisoner releases are ordered by the courts rather than by the UKBA. Of the 1,211 foreign national prisoners who were released into Britain between February 2010 and January 2011, only 109 were released by the UKBA. The remaining 1,102 prisoners were

the statistics quoted by staff are accurate, or whether they represent inflated rumours about the ineffectiveness of the deportation system.[18] Either way, Canterbury staff members believed that the majority of incarcerated foreign nationals ended up living in the United Kingdom.

This belief highlights the degree to which the foreign-only prison was like any other penal institution. Despite its unique mission, Canterbury held prisoners with concerns that British national prisoners shared, including distance from family, dynamics with cellmates, and life after release. To the surprise of some prison staff, Canterbury's prisoners also had many of the same health concerns as their British counterparts. 'I thought they would present different health issues', Canterbury's health manager told me:

> I thought the Eastern Europeans would have higher rates of TB. I was concerned about asthma with Asians and HIV in the African population. But no, the numbers aren't there.

The Safer Custody representative, who was responsible for violence reduction and self-harm prevention, made a similar discovery:

> They don't get drugs because there are no links to the community and they have fewer visits. But it's really difficult to say they're any different from an indigenous population.

It is worth pausing to consider this officer's use of the term 'indigenous'. More often employed to describe colonized populations, here 'indigenous' sets foreign nationals against an imagined group

released after bringing their appeals to the Courts and Tribunal Service. The *Vine Report*, p. 22.

[18] To be clear, the *Vine Report* is not necessarily at odds with these prison staff members' quoted statistics on deportation. According to that report, the Facilitated Returns Scheme (FRS) accounted for 49 per cent of the total 5,235 deportations of foreign national prisoners in 2010. That leaves 2,565 prisoners who did not elect to return to their 'home' countries under the FRS programme in 2010. If you consider only those prisoners, the rate of release for foreign national prisoners in 2010 would be 47 per cent (based on 1,211 releases between February 2010 and January 2011). *Vine Report*, p. 11. That figure is much closer to the deportation numbers that staff members quoted in interviews. When considering these claims, it is also important to note that the *Vine Report* refers to the total population of foreign national prisoners in the penal and immigration estates, while HMP Canterbury held only foreign national prisoners facing deportation who were within five years of the end of their criminal sentences.

of people who have a claim to the United Kingdom. This diction naturalizes Britishness when the country's contours are in fact deeply contested. The officer's comments also put conversations about prison violence into perspective. Outside HMP Canterbury, prison staff and officials often told me that foreign nationals constitute a security threat and present greater mental and physical health challenges than the rest of the prison population. Staff cited these challenges as one justification for the stand-alone all-foreign prison. Yet, in that 'foreign' space, non-citizens turned out to be the same as prisoners everywhere.

What made these prisoners different was not where they were born, but where they were incarcerated. Canterbury looked like a classic nineteenth-century prison, but the facility was defined by the categories of people it confined: non-citizen; foreigner; foreign national; detainee. Unlike other penal institutions, which are organized around security classifications and programming capacities, Canterbury's population and daily operations hinged on citizenship. The prison was a condensed and controlled experiment into what happens when foreignness becomes the dominant feature of punishment.

One palpable result of that project was that prisoners came to believe they were being punished for their citizenship status rather than their crimes. In the 'mixed' foreign and British national prisons I visited, prisoners typically described punishment as a by-product of the penal regime, through references to their loss of liberty or the conditions behind bars. In Canterbury, in contrast, prisoners tended to think they were being punished for who they were:

> They just want you to feel punishment. They just want to punish foreign nationals. (Anonymous)

> It does feel like punishment for being foreign a bit, because there are a number of differences in this prison. Once you're branded a foreign national, it is irrelevant where your family is...Education isn't the same...I felt, yeah, I was being punished because I was tagged as a foreign national. (Rus)

> Punishment is harder for foreigner nationals at sentencing. (Anonymous)

> I feel different being in a foreign national prison. I feel segregated. Mixing up with other people is more relaxing, more social...I'm punished by being here. (Noishime)

I think they're just trying to keep all the foreigners in one boundary. I am 135 miles from my family because I am a foreign national. (Anonymous)

Punishment? Yes definitely. That's their tactic. Immigration separates you from your family—literally, they say that—so you just sign and go. (Anonymous)

I think all 300 prisoners here would say they're being punished because they're foreign. (George)

In each of these accounts, the punitive aspect of incarceration stemmed from prisoners' putative or actual lack of British citizenship. Prisoners who did not identity themselves as foreigners found this particularly upsetting; they often reminisced about life in prisons where foreignness 'didn't matter so much'. 'I was happy at Scrubs', one prisoner told me, 'then I have to come here, and now I feel different'. Other prisoners, especially those who conceived of themselves as foreign, wanted to be housed in Canterbury. One man said he liked being in an institution where people recognized his national identity: 'The difference is in Belmarsh no one would know I'm from Ghana.'[19]

There was variation in whether prisoners preferred incarceration in a foreign-only prison, but most agreed that the conditions in Canterbury were worse than in other facilities. Their grievances did not centre on prison officers—Canterbury's staff was notably well liked and attuned to the needs of the population—nor on access to immigration caseworkers, which was a concern in many 'mixed' prisons. Instead, prisoners in Canterbury felt that the facility itself got short shrift. 'There's not the quality of education here, probably because it's a foreign national prison', one prisoner explained. He continued:

I don't have access to the courses I need for my sentence plan. They think all of these people are going home, but it's like any other prison. Enhanced thinking skills, victim awareness; they're not here. It's just alcohol and drug related.

Inadequate service provision was a recurring theme. 'Facility-wise, the budget is the big difference because it's foreign national prison', a prisoner from Pakistan explained. 'In Bullingdon, you get toiletries every day. Here it's once a week.' Another prisoner said

[19] 'Scrubs' refers to HMP Wormwood Scrubs, a Category B prison in west London. HMP Belmarsh is a Category A prison in south-east London.

Canterbury was a hand-me-down institution: 'we only get gym facilities from other prisoners who have discarded them. They're making us second rate prisoners.' His friend, who also asked to remain anonymous, agreed: 'There is nothing like rehabilitation in this prison and the earlier this charade is stopped the better.'

Like prisoners' testimonies about discrimination, these charges raise questions about truth, trust, and the ethnographer's epistemological role. In my experience, most prisoners describe their incarceration regime as worse than others. Prisoners outside Canterbury regularly told me how much better life was in all-foreign prisons, where people shared anxieties about deportation, and in immigration detention centres, where prisoners could more easily communicate with their families and solicitors. These claims are one of the ways that prisoners make sense of their imprisonment and imagine a better world. They are important coping mechanisms, and in that sense, are true for the prisoners making them no matter where they are incarcerated.

In the case of Canterbury, claims about poor conditions also reflected the prison's relative position in the penal bureaucracy. According to one prison official, 'for funding, Canterbury is at the bottom of the list'. Staff reported that the prison did not receive support for anger management or vocational classes because Canterbury had a theoretically exceptional population of prisoners who would not return to British society. As one prison official put it:

> NOMS [the National Offender Management Service] said what they are doing is reducing reoffending. These people aren't ending up on the stats. Why give them services that won't affect the stats? It's an informed decision.

A staff member at Canterbury echoed this account, explaining that the 'foreign national issue gets pushed under the carpet'. He added:

> They're assumed deportable, but 60 per cent aren't, so they just don't get services. They say foreign nationals must receive exactly the same service, but I know for a fact that they don't.

The cumulative result of this approach to foreign nationals was a system distinguished by what one prison official called 'second-class service to foreigners'.

This second-class system provides a window into the nationalist boundaries of the penal project. The paucity of rehabilitative programmes in Canterbury stems from the Prison Service's reliance on performance metrics, and specifically, on metrics that exclude non-citizens. The absence of anger management and bricklaying courses in the foreign-only prison demonstrates not only the dominance of actuarial logic in prison management, but also the degree to which that logic is bound to the nation-state. The implicit assumption here is that the prison is made for the British polity. The reality is that the prison *makes* the British polity through practices like finding foreigners and placing them in specialized institutions.[20]

Prisoners often told me that they understood foreignness in terms of cultural belonging rather than legal status. Many non-citizen prisoners identified with British culture, and as residents of Scotland, Northern Ireland, and Wales would remind prison officials, Britishness is a disputed idea. The British polity does not exist as a stable entity to be policed. Practices of policing and punishment create the boundaries of Britain. In identifying people as foreigners—people who do not conceive of themselves that way—the Prison Service and the Border Agency refine the concept of British citizenship. By placing those 'foreigners' in separate facilities, these agencies telegraph that foreign nationals do not belong in the country, nor even in its regular prisons.

The prison's role in creating citizens became particularly clear when HMP Canterbury attempted to judge itself. In the Prison Service lexicon, the main measure for evaluating prisons is the key performance indicator, or KPI. Prisons in the British penal estate operate along a shared set of KPIs for everything from health care provision to resettlement programmes.[21] These indicators tend to be hyper-quantitative—one KPI, for instance, is that 'the rate of

[20] This claim about the production of citizens in prisons complements Catherine Dauvergne's work on migration. Dauvergne argues that 'the contemporary crackdown on extralegal migration' creates a class of unwanted people whose 'illegality' legitimates the sovereign state. See Catherine Dauvergne, *Making People Illegal: What Globalization Means for Migration and Law* (Cambridge: Cambridge University Press, 2008), p. 47. My argument is that the crackdown Dauvergne critiques works not only to make people illegal, but to construct citizens as well.

[21] Prison Service Order 7100 lays out many of the Prison Service's key performance indicators and targets. See Her Majesty's Prison Service, *Prison Service Order 7100: Key Performance Indicators, Key Performance Targets and Additional Measures* (London: MoJ, 2007).

escapes . . . expressed as a percentage of the average prison population is lower than 0.05 per cent'.[22] KPIs provide a way for prisons to audit themselves and to track their effectiveness through a more localized metric than crime or recidivism rates.

Despite its small size and dedicated staff, Canterbury regularly failed certain KPIs: making contacts to help prisoners find jobs after release; providing offenders with assistance opening a bank account; maintaining facility capacity. Canterbury struggled to meet these metrics because its prisoners were frequently transferred to detention centres and were ineligible for bank accounts and 'British' jobs. That is to say, the prison failed where it could not succeed because the measurements were made for citizens. Staff members tried to ameliorate this situation by thinking outside the typical constraints of the penal institution. Canterbury's sub-par performance metrics prompted a series of questions in one meeting of the prison's managers:

> Would we facilitate evening visits for a family member who had flown in from Sierra Leone and it was the only time they could visit?

No, the group agreed, that would be too complicated and would necessitate evening shifts for visits. 'Do we want to do parenting courses?' One staff member thought not:

> The culture is so different. Some of these guys think nothing of beating their children.

The staff members agreed against offering the course and moved on.

> Do we need a global resettlement centre?
>
> Can we facilitate communication with the Congo or Somalia?

After each question, the managers debated whether the prison could afford specialized programmes and policies for non-citizens. Invariably, the answer was no. Foreign nationals confused the system, demanding services—night-time visits, global resettlement—that were new, unusual, and in some cases downright unacceptable.

[22] Enver Solomon, *A Measure of Success: An Analysis of the Prison Service's Performance against its Key Performance Indicators 2003–2004* (London: Prison Reform Trust, 2004), p. 7.

This vignette captures the conceptual and practical boundaries of the British prison. Both as an idea and as a set of practices, the prison is a place where citizens are the imagined recipients of the many services involved in incarceration. Familiar with the challenges foreign nationals experience and pose, some of Canterbury's staff sensed a problem with this approach. Regardless of where prisoners end up, 'they're people worth helping', one officer explained. He wondered why resettlement should matter less in a foreign national prison. 'You don't want to leave a guy to rape someone there either, do you?'

Such questions fall outside prison policies and performance metrics. In doing so, they illustrate how significantly prisons would have to change if punishment were not presumed to be a national practice. The traditional line-up of prison services did not begin to encompass the full range of prisoners' experiences in Canterbury. Prisoners needed programmes that operated in a global frame: some wanted to make international phone calls; some spoke no English and asked for a better foreign language library collection; some worried about their deportation dates and whether their home countries had repatriation agreements with the British government. One response to these concerns is to ask what programmes, what budget, and what sort of political will a prison would need to provide something other than second-class service. Another is to ask what values are assumed and imparted in places like Canterbury.

Foreign national prisoners have distinct needs, but they are not simply a 'special needs' population. These prisoners' concerns reflect the nationalist presumptions on which punishment depends. The fact that British prison officials cannot think beyond the country's borders to, for instance, the problem of reoffending in the Congo, suggests that punishment is a precarious project in any context. How, if imprisonment does not stop reoffending 'out there', are we so convinced that it works in Britain, or at all? Scepticism about global resettlement and long-distance phone calls can quickly become a critique of incarceration's utility as a mode of punishment.

Focusing on foreign-only prisons also raises questions about the vision of citizenship implicit in incarceration. In HMP Canterbury, imprisonment was a self-consciously domestic practice, a way to reinforce the tenuous link between punishment and the polity. Canterbury was also a space where prisoners received a set of lessons about the meaning of British citizenship. The Prison Service not only identified Canterbury's population as foreign and segregated them from the rest of the prison population. Staff also enrolled prisoners in education courses where they learned good grammar, proper pronunciation, and above all, what it takes to belong in Britain. This didactic, nationalist aspect of incarceration came to life in Canterbury's English language class.

Practise Your English

Though only a small piece of the prison regime, education courses are a critical part of the experience of incarceration. Many prisoners told me that classroom time was essential to their survival. Noishime explained:

> The education course keeps me out of my cell. If you stay in your cell, everything comes back, the stress, the depression... Your whole life starts coming in, you start getting more depressed... You have to try to fight.

Education programmes offered Noishime a reprieve from the simultaneous anxieties of incarceration and potential deportation. These courses provide a glimpse into what it means to be—and to become—British behind bars.

Of all the courses offered in Canterbury, English as a Second Language was especially laden with references to national culture. The course I observed took place in a classroom adorned with posters celebrating the prison's international population. 'I am Romanian', 'I am Turkish', 'I am Russian', posters read. Around the room, signs declared their creator's origins in the Congo, China, Lithuania, and Italy. Prisoners conversed with each other in Arabic, French, and Hindi. With their teacher, however, they spoke English. She was keen on this and reprimanded me when I spoke French with a prisoner from the Congo.

The class began with a short lecture on the import of learning English, then turned to a discussion of volunteerism, the topic of the day.

> How many of you have volunteers in your country?

All but one of the men raised their hands. The teacher turned to the lone holdout:

In Fred's country, they don't appear to have a history of helping people and volunteer work. Everyone else does.

The prisoners seemed unconcerned as she continued:

This country has a huge history of volunteering. Do you know why volunteering is important?

When the men did not reply, the teacher offered her own answer:

If a lot of people get involved in volunteering, it will help integration, but a lot of groups are specific to ethnicities. If you volunteer for a Pakistani group, you won't help other people. But if you volunteer for Red Cross at the hospital, that will be better. If there was more volunteering in your country, do you think it would be a better place to live?

This was a rhetorical question, but an Algerian prisoner disagreed.

No.

The teacher took his response as an opportunity to expand her argument, and an exchange ensued:

TEACHER: This country has a big thing for helping disabled people. Who helps people who can't see and hear in your country?
PRISONER: People help people in Algeria.
TEACHER: Yes, but it's just people helping people and not an organization. So do you think that's better?
PRISONER: Yes.
TEACHER (*flustered*): Okay, well why don't you group-talk about it then. Practise your English.

She turned to Fred, who was born in the Congo. He seemed a more willing participant.

Do people not help each other where you are from?

Fred's reply was too soft for me to hear from the back of the room. I only caught his instructor's response:

Oh, well, yes, it's been very difficult with the fighting.

With that, she returned to the theme of the course. 'Now Fred, the more you practise your English the better your English will get.'

Courses like this one construct a very specific understanding of British national belonging. This teacher's presentation on volunteering suggested that to be British is to be involved in the community in a particular way, namely, through organizations like the Red Cross.

Her delivery of this message felt like a satire of British culture—'but that's just helping people and not an organization!' the British bureaucrat protests. The implicit claims here are both normative and paternalistic: bureaucracy is better than kinship; integration is preferable to 'ethnic' separation. In sum, it would be better if your country were more like ours, and to be a part of ours you ought to conform. Conforming, moreover, means more than just applying for citizenship and stating a desire to reside in the United Kingdom. To be a true citizen, a person must accept and reproduce the British vision of social structure and community involvement.

This was only one class in one prison. This scene is not necessarily repeated in every institution, but it does capture how imprisonment can be used to craft citizens. In recent years, the British government has placed a growing emphasis on migrants' acceptance of British values and customs.[23] Through measures like the citizenship test, which was introduced in 2002, those seeking to join the British polity are increasingly required to demonstrate their familiarity with aspects of British culture such as Mothering Sunday or the constitution of Parliament.[24] These requirements infuse the concept of citizenship with cultural norms about the meaning of Britishness and make 'knowledge about life in the United Kingdom' one barrier to entry.[25]

Prisoners contested this approach to citizenship. Like the practice of finding foreigners, the effort to teach prisoners about British citizenship was met with resistance. No, the Algerian prisoner replied, organizational volunteering is not better than familial aid. No, the Congo would not be better off if it looked more like the United Kingdom. Prisoners in Canterbury disagreed about what community involvement should look like and how a good citizen would relate to the state. In return, they were taught that one model of national belonging was best and that to be British they had to accept a version of political membership that was imbued with very particular social norms. Citizenship was constructed narrowly and slowly, through a series of rocky interactions between prisoners and staff.

In the end, this process changed how prisoners saw themselves. Several of the people I interviewed told me that the experience of

[23] Zedner, 'Security, the State, and the Citizen', p. 387.

[24] The citizenship test was introduced by the Nationality, Immigration and Asylum Act of 2002. The Borders, Citizenship and Immigration Act of 2009 contains similar provisions requiring familiarity with British culture.

[25] Zedner, 'Security, the State, and the Citizen', p. 384.

being classified and treated as a foreigner had altered their identity. Damien was one of these people. Like many of the prisoners I met, he had always believed that he was British and did not expect problems with immigration when he was arrested. Damien was born in Jamaica and had migrated to England with his aunt before his twelfth birthday. A year after he came to London, Damien's mother, who still lived in Jamaica, died. When I asked him about her death, Damien replied with a question: 'They don't care, do they?' This answer hung in the air as he recounted his story.

After moving to London, Damien began to attend British schools and make British friends. He picked up a British accent, married a British citizen, and had a son. Doctors diagnosed Damien's son with a serious skin disease shortly after his birth. A year later, his wife was diagnosed with cancer. Damien dealt drugs to make money:

> My partner earns £100 a week on disability. If she comes to visit, pays the train fare, then my kid goes without food for a week. I was selling drugs, but at least I was working for my family.

Damien was arrested and imprisoned for drug possession in 2008. At the end of his criminal term, he was transferred to an immigration 'removal' centre (IRC), where the government detained him under immigration powers. After spending a year in the IRC without any movement in his immigration case, Damien felt hopeless. He asked to see UKBA officials to discuss his case, but got no reply. After several weeks, Damien placed a razor in his mouth and demanded a meeting with immigration authorities. IRC staff attempted to restrain him, and in the fight that followed, Damien swallowed the razor. He was recovering from the injuries to his stomach when we first met.

I introduced myself to Damien in an immigration meeting at a Category A prison. He had recently been transferred back into the penal estate for the 'problems' he had caused in the IRC. Damien agreed to speak with me after I described my research and talked with a few other prisoners. Initially, he told me that he was British. 'I'm never going to Jamaica anyway. I'm not dumb', he said. 'Don't let my hair fool you.'[26] A month later, Damien was concerned that he might actually be deported and that his son would be left without a father. 'You're just playing the same tune in my head that

[26] Chapter 5 examines the relationship between race, nationality, and self-presentation.

plays in my son's head', Damien told me. I asked him what that meant and he explained:

> My partner has cancer. She's not expected to pass thirty-two, thirty-five. My son's not gonna have a mom, not gonna know where his dad is. How are you going to explain to that young man where his dad is?

This question weighed on Damien during his imprisonment and informed his prolonged resistance to deportation.

Slowly, Damien's perspective shifted. I returned to see him once a month. Each visit, his outlook was different. The third time Damien and I met, he said he no longer felt British. Life behind bars had changed his mind:

> It wasn't until I got to prison that I realized I wasn't British. When all this started, they made me realize I wasn't British.

More than a year of indefinite detention had altered Damien's identity. Now, he said, he knew he was 'not really British'. I last saw Damien a few months later, again in an immigration meeting. Two days earlier, he had agreed to return to Jamaica. The last thing Damien told me was a joke: 'Seventeen years of bad weather is enough.'

Damien's story is neither exceptional nor, in the general scheme of studying deportation, is it unusually sad. He was not a refugee displaced by genocide, a foreigner with no family, or a prisoner whose only crime was illegal entry. Damien was guilty of the crime of drug possession and was, by all accounts, born on the island of Jamaica. He was one of many prisoners who threatened and enacted self-harm in the context of his immigration case, and unlike some of them, he survived to tell his tale.[27] Damien was, in other words, a person whose file might go unnoticed by Border Agency caseworkers and prison staff. It is precisely this ordinariness that makes him compelling. Damien's narrative captures how changing prisoners' identities becomes a routine part of incarceration.

[27] For a study of suicides among the foreign national prisoner population, see Jo Borrill and Donna A. Taylor, 'Suicides by Foreign National Prisoners in England and Wales 2007: Mental and Cultural Issues', *Forensic Psychiatry and Psychology* 20, no. 6 (Nov. 2009): pp. 886–905.

Criminologists have long noted that the practice of imprisonment operates on and through individual identity.[28] Drawing on ethnographic research, scholars such as Pat Carlen, Mary Bosworth, and Eamonn Carrabine have demonstrated that the effects of incarceration are realized in the transformation of a person's sense of self.[29] Under conditions of mass mobility, this process plays out around the idea of citizenship. The experience of incarceration teaches prisoners like Damien that, despite whatever they believe, they are not really British. Imprisonment is the practice through which those behind bars learn that the law determines who they are.

Most of the prisoners I interviewed discovered that they felt less British over time. Some found the opposite. George, for example, had always conceived of himself as Ghanaian despite possessing a British passport and living in the United Kingdom for decades. He felt different behind bars:

> If you asked me before I would've said I was Ghanaian. If you asked my mindset, my identity, I would've said Ghanaian. But since being here I've realized I'm not Ghanaian; I don't fit in with the Ghanaians. But I'm not English. It messes with my identity. I've started questioning who exactly I am. I'm not Ghanaian; we have totally different aspirations. Before I would've said, 'no, I'm not English'. But I'm bloody English now and I have to accept it.

George served his time in Canterbury alongside many Ghanaian nationals. Life in the 'all-foreign' prison forced him to accept his Britishness.

[28] See, e.g. Mary Bosworth, *Engendering Resistance: Agency and Power in Women's Prisons* (London: Ashgate, 1999); Pat Carlen, *Women's Imprisonment: A Study in Social Control* (London: Routledge, 1983); Eamonn Carrabine, *Power, Discourse, and Resistance: A Genealogy of the Strangeways Prison Riot* (Aldershot: Ashgate Publishing, 2004); Eamonn Carrabine and Mary Bosworth, 'Reassessing Resistance: Race, Gender, and Sexuality in Prison', *Punishment and Society* 3, no. 4 (October 2001): 501–15; Ben Crewe, 'Power, Resistance and Adaptation in the Late-Modern Prison', *British Journal of Criminology* 47, no 2 (March 2007): 256–75.

[29] Bosworth, *Engendering Resistance*; Carlen, *Women's Imprisonment*; Carrabine, *Power, Discourse, and Resistance*.

For other prisoners, incarceration erased any notion of national belonging. Patrick explained:

> I wanna go home to my family. That's the only home I know. I don't know what they're thinking. If I went to Congo, they'd call me a foreigner. Here I'm a foreigner; there I'm a foreigner. I don't know.

At the conclusion of four years behind bars, Patrick was left feeling that he did not belong anywhere. He shared this sense of perpetual alienation with many prisoners who did not remember living where they were born—people like Rus and George, who immigrated as infants and could not speak the language of their birthplaces.[30]

Whether it makes prisoners British or foreign, imprisonment is transformative. People like Damien, George, and Patrick enter the penal institution with one idea about who they are. They leave prison with very different answers to that question. Through education courses and reception questionnaires, incarceration displaces prisoners' national identities and ascribes new ones—those in line with the law—onto them. Penal practices teach prisoners that they were wrong, that they did not understand what it takes to be a British citizen. When magnified across the prison estate, these lessons situate the prison as a material site at which the epistemological boundaries of the citizen are etched. Today's prisons not only incapacitate and rehabilitate prisoners. They alter who prisoners are and what being British really means.

Conclusion

Studying prison is often, if not always, a way to ask how societies determine their own boundaries. Prisons are places where polities sort out who belongs, who should be exiled, and when it is appropriate to return to a community. Questions about the meaning of citizenship flow naturally from this inquiry. More than thirty years ago, Foucault argued that prisons mediate between sovereign and subject, forging good citizens through discipline.[31] More recently, Jonathan Simon has suggested that prisons embody the core tenets

[30] Abdelmalek Sayad situates the problem of perpetual foreignness as one of the central tensions of migration. Abdelmalek Sayad, *The Suffering of the Immigrant*, trans. David Macey (Cambridge: Polity Press, 2004).

[31] Michel Foucault, *Discipline and Punish: The Birth of the Prison*, trans. Alan Sheridan (New York, NY: Vintage Books, 1977).

and contradictions of modern democracy.[32] Simon notes that the penal institution evolved from liberal democracy and, since its inception, has been a place where governments reproduce ideas about citizenship.[33] Like many criminologists and political theorists, he contends that the prison is a projection of the norms that constitute the sovereign state.[34]

The claim that prisons make citizens is thus not particularly radical. One might argue that it is a founding assertion of critical criminology. What is noteworthy, though, is that contemporary prisons endorse a different model of citizenship than penal institutions of the past. Simon hinted at this phenomenon in his work on immigration detention in the late 1990s.[35] Citing the rise of globalization and the growth of mass imprisonment in the United States, Simon argued that twenty-first-century prisons were caught between an undemocratic philosophy of containment and the democratic principles from which the penal institution emerged.[36]

This tension surfaces, albeit in a slightly different form, in the British penal estate. Though he does not articulate in these terms, Simon's claim is essentially that the prison is becoming a new sort of place, one less concerned than before with reforming citizens and returning them to the polity.[37] Where the modern prison aimed to discipline criminals, and in that sense presumed their political membership, twenty-first-century prisons distinguish citizens from foreigners and emphasize that non-citizens do not belong. In this framework, the prisoner is not so much presumed reformable as assumed deportable. The project of penality is to identify and reinforce the nation-state, not only by reforming its deviant members but by determining its edges as well.

[32] Jonathan Simon, 'Refugees in a Carceral Age: The Rebirth of Immigration Prisons in the United States', *Public Culture* 10, no. 3 (Spring 1998): pp. 577–607.

[33] Simon, 'Refugees in a Carceral Age', p. 604.

[34] Simon, 'Refugees in a Carceral Age'. For other work on this issue, see Thomas Dumm, *Democracy and Punishment: Disciplinary Origins of the United States* (Madison, WI: University of Wisconsin Press, 1987); David Garland, *Punishment and Welfare* (Brookfield, VT: Gower Publishing, 1985).

[35] See Simon, 'Refugees in a Carceral Age'.

[36] Simon, 'Refugees in a Carceral Age'.

[37] Simon, 'Refugees in a Carceral Age'; see also Mary Bosworth and Emma Kaufman, 'Foreigners in a Carceral Age: Immigration and Imprisonment in the United States', *Stanford Law and Policy Review* 22, no. 1 (May 2011): pp. 429–54.

This project has a substantive effect on the meaning of citizenship. Historically, Anglo-American law has cast citizenship as a marker of 'civil, political, and social rights'.[38] Citizenship has long been an exclusive concept—some people are citizens, some are not—but in its classic iteration, citizenship is a form of enduring membership born from participation in a polity. This is the idea around which both the liberal state and the modern prison developed. In recent years, however, that model has been eclipsed by a new formulation in which citizenship is, as the Home Office puts it, 'something to be earned'.[39] Lucia Zedner has critiqued this vision of political membership, noting that it makes citizenship an especially harsh means of social control. As she explains it, 'the conditional nature of contemporary citizenship…becomes a potent tool by which those at the margins of the political community are policed by the state'.[40]

Zedner stands alongside several theorists, including Nancy Fraser and Wendy Brown, who have developed insightful arguments about the relationship between globalization, political participation, and crime control.[41] These scholars contend that citizenship changes with the times and, in an age of 'waning sovereignty', has become a technique of exclusion.[42] The foreign-only prison brings this transformation into being. Prisoners like Noishime, Patrick, and Damien demonstrate that incarceration is one way that citizenship becomes a contingent status. These prisoners' stories implicate prisons in the enforcement of normative ideas about political membership, and specifically, in creating the sense that citizenship is both a privilege and goal.

Noishime gave voice to this particular feeling. When I asked him what he would do if he were released, Noishime told me that he would pursue British citizenship:

> If I get out, I'll go for British citizenship. If I get citizenship, I won't be a foreign national. I'll neutralize myself.

[38] Zedner, 'Security, the State, and the Citizen', p. 382.

[39] Home Office, *Fairer, Faster, Firmer: A Modern Approach to Immigration and Asylum* (London: HMSO, 1998); see also Zedner, 'Security, the State, and the Citizen', p. 386.

[40] Zedner, 'Security, the State, and the Citizen', p. 382.

[41] Wendy Brown, *Walled States, Waning Sovereignty* (Cambridge, MA: Zone Books, 2010); Nancy Fraser, *Scales of Justice: Reimagining Political Space in a Globalizing World* (Cambridge: Polity Press, 2010). See also Michael Hardt and Antonio Negri, *Empire* (Cambridge, MA: Harvard University Press, 2001).

[42] Brown, *Walled States, Waning Sovereignty*.

Noishime's plan illustrates the degree to which citizenship has become an aspiration in prison. For him, and for many foreign nationals, British citizenship is a way to avoid the dual threats of deportation and discrimination. Citizenship is a means to a less unhappy life and to a new identity. It is a way to 'neutralize' the features of one's self that prison policies—and through them, the British state—have deemed unacceptable. The problem, as we will learn in Chapter 5, is that those features often cannot be erased, for the practice of making citizens is linked to the legacy of British racism.

5

The Queen's English

Nella Larsen's 1929 novel *Passing* introduces readers to Irene and Clare, two young girls from interracial families. When Clare's father dies, she moves to live with her two white aunts, who raise her in their white community. After finishing school, Clare marries a racist man who believes that she is white. Irene moves to Harlem, where she marries a black doctor and identifies as African-American.

Years later, the two friends have a chance meeting in the rooftop restaurant of the Drayton, a Chicago hotel. Both women are passing as white in the racist establishment. Clare stares at Irene, recognizing her from the distant past. Irene feels Clare's gaze and, sensing that she does not belong, 'anger, scorn, and fear slide over her'.[1] For a moment, the reader is caught with Irene in the fear that her 'real' race will be found out. Regardless of our own identities, we are gripped by the high stakes of racial performance.

Now a canonical text in critical theory courses, *Passing* depicts the experience of identity in a society structured on racist and heteronormative beliefs. Larsen's novel captures the ambiguity of race, class, and gender in the United States of the late 1920s. The power of her narrative lies in what remains unsaid, in the subtle ways that her characters subvert social norms, and in the questions her plot raises: What does it mean to be black or white? When and where does race matter? How do societies determine who belongs? This chapter asks each of those questions in the context of the twenty-first-century British prison—a very different space than the one Larsen explored eighty years ago, but one in which her message resonates with equal force. Turning to the testimonies of prisoners incarcerated as foreigners, I examine how identity gets created and contested behind bars.

[1] Nella Larsen, *Passing* (New York, NY: Penguin Classics, 2003), p. 16.

The first half of the chapter explores how people inside British prisons understand race. In the five institutions I visited, no two people had the same answer to questions about race and ethnicity. Prisoners described racial identity as dependent on past experience and said that race was a particularly flexible concept in the close confines of the prison. At the same time, racism provided a powerful framework for prisoners seeking to explain their incarceration. The beginning of the chapter contends with the simultaneous contingency and relevance of race.

The second half of the chapter considers how penal policies affect identity dynamics. The British policy on non-citizens, which is known as hubs and spokes, categorizes both prisoners and prisons by citizenship status. In practice, this policy has encouraged widespread racial profiling. It has also prompted creative forms of coping and evasion by prisoners seeking to subvert border control. This chapter documents prisoners' responses to hubs and spokes, which range from increased empathy and attempts to mimic Britishness to heightened claims of gender conformity among prisoners whose national identities have been challenged. Drawing on testimonies, the chapter asks whether the responses to hubs and spokes are modes of resistance, compliance, or both. Ultimately, I argue that the new policy on citizenship has reconstituted the relationship between identity and confinement.

Race and Nation

The study of race has a rich history in the United Kingdom. In the late 1970s and early 1980s, postcolonial theorists began to argue that policing practices built racist sentiment into the structure of the British justice system. Drawing on Marx and Freud, scholars such as Stuart Hall and Paul Gilroy asserted that punishment is a form of social control and that state power disproportionately targets non-white migrants from former colonies.[2] This argument percolated in legal and sociological scholarship throughout the

[2] See, e.g. Paul Gilroy, *There Ain't No Black in the Union Jack: The Cultural Politics of Race and Nation* (Abingdon: Routledge, 1987); Stuart Hall, Chas Critcher, Tony Jefferson, John N. Clark, and Brian Roberts, *Policing the Crisis: Mugging, the State, and Law and Order* (London: Palgrave MacMillan, 1978).

1980s. It resurfaced in a particularly poignant form in 1993 with the death of Stephen Lawrence.

Lawrence, a black British nineteen-year-old, was killed by a group of white teenagers while he waited for a London bus. The government delayed and mishandled the investigation of his murder, prompting a public outcry. In the wake of the scandal surrounding Lawrence's death, High Court judge William Macpherson undertook a study of racism in the Metropolitan Police Force and the Crown Prosecution Service.[3] In 1999, nearly two years after his investigation began, MacPherson concluded that the British police force was 'institutionally racist'.[4] This claim reverberated through British culture as advocacy groups and policymakers debated whether an institution can discriminate.[5] The BBC has since called the Lawrence murder 'one of the most important moments in the modern history of criminal justice in Britain'.[6]

In academic circles, the Lawrence inquiry intersected with a long-standing debate about the nature of British race relations. For decades, criminologists have asked how people experience race,[7] and in the case of prisons, whether prisoners' identities are

[3] William MacPherson, *The Stephen Lawrence Inquiry: Report of an Inquiry by Sir William Macpherson of Cluny*, CM4262-1 (London: HMSO, 1999).

[4] MacPherson, *The Stephen Lawrence Inquiry.*

[5] There is a robust body of criminological writing on the Lawrence Inquiry and its aftermath. See, e.g. Lee Bridges, 'The Lawrence Inquiry—Incompetence, Corruption, and Institutional Racism', *Journal of Law and Society* 26, no. 3 (September 1999): pp. 289–322; Norman Dennis, George Erdos, and Ahmed Al-Shahi, *Racist Murder and Pressure Group Politics: The Macpherson Report and the Police* (London: Institute for the Study of Civil Society, 2000); Janet Foster, Tim Newburn, and Anna Souhami, *Assessing the Impact of the Stephen Lawrence Inquiry*, Home Office Research Study 294, (London: Home Office, 2005); John Lea, 'The Macpherson Report and the Question of Institutional Racism', *The Howard Journal* 39, no. 3 (August 2000): pp. 218–33; John Solomos, 'Social Research and the Stephen Lawrence Inquiry', *Sociological Research Online* 4, no. 1 (1999).

[6] 'Q&A: Stephen Lawrence murder', *BBC News*, 5 May 2004, <http://news.bbc.co.uk/2/hi/uk_news/3685733.stm>.

[7] See, e.g. Leonidas Cheliotis and Alison Liebling, 'Race Matters in British Prisoners: Towards a Research Agenda', *British Journal of Criminology* 46, no. 2 (2006): pp. 286–317; Ben Crewe, *The Prisoner Society: Power, Adaptation, and Social Life in an English Prison* (Oxford: Oxford University Press, 2009); Elaine Genders and Elaine Player, *Race Relations in Prison* (Oxford: Clarendon Press, 1989); Philip Goodman, 'It's Just Black, White, or Hispanic: An Observational Study of Racializing Moves in California's Segregated Prison Reception Centers', *Law and Society Review* 42, no. 4 (December 2008): pp. 735–70; Coretta Phillips,

imported from the outside world or derived from the isolated conditions of confinement.[8] The tension between these two views, which are known as the importation and deprivation theories of imprisonment, has softened in recent years as criminologists have argued that incarceration both reaffirms *and* undermines racial tropes.[9] Ethnographers Coretta Phillips and Rod Earle note that existing racial ties and identities are often subsumed within broader 'territorial allegiances', which develop from 'outside' society but 'permeate the prison' and take unique forms behind bars.[10]

'Ethnicity, Identity, and Community Cohesion in Prison', in Margaret Wetherell, Michelynn Lafleche, and Robert Berkeley, eds, *Identity, Ethnic Diversity, and Community Cohesion* (London: Sage Publications Ltd, 2007); David Wilson, '"Keeping Quiet" or "Going Nuts": Some Emerging Strategies Used by Young Black People in Custody at a Time of Childhood Being Re-constructed', *Howard Journal of Criminal Justice* 42, no. 5 (December 2003): pp. 411–25.

[8] See Francis Cullen and Pamela Vilcox, eds, *Encyclopedia of Criminological Theory, Volume 1* (London: Sage Publications Ltd, 2010).

[9] See Mary Bosworth, Benjamin Bowling, and Maggy Lee, 'Globalization, Ethnicity and Racism: An Introduction', *Theoretical Criminology* 12, no. 3 (Month 2008): pp. 263–73; Kimmett Edgar and Carol Martin, *Perceptions of Race and Conflict: Perspectives of Minority Ethnic Prisoners and of Prison Officers*, RDS Online Report 11/04 (London: Home Office, 2004); Loraine Gelsthorpe, 'The Experiences of Female Minority Ethnic Offenders: The Other "Other"', in Sam Lewis, Peter Raynor, David Smith, and Ali Wardak, eds, *Race and Probation* (Devon: Willan, 2005); Kathleen McDermott, 'We Have No Problem: The Experience of Racism in Prison', *New Community* 16, no. 2 (1990): pp. 213–28; Coretta Philips and Rod Earle, 'Reading Difference Differently? Identity, Epistemology and Prison Ethnography', *British Journal of Criminology* 50, no. 2 (March 2010): 360–78; Coretta Phillips and Rod Earle, 'Cultural Diversity, Ethnicity, and Race Relations in Prison', in Ben Crewe and Jamie Bennett, eds, *The Prisoner* (London: Routledge, 2011), pp. 117–30; Coretta Phillips, '"It Ain't Nothing like America with the Bloods and the Crips": Gang Narratives inside Two English Prisons', *Punishment and Society* 14, no. 1 (January 2012): pp. 51–68; Coretta Phillips and Rod Earle, 'Negotiating Identities: Ethnicity and Social Relations in a Young Offenders' Institution', *Theoretical Criminology* 12, no. 3 (August 2008): pp. 313–31.

[10] Phillips, 'It Ain't Nothing like America with the Bloods and the Crips', p. 57; see also Martha Henderson, Francis Cullen, and Leo Carroll, 'Race, Rights, and Order in Prison: A National Survey of Wardens on the Racial Integration of Prison Cells', *Prison Journal* 80, no. 3 (September 2000): pp. 295–308. For the American counterpoint, see Philip Goodman, 'It's Just Black, White, or Hispanic'. Goodman presents a rigid account of race in the California prison system. See also Juanita Diaz-Cotto, *Gender, Ethnicity, and the State: Latina and Latino Prison Politics* (Albany, NY: SUNY Press, 1996).

Phillips and Earle conclude that the meaning of race is simultaneously dependent on features of life beyond prison and constituted from the particular context of the penal institution.[11]

This contextual account of race resonates with my fieldwork in British prisons. In the five institutions I visited, prisoners offered a wide variety of answers to questions about the meaning of race. When I asked what their races were, some prisoners told me they were 'black' or 'white'. Others said they were 'Jamaican', 'British', or simply, 'it depends'. Several South Asian prisoners, such as Rus, identified themselves as 'coloured'. Some prisoners said they were 'white Polish' or 'Lithuanian'. One man looked at me puzzled when I asked about race. 'I don't have a race', he replied. In a year of fieldwork, I never found two people who articulated race the same way.

Prisoners had equally fluid views of race relations. In interviews, I often asked how race affected prisoners' friendships with each other and interactions with prison staff. Prisoners' responses suggest that race bends with context. One man, an eighteen-year-old born in Kigali and raised in London, told me, 'depends, innit. You could be friends, but at the end of the day, it depends what the situation is.' Gus, in contrast, reported that 'races stick together: Chinese, Arabs, Muslims, Africans'.[12] Thomas offered a slightly different account of the prison hierarchy: 'An English guy with an English accent gets more respect than any foreigner.' Then, laughing and shaking his head, he added, 'the white man is in the best position. Always.' Noishime described a similar spectrum: 'The way I see it, we're categorized. If you're a white foreigner you get less than British prisoners, but more than Africans.'

These descriptions hint at the sheer power of the prison environment. While identity is intersectional and precarious in any social space, race appeared to become especially slippery in the small and intensely hierarchical world of the prison. Many prisoners said that incarceration reshaped racial divisions that were entrenched

[11] See Phillips, 'It Ain't Nothing like America with the Bloods and the Crips'; Phillips and Earle, 'Reading Difference Differently?'; Phillips and Earle, 'Cultural Diversity, Ethnicity, and Race Relations in Prison'.

[12] For more on the relationship between race and religion, see Phillips, 'It Ain't Nothing like America with the Bloods and the Crips'; and HM Inspectorate of Prisons, *Muslim Prisoners' Experiences: A Thematic Review* (London: HMIP, 2010). Mark Hamm has also written about this topic. Mark Hamm, 'Prison Island in the Age of Sacred Terror', *British Journal of Criminology* 49, no. 5 (2009): pp. 667–85.

in British society. A Nigerian prisoner named Tosin told me that in the confines of the prison, 'white guys can talk with blacks, share milk, do sports, shake hands'. Another prisoner explained that imprisonment erased national and cultural boundaries, making race a more salient social force:

In a crowded situation, Africans and West Indians will get along. In London, with the more diverse population, it's different. But in prison black people will all group together.

Phillips and Earle have written about the relationship between the diversity of places like London and the experience of race in British prisons.[13] They point out that interaction across racial and ethnic boundaries is a defining feature of life in dense urban spaces, especially for young people, and that this familiarity with difference informs identification processes in prison.[14] One prisoner I met, who was born in Zimbabwe, echoed this account. He argued that a prisoner's race and nationality 'depends on the group':

Race doesn't matter here as much as in the US. If you're with somebody from Africa you're going to connect. One guy on my wing from Kenya relates to Jamaicans because he grew up in London. It just depends on the group. Depends on your nature as well.[15]

In this testimony, imprisonment reconfigures and in some sense relaxes existing modes of identification. Augustus saw this as the principal effect of incarceration:

In prison, it's not about race so much; it's about the position you're in. If you come from a poor place, you have a rough upbringing, then you can get along irrespective of colour. You do the same things: smoke cannabis, do drugs, go to school together. You forget the person is black or white.

[13] Phillips and Earle, 'Reading Difference Differently?'; Phillips and Earle, 'Cultural Diversity, Ethnicity, and Race Relations in Prison'.

[14] Phillips and Earle, 'Cultural Diversity, Ethnicity, and Race Relations in Prison'.

[15] This testimony raises questions about the difference between British and American prisons. The scholarship on America penal institutions suggests that race operates in a much more static way in the United States than in Britain. See Philip Goodman, 'It's Just Black, White, or Hispanic'; Diaz-Cotto, *Gender, Ethnicity, and the State*; Henderson, Cullen, and Carroll, 'Race, Rights, and Order in Prison'. Goodman's work on the California prison system portrays the divisions between 'black, white, and Hispanic' as thoroughly entrenched in the American penal project.

For Augustus, race was contingent on experience.

Yet, alongside this contingency, there was also a persistent sense that race mattered to prison life. Prisoners often told me that discriminatory beliefs about race shaped their treatment. One man, who was from Jamaica, said that, 'prison is an institution of racism. It's the most institution of racism you can come across. It's not like this in the outside world.' Rus drew a similar conclusion from confinement: 'Being in prison has made me realize it's about the colour of your skin.'

The relevance of race is not lost on the Prison Service. British prisons have been publishing race relations statements on prison walls for years. The Prison Service first began this practice in the late 1980s in response to concerns about brutality and harassment by prison officers.[16] Those concerns grew, as did the Prison Service's emphasis on race, after Zahid Mubarak's death in 2000. Mubarak, a Pakistani-British prisoner, was nineteen years old when his cellmate scrawled racist notes on the wall and then murdered him. He died five hours from the end of a three-month sentence for stealing £6 worth of razor blades. Mubarek's murder sparked a four-year public inquiry and an investigation by the Commission for Racial Equality.[17] More than ten years on, many prisoners saw the race relations policies that emerged from the murder as an empty promise. 'Just look at those boards', one man said, pointing to the race relations statement that was prominently posted on the wall. 'None of the bullshit that it says on the boards is real.'

[16] See Paul Gordon, *White Law: Racism in the Police, Courts, and Prisons* (London: Pluto, 1983); see also National Association for the Care and Resettlement of Offenders, *Race and Prisons: A Snapshot Survey* (London: NACRO, 2000); Genders and Player, *Race Relations in Prison*.

[17] Zahid Mubarek was murdered on 21 March 2000 at the Feltham Young Offender's Institution in London. See Community for Racial Equality, *A Formal Investigation by the Commission for Racial Equality into HM Prison Service of England and Wales—Part 1: The Murder of Zahid Mubarek* (London: CRE, 2003); Community for Racial Equality, *A Formal Investigation by the Commission for Racial Equality into HM Prison Service of England and Wales—Part 2: Racial Equality in Prisons* (London: CRE, 2003); Brian Keith, *Report of the Zahid Mubarak Inquiry, Vols I–II* (London: House of Commons, 2006). Both inquiries found that Mubarek's death was the result of his cellmate's racism as well as failures on the part of the Prison Service.

Instead, prisoners described an institution in which perceptions of race determined the quality of their daily lives. A few of the people I interviewed pointed to specific instances of racism, such as the man who reported being called a 'black bastard' by an officer and the prisoner who was told by staff to 'turn down the jungle music' coming from his cell. More frequently, prisoners invoked the idea of racism to describe the frustrations of incarceration. 'Racism is very rampant', one prisoner told me, 'like, I've been asking to go to the doctor for weeks.' Thomas, who had been imprisoned for ten years, told me, 'black people have it hard. White people ask for something...get it right away. Blacks get it two days later.' Rus also focused on the disparities in treatment by staff. Born in Bangladesh but now a British citizen, Rus said that 'white guys can wear sandals on the landing, but we can't'. He reported that 'Englishmen' get more favours from line officers than 'people like me'. 'Me and a white Englishman, the priority goes to him', Rus explained:

> Like my tin of tuna this morning. I couldn't get a can opener to open it from the guard, then a white guy gets it opened. It's the colour thing. All the white people work at the servery. They only sort out their own people and who they get along with. They wouldn't hesitate to put me on basic. I applied and never got enhanced. You have to chase it up.[18]

'Basically, the officers are racist', he concluded. 'They won't put it directly, but they put it indirectly.'

The law does not offer a clear or compelling response to these testimonies. As a legal matter, it is exceedingly difficult to prove that slow medical care, delays in prisoners' requests, job assignments, or uniform regulations are motivated by racism.[19] It is also

[18] Rus is referring in this quotation to the Incentives and Earned Privileges (IEP) Scheme, which the Prison Service introduced in 1995 as a way to incentivize good behaviour and encourage prison order. Under that scheme, prisoners can earn 'privileges' such as extra visits, wearing their own clothes, and time out of their cells. This scheme has three levels—Enhanced, Standard, and Basic—the last of which is generally considered a punishment. For a fuller discussion of IEP, see Alison Liebling, *Prisons and Their Moral Performance: A Study of Values, Quality, and Prison Life* (Oxford: Oxford University Press, 2005).

[19] My claim is not that race is irrelevant to any aspect of prison life, but rather that scholars cannot know for sure if particular job assignments or medical decisions result from racism. Coretta Phillips has written about this epistemological puzzle. Coretta Phillips, 'Institutional racism and Ethnic Inequalities: An Expanded Multi-Level Framework', *Journal of Social Policy* 40, no. 1 (2011): pp. 173–92. Phillips endorses a 'multi-level framework' for examining

worth emphasizing that these prisoners' claims were expressed to me, a white woman, in the context of one-on-one interviews in which I was asking about race relations. My position in these conversations matters. It may be that prisoners commented on race because I raised the issue. Prisoners' descriptions of racism might have been different if they were speaking to someone they perceived as non-white. Nonetheless, it remains the case that prisoners chose to articulate their experiences as they did. Racism was the framework through which prisoners represented their lives to me.

Racism also surfaced in prisoners' discussions of the outside world. Often, prisoners presented their incarceration as just one example of the alienating experience of being black in Britain. Early in my fieldwork, I interviewed a man who asked to be called System. When I asked him why he chose that pseudonym, he replied, 'That's my name because that's who brought me up.' System offered this account of his conviction on drug charges:

> I felt like shit standing in front of twelve people trying to justify my life. Twelve fucking white people. How can I judge, can they judge? Me and my wife see things differently. Black people—Jamaican black people—them friend mean a lot. You pass by and think we're having a fight. Five white men standing together isn't a crime; three black people it's a crime because . . . black people up to no good. A black man in a nice car—you think footballer . . . or what? Black people aren't supposed to do these things unless they're professional and well known.

System told me that black British people are viewed through the dual assumptions that race is linked to crime and wealth is 'supposed to be white'. As he put in another interview:

> I'm treated this way because I'm a Jamaican. I'm black. They know they have a case because I'm Jamaican. In the dictionary it say that Jamaicans are yardies and are related to drugs.

Rus, who was also incarcerated on drug charges, had a similar assessment of British culture. Born in Bangladesh, Rus considered

institutional racism. Other scholars have attempted to document systematic inequities in work allocation in prisons. See, e.g. Hindpal Singh Bhui, *Going the Distance: Developing Effective Policy and Practice with Foreign National Prisoners* (London: Prison Reform Trust, 2004); Jeremy Coid, Ann Petruckevitch, Paul Bebbington, Traolach Brugha, Dinesh Bhugra, Rachel Jenkins, Mike Farrell, Glyn Lewis, and Nicola Singleton, 'Ethnic Differences in Prisoners 1: Criminality and Psychiatric Morbidity', *British Journal of Psychiatry* 181 (2002): pp. 473–80.

himself to be black and to be part of a growing community of 'coloured people' in the United Kingdom. 'This country is more coloured people than white now', he told me:

> Twenty years ago, my dad used to tell me to stay away from the white neighbourhoods. Now a white boy can't say nothing to me.

Still, Rus said, mainstream British society remained more concerned with 'white people's problems' than the issues that affect black communities. 'Like the Stephen Lawrence thing', he said. 'You heard about it, but then never again. Then a girl gets kidnapped in Portugal and it's still on the news.'[20] In our last interview, Rus sighed and shook his head. 'I don't know. I think I should bleach my skin and become white. Life would be easier in this country.'

Rus and System were deeply critical of the relationship between incarceration and British racism. Damien was too, but he had a slightly different perspective on British culture. Damien was born in Jamaica and had grown up in Britain. At least at the beginning of his prison term, Damien saw himself as a British person. He argued that racism is one aspect of a larger aversion to difference in British society: 'English people don't like difference, or going against the grain. In any way.' In this account, nonconformity is the 'problem' and race is one of its dimensions. Damien argued that, in Britain, being black is itself an affront to the norm.

Criminologists have explored this conceptual tension between blackness and Britishness.[21] Following a line of thought pioneered by Stuart Hall, scholars such as Paul Gilroy and Benjamin Bowling have argued that British racism is closely linked to the creation of

[20] Rus was referring to the death of Stephen Lawrence and to the case of Madeleine McCann, a white British three-year-old whose disappearance during a holiday to Portugal in 2007 was widely reported in the British press. See BBC, 'Holiday Girl Abducted, Police Say', *BBC News Online*, 5 May 2007, <http://news.bbc.co.uk/2/hi/europe/6627605.stm>; Daily Mail, 'In Pictures, the 120 Metre Route to Check on Madeleine', *Mail Online*, 10 August 2007, <http://www.dailymail.co.uk/news/article-474428/In-pictures-120-metre-route-check-Madeleine.html>; Richard Edwards, 'Madeleine McCann's Parents Deny Suspicions', *The Telegraph Online*, 8 August 2007, <http://www.telegraph.co.uk/news/worldnews/1559688/Madeleine-McCanns-parents-deny-suspicions.html>.

[21] See, e.g. Benjamin Bowling, *Violent Racism: Victimization, Policing and Social Context* (Oxford: Clarendon Press, 1998); Phillips, 'Ethnicity, Identity, and Community Cohesion in Prison', pp. 75–86.

a post-imperial British nationalism.[22] Gilroy explains that xenophobia and racism developed in tandem in the aftermath of British colonialism and cannot be dissociated from one another. In his account, as Britain's Empire changed shape, politicians and the press began to frame 'black settlement' as an invasion from foreign lands.[23] This formulation constructed 'the black presence...as a problem against which a homogenous, white, national "we" could be unified'.[24] Nationalism and racism were articulated in and through each other in the wake of the British Empire. They were, and still are, 'densely interwoven' concepts.[25]

Gilroy's thesis has generated a wide body of scholarship over the past four decades.[26] Across history, sociology, anthropology, and political science, academics have drawn on Gilroy's ideas—and in particular, on his writing in *There Ain't No Black in the Union Jack*—to refine the critique of British nationalism. Together, these studies make a compelling case that post-war political discourses positioned black migrants as '"bad stock" assimilating into British culture'.[27] This account contextualizes the testimonies I witnessed

[22] See Hall, Critcher, Jefferson, Clark, and Roberts, *Policing the Crisis*.

[23] Gilroy, *There Ain't No Black in the Union Jack*, pp. 53, 101. Gilroy cites sources such as Enoch Powell's 1968 Rivers of Blood speech, in which the Conservative MP warned that Commonwealth migration would bring 'tragic and intractable' violence. See Enoch Powell, *Freedom and Reality* (Kingswood: Elliot Right Way Books, 1969).

[24] Gilroy, *There Ain't No Black in the Union Jack*, p. 49.

[25] Gilroy, *There Ain't No Black in the Union Jack*, p. xxiii.

[26] Since its publication, Gilroy's writing on British colonialism has informed studies of violence, housing conditions, and educational achievement. See, e.g. Kjartan Sveinsson, *A Tale of Two Englands: 'Race' and Violent Crime in the Media* (London: Runnymede Trust, 2008); Ernest Cashmore, 'The Experiences of Ethnic Minority Police Officers in Britain: Under-Recruitment and Racial Profiling in a Performance Culture', *Ethnic and Racial Studies* 24, no. 4 (2001): pp. 642–59; Jane Lakey, 'Neighborhoods and Housing', in Tariq Modood, Richard Berthoud, Jane Lakey, James Nazroo, Patten Smith, Satnam Virdee, and Sharon Beishon, eds, *Ethnic Minorities in Britain: Diversity and Disadvantage* (London: Policy Studies Institute, 1997); David Gillborn, *Racism and Education: Coincidence or Conspiracy* (London: Routledge, 2008); Chris Searle, *An Exclusive Education: Race, Class, and Exclusion in British Schools* (London: Lawrence and Wishart, 2001).

[27] Coretta Phillips and Benjamin Bowling, 'Ethnicities, Racism, Crime, and Criminal Justice', in Mike Maguire, Rod Morgan, and Robert Reiner, eds, *The Oxford Handbook of Criminology* (Oxford: Oxford University Press, 2007), p. 423; see also Kathleen Chater, *Untold Histories: Black People in England and Wales During the Period of the British Slave Trade, c. 1660–1807*

in British prisons. Scholarship that situates British racism in its social and political moment helps to explain why so many prisoners and staff blurred nationality, ethnicity, and race when describing incarceration. It is impossible to separate race and nation from each other or from prison policy. In Britain, the meaning of race emerges from a long pattern of excluding certain migrant groups, treating minority communities as a problem, and 'identifying criminals as alien'.[28]

Obvious Evidence

The fraught relationship between race and nation lies just below the surface of the policy on foreign national prisoners. Chapter 4 described how prisoners wind up on the UKBA's radar. That chapter explained that prison and immigration officers screen prisoners and categorize them as either British or foreign nationals. It is not always clear who is responsible for this effort to find 'foreigners'. In some of the prisons I visited, 'embedded' UK border agents conducted the immigration screenings. In most cases, however, the obligation to identify non-citizens fell to prison staff.

At the time of my research, the Prison Service explicitly encouraged its officers to refer anyone who 'seemed to be' foreign to immigration authorities in order to avoid 'mistakes'.[29] Implementation

(Manchester: Manchester University Press, 2009); David Killingray, '"A Good West Indian, a Good African, and, in Short, a Good Britisher": Black and British in a Colour-Conscious Empire, 1760–1950', *Journal of Imperial and Commonwealth History* 36, no. 3 (2009): pp. 363–81; Panikos Panayi, *An Immigration History of Britain: Multicultural Racism Since 1800* (London: Harlow Longman, 2010); Olufemi Taiwo, 'Reading the Colonizer's Mind: Lord Lugard and the Philosophical Foundations of British Colonialism', in Susan Babbitt and Sue Campbell, eds, *Racism and Philosophy* (Ithaca, NY: Cornell University Press, 1999), pp. 157–88.

[28] Phillips and Bowling, 'Ethnicities, Racism, Crime, and Criminal Justice', p. 423; see also Bowling, *Violent Racism*; Peter Fryer, *Staying Power: The History of Black People in Britain* (London: Pluto, 1984).

[29] Prison Service Order 4630 mandates that prison staff report to the UKBA 'when there is reason to suspect that the prisoner is a foreign national', HM Prison Service, *Prison Service Order 4630: Immigration and Foreign Nationals in Prison* (London: MoJ, 2008), p. 7. The hubs and spokes agreement also defines the term foreign national prisoner 'in its broadest sense', as 'a remand, sentenced or time-served detained prisoner...known or believed to be a foreign national'. Ministry of Justice (MoJ) and United Kingdom Border Agency (UKBA), *Service*

of this ambiguous policy hinged on prison staff members' discretion and assumptions. Some prison officers described using information about a prisoner's birthplace to identify non-citizens. Others said they relied on what one prison official called 'the telltale signs' of foreign nationality: ethnicity; accent; name; dress; religious identification; and even association with other 'identified foreigners'. Prison staff told me that they often referred prisoners to the UKBA 'just to be safe'. One officer explained that he took a 'loose' approach to avoid problems:

> One of the problems is the problem of nationality because it is self-declared. At the end of the day, it's not foolproof. You look for obvious evidence. Someone could slip through, or the reverse could happen.

In general, prison officers were relatively open about identifying foreign nationals based on their beliefs about what foreignness looked, sounded, and seemed like to them. Immigration agents who worked in prisons concurred with this description, but argued that failures in the referral process stemmed from poor training. One UKBA officer explained:

> Sure, some people slip through. It's the Prison Service... You could slip through... That's how we end up with some Brits. They're not trained to recognize foreigners. We've got the instruments to determine who is a real Brit.

This border agent argued that reliable instruments to determine who is a 'real Brit' exist. He claimed that the Border Agency's possession of such instruments made it the only legitimate 'border control operation'.

This claim contrasted with the interactions I observed. During the course of my fieldwork, I visited many immigration 'surgeries', the mandatory sessions in which prisoners meet with UKBA and Prison Service officials. In those meetings, both immigration and prison staff members relied on racialized assumptions to decide whether prisoners qualified as foreign nationals. In one exchange I observed, a black British national prisoner sat down to speak with a UKBA officer. The prisoner was in his mid- to late fifties. He told the border agent that he had a British passport and had lived in the country for twenty-six years. The border agent challenged

Level Agreement to Support the Effective and Speedy Removal of Foreign National Prisoners (London: MoJ and UKBA, 2009), p. 4.

him: 'But I see you have a strong Nigerian accent.' The prisoner retorted, 'That has nothing to do with you.'

Interactions like these made many prisoners feel that race was the real focus of border control. During a group interview at HMP Canterbury, one man pointed to his friend, a black British citizen who prison staff had misidentified as a foreign national. That prisoner asked:

> Who are the real foreigners? It's about colour. Look at him. He's British, but because of his colour he's here.[30]

When I asked how staff identified foreign nationals in a different interview, Roland, a migrant from Nigeria, said 'very easy. Colour can tell number one.' Patrick, a non-citizen born in the Congo, summarized the immigration referral process with a joke: 'if you're black, you're going back'.

Long-time residents of the United Kingdom were the most critical of the role that race played in the referral process. George, one of the oldest prisoners I interviewed, had lived in the United Kingdom for thirty-six years when we met. He had noticed a shift in attitudes towards migrants during that time:

> What is this fortress Europe mentality we're getting? You can't help but notice, well, European people are white people. Europe has all the wealth and is trying to fend everybody else off. I see what's happening to me as political.

George understood his imprisonment as a manifestation of 'fortress Europe', an approach to immigration that many criminologists have critiqued.[31] Greek criminologist Vassilis Karydis describes 'fortress Europe' as a collection of laws and migration

[30] HMP Canterbury has since ceased to be a prison devoted to confining foreign nationals. See Chapter 3 for a fuller description of the hubs and spokes system and Chapter 4 for an account of life in HMP Canterbury.

[31] See, e.g. Alessandro De Giorgi, 'Immigration Control, Post-Fordism, and Less Eligibility: A Materialist Critique of the Criminalization of Immigrants across Europe', *Punishment and Society* 12, no. 2 (2010): pp. 147–67; Nicola Lacey, *The Prisoner's Dilemma: Political Economy and Punishment in Contemporary Democracies* (Cambridge: Cambridge University Press, 2008); Vassilis Karydis, 'Criminality of Criminalization of Migrants in Greece? An Attempt at Synthesis', in Vincenzo Ruggiero, Nigel South, and Ian Taylor, eds, *The New European Criminology: Crime and Social Order in Europe* (London: Routledge, 1998), pp. 350–67; Loic Wacquant, 'Suitable Enemies: Foreigners and Immigrants in the Prisons of Europe', *Punishment and Society* 1, no. 2 (October 1999): pp. 215–22.

policies that emphasize the 'protection of the single European entity from illegal migration and irregular asylum seekers'.[32] Karydis argues that migration control rhetoric pits migrants from North Africa, South Asia, the West Indies, and the Middle East against a unified—and implicitly white—Europe.[33] George echoed these ideas and connected the 'fortress mentality' to inequalities in the global distribution of wealth.

George was careful, however, to distinguish the purpose of migration control from his daily experience in prison. Describing himself as a 'lifetime Brit', George said that prison staff treated him 'as a British person' even though they had referred him to the UKBA. He explained that it was typical for staff to send many prisoners' names to immigration 'just to be safe' but then to treat only a smaller subset of prisoners 'as real foreigners'. Another prisoner described a similar pattern. During a group discussion, he listened as a Jamaican national who had recently immigrated to the United Kingdom recounted having his stereo taken by prison staff. 'I wouldn't experience that', the first man said:

> I notice differences in how the officers speak to me because of my accent. I think it goes deeper than communication. They don't perceive me as much as a foreign national. Their reaction to a Jamaican inmate with a thick accent is different.

This testimony captures the connection between national identity and affect. Many prisoners said that being foreign was a matter of speech and self-presentation rather than legal status. One prisoner, who I met in an immigration meeting, smiled when I asked him how he had wound up in a 'surgery' for non-citizens: 'It's simple. If your accent is not the Queen's English, you'll be in here.'

[32] Karydis, 'Criminality of Criminalization of Migrants in Greece?', p. 351. Phil Marfleet argues that the notion of a 'fortress Europe' echoes racist ideologies that 'underpinned Europe's rival nationalisms' and the rise of Nazism in the twentieth century. Phil Marfleet, 'Nationalism and Internationalism in the New Europe', *International Socialism Journal* 84 (1999).

[33] Citizens from the EU are not always white and the term 'white' is itself an historical construction. The concept of a 'fortress Europe' relies upon a long-standing myth that Europe is a white region. As Coretta Phillips and Ben Bowling note, this myth has been a 'theme of racist thinking' since the Enlightenment. Phillips and Bowling, 'Ethnicities, Racism, Crime, and Criminal Justice', p. 422.

Many of the prisoners who attend immigration surgeries will not be deported from the United Kingdom. The 2007 Border Act establishes specific criteria for automatic removal, which include a prisoner's sentence length and prior criminal record.[34] These criteria mean that a number of prisoners who staff identify as foreign nationals do not leave Britain, either because they do not qualify for deportation or because they assert some grounds for relief. There is, in other words, a notable gap between the group of prisoners who are classified as non-citizens and those who are actually expelled. Finding foreigners is a sociological phenomenon—and a government project—of its own.

This project is not wholly determined by race. In the midst of this account of racial profiling, it is crucial to note that many of the prisoners identified as foreign nationals are Eastern European. The people in Britain's prisons come from Poland, Romania, and Lithuania as well as Jamaica and the United Kingdom.[35] To the extent that Eastern European migrants are perceived as white and classified as non-citizens, race is not the only proxy for foreignness behind bars. But race is one crucial barometer for Britishness.

From day to day, prison and immigration officials depend on racialized generalizations in order to do their jobs. For the most part, the prisoners who pass through reception without question are white men and women with British accents. Other prisoners—those who 'look and sound foreign' but turn out to be British nationals—become exceptions to a rule about who 'obviously' belongs in Britain. The hubs and spokes policy thus transforms nationality into a placeholder for racialized ideas about the character of Britishness. In practice, this policy suggests that British national identity is identifiable and is essentially white.

These ideas were on display during one of my visits to a prison in the north-east. As I waited for prisoners to come to that week's immigration meeting, I overheard two border agents discussing a prisoner who their colleague had classified as a foreign national.

[34] Under the 2007 Border Act, all non-citizen prisoners are automatically considered for deportation, while non-European foreign nationals sentenced to at least one year and European Economic Area (EEA) nationals sentenced to at least two years face mandatory deportation. These guidelines determine which prisoners will face deportation but they do not dictate which prisoners will ultimately be deported.

[35] For a breakdown of the prison population by nationality at the time of my fieldwork, see Ministry of Justice (MoJ), *Offender Management Caseload Statistics 2009* (London: Ministry of Justice, 2010).

'Is he EEA?', one staff member asked, referring to prisoners from the European Economic Area.[36]

'No, he's not European...he's *foreign national* foreign national', the other agent replied, stressing the term to imply a distinction between being really and only technically foreign.

In this exchange, the term 'foreign' referred not to a legal status, but to a group of non-European and largely non-white people in the prison population. When repeated across the prison system, conversations like these turn hubs and spokes into a vehicle for profiling. Over time, the repetition of these practices creates, and continually recreates, a racialized vision of British citizenship.

This picture of citizenship clashes with the government's stated policies. Great Britain is and has always been a highly diverse society, and at least publicly, the government has long championed that diversity.[37] Though it has never been very clearly defined, 'multicultural

[36] The acronym 'EEA' refers to the European Economic Area. Under the UK Borders Act 2007, the rules for automatic deportation are different for EU, EEA, and non-European nationals. Eligibility for the Facilitated Returns Scheme, a programme that provides cash and grants to prisoners who volunteer to be deported, also varies depending on a prisoners' country of origin.

[37] For accounts of Britain's long-standing diversity, see Philip Baker and Yasir Mohieldeen, 'The Languages of London's Schoolchildren', in Philip Baker and John Eversley, eds, *Multilingual Capital* (London: Battlebridge, 2000), pp. 5–60; Colin Holmes, 'Cosmopolitan London', in Anne Kershen, ed., *London: The Promised Land?* (Aldershot: Avebury, 1997), pp. 10–37; and Steven Vertovec, 'Super-diversity and Its Implications', *Ethnic and Racial Studies* 30, no. 6 (2007): pp. 1024–54. There is some reason to believe that the government is moving away from its public commitment to 'multiculturalism'. In February 2011, for instance, Prime Minister David Cameron declared that, 'multiculturalism has failed'. MSNBC, 'British PM: Multiculturalism Has Failed', *MSNBC Online*, 06 February 2011, <http://www.msnbc.msn.com/id/41444364/ns/world_news-europe/t/british-pm-multiculturalism-has-failed/#.TzL5EyOJ_J8>. At the time, Cameron blamed the 'multicultural agenda' for 'Islamic extremism'. However, Cameron interprets 'multiculturalism' to mean the separation and isolation of ethnic communities within Great Britain. The fact remains that the British government has long upheld an official policy of 'multiculturalism', defined as the celebration of distinct cultures within one country. See Foreign and Commonwealth Office, 'Kwame Kwei-Armah on Multicultural Britain' 28 March 2011, <https://www.gov.uk/government/news/kwame-kwei-armah-on-multicultural-britain>; Stuart Hall, 'Conclusion: The Multicultural Question', in Barnor Hesse, ed., *UN/Settled Multiculturalisms: Diasporas, Entanglement, Transruptions* (London: Zed Books, 2001), pp. 209–41.

Britain' has been a standard phrase in both Home Office and Foreign and Commonwealth Office documents since the late seventies, and particularly since Tony Blair took office in 1997.[38] As recently as 2012, the government touted the 'multicultural' character of British society as a selling point in tourism materials.[39] This public discourse conflicts with the government's approach to foreignness in prison. In penal institutions, non-white prisoners become presumptive non-citizens.

Prison policies thus make race matter. While prisoners have varied, contextual, and fluid conceptions of what race means to them, they live in a system that relies on and reiterates a particular vision of race. In practice, the hubs and spokes policy cements a crude analogy in which race and nationality are always already aligned.[40] This process has significant ramifications on the meaning and possibilities of racial identity in prisons. Through a series of local interactions between prisoners and staff, the effort to classify foreigners has entrenched the view of British citizenship that Paul Gilroy indicted forty years ago.

Modes of Resistance

The story of hubs and spokes does not end with racial profiling. While it has made race more rigid, the new policy on non-citizens has also prompted creative forms of resistance and critique. Inside prisons, the government's myopic focus on foreignness has relaxed certain penal mores, and at least in some cases, has encouraged nuanced strategies of denial and cooperation. Prisoners' varied responses to hubs and spokes suggest that citizenship paranoia has not only altered prison geography by shifting the organization, location, and culture of penal institutions. The policy has also changed how prisoners experience and survive incarceration.

[38] See Bridget Anderson and Emanuela Paoletti, 'Citizenship, Deportation, and the Boundaries of Belonging', *Citizenship Studies* 15, no. 5 (2011): pp. 547–63; Hall, 'Conclusion: The Multicultural Question'; Homi Bhabha, *The Location of Culture* (London: Routledge, 1994).

[39] Foreign and Commonwealth Office, 'Kwame Kwei-Armah on Multicultural Britain'.

[40] Postcolonial and critical race theorists have long argued that race is not a biological fact but a politicized, contingent, and fundamentally unstable idea. See Paul Gilroy, *Postcolonial Melancholia* (New York, NY: Columbia University Press, 2006), p. 14; Hall, 'Conclusion: The Multicultural Question', pp. 209–15.

The most palpable reaction to hubs and spokes was a strong chord of empathy between prisoners slated for deportation. In immigration meetings, prisoners from Lithuania, Nigeria, Sri Lanka, and Jamaica conversed with one another about the challenges of life as a foreigner. Some of these prisoners told their migration stories, recounting their lives before incarceration and comparing their experiences in the United Kingdom. Others shared information about their immigration cases and traded telephone numbers for lawyers. After watching these exchanges, I turned to a prisoner and noted that everyone in the meeting was talking to each other. He said the space was unusual: 'it's relaxed in here because we're all in the same boat'. In moments like these, the hubs and spokes policy carved out lines of identification that crossed, complicated, and softened racial boundaries. Throughout my fieldwork, mandatory immigration meetings and 'foreign-only' prisons seemed to allow—and sometimes to force—prisoners who might otherwise face imprisonment separately to see themselves as part of the same experience. These men did not necessarily forge friendships, but under the pressure of a new prison policy, they sympathized with each other.[41]

Patrick described how these empathetic interactions unfold. He told me that being classified as a potential foreign national enabled identification 'across races' because:

> You think, I could be with you for a while. We could just be going to Colnbrook or Dover. You're facing the same struggles as me.[42]

Other prisoners said they bonded with fellow foreigners. One man, who I met in an all-foreign prison, told me that being grouped with other non-citizens created a sense of solidarity that superseded race or nationality. He explained:

> There are people here from Iraq, Afghanistan, people who know their families have been killed. I feel for them. In the previous prison, you don't talk about immigration topics. In this prison, you're all going through the

[41] My research was limited by the fact that I did not have access to prison wings in most prisons. I did spend time observing the wings, as well as the library and education facilities, in the Category C facility I visited, but for the most part I did not see prisoners interact with one another outside the interview spaces where I met them. Chapter 2 considers these and other limitations of prison ethnography.

[42] Colnbrook and Dover are two Immigration Removal Centres run by the UK Border Agency.

same things, so you can talk about your immigration cases on the wings. In this boundary, we know we are all foreign nationals. In an English prison you get an inferiority complex about not being born here. Here you're all the same.

While this prisoner focused on the qualities of life in an 'all-foreign' prison environment, his claims echoed testimonies that I heard from prisoners in other facilities. In one Category A prison, a misidentified British citizen said that being 'flagged foreign' had changed his approach to the people around him. He told me that despite his citizenship status, 'I find myself pulled toward them. I find myself in the same boat as the people being deported.' Damien agreed. He found that identifying with other foreign nationals was a way to connect with fellow prisoners and to cope with life in the penal institution.

He described this strategy when I asked how he handled the stresses of incarceration:

I give help to other foreign nationals; I listen to their cases. I get on with everybody. If you don't speak English, I try to point you in the right direction. Everyone's got the same issue. We're all vulnerable in here.

Damien's reply suggests that hubs and spokes has recalibrated prisoners' identities, opening and demanding new methods of 'psychological survival'.[43] While the policy on non-citizens has alienated people, it has also enabled empathy by creating a sub-criminal class of prisoners who do not belong.

The hubs and spokes policy has also inspired new forms of subversion. In interviews, several prisoners said they had tried to avoid deportation by posing as British citizens when they came into the prison system. As they described it, this effort involved taking on pseudonyms that sound 'less foreign' and affecting British accents. Gus explained that 'foreigners' accents 'shine on them like a big torch' and that sounding British was the key to evading immigration authorities. Another prisoner told me that he had witnessed attempts to 'talk English' many times and had tried to speak with an accent when he was first incarcerated. He explained the process:

At reception, people are onto how it works, so they'll say they're English, act English. But they'll watch you on the wings to see who you associate

[43] Stanley Cohen and Laurie Taylor, *Psychological Survival: The Experience of Long-Term Imprisonment* (New York, NY: Vintage, 1974).

with and listen to your phone calls. They have set officers to deal with this on the wing. They're all working together, the Home Office and the Prison Service. It's all in conjunction.

Another prisoner said that having the right accent is a way to 'blend in' to British society:

Polish people, Czechs, Croatians. That influx of people, they tend not to blend into this country. Blacks and second-generation immigrants can blend in. That's the difference between being English and not—when you sound English. That's when people become blind to colour. Your children go to school, watch soap operas, become fully integrated English people. They can walk along and marry an English girl.

For this prisoner, sounding English was a strategy to overcome racial discrimination.

John, a prisoner I met in a Category A prison, learned this tactic outside prison. John left Nigeria in 2001 after his family died in what he described as 'a massacre at a church'. During that massacre, John watched as his sister was doused with petroleum and set on fire. He fled the church, then the country, and settled on the United Kingdom as his new home. Upon arriving in London, John quickly taught himself a British accent. He credited that accent with helping him 'run far away and forget about home'. Another prisoner, Eman, described his accent as a survival tool. Eman was born in Rwanda and identified as a foreign national when he entered prison. He did not see himself as a foreigner, in part because he spoke with a British accent. 'I'm not a foreigner', Eman told me. 'I'm a free person. As long as I can speak, I'm black British.'

John and Eman link British prisons to ethno-sectarian violence in countries thousands of miles from the United Kingdom. On a more local level, their testimonies also capture how crucial physicality, affect, and speech are for foreign national prisoners. The way prisoners present themselves matters not only to social dynamics in the penal institution, but also to their futures beyond prison walls. Faced with the prospect of deportation, and with the more immediate stigma of being foreign, many prisoners affect a British identity. Like the characters in Nella Larsen's novel, they pass and perform, mimic and imitate 'British behaviour' to avoid migration control.

There are multiple ways to interpret these acts of passing. On one hand, prisoners' efforts to seem British reflect the force of state power. While it is impossible to know if prisoners actually slip through the hubs and spokes system, the mere existence of a group of people who imitate Britishness demonstrates how limited identity is in prison. When they enter the penal estate, prisoners cannot be identified with one nation and legally aligned with another, at least not when interacting with prison authorities. In the context of hubs and spokes, prisoners can only have one nationality; they cannot be 'a little more British than Jamaican' or 'foreign and British' at the same time. These descriptions may capture the realities of prisoners' lives, but in prison, identity has to be fixed.

On the other hand, Eman and John tell narratives of resistance. Though accounts of passing highlight the demand for conformity, they also undermine the dictates of border control. Feminists and queer theorists understand the practice of passing as precisely such a subversion strategy.[44] Philosophers such as Judith Butler, Eve Sedgwick, and Michael Warner argue that the performance of identity is a creative response to hierarchical power structures.[45]

[44] I have chosen to combine the scholarship on identity under the heading 'feminist and queer theory'. There are active debates about whether the writing on performativity and passing can be classified as feminist and whether queer theory is a development or a diversion away from the core ideas of the feminist movement. See, e.g. David Eng, Judith Halberstam, and Jose Munoz, 'Introduction: What's Queer about Queer Studies Now?', *Social Text* 84, no. 5 (2005): pp. 1–17; Joshua Gamson, 'Sexualities, Queer Theory, and Qualitative Research', in Norman Denzin and Yvonna Lincoln, eds, *Handbook of Qualitative Research*, 2nd ed. (London: Sage, 2000), pp. 347–65; Annamarie Jagose, *Queer Theory: An Introduction* (New York, NY: New York University Press, 1996); William Turner, *A Genealogy of Queer Theory* (Philadelphia, PA: Temple University Press, 2000); Michael Warner, *The Trouble with Normal: Sex, Politics, and the Ethics of Queer Life* (New York, NY: Free Press, 1999). I have written about these debates with Mary Bosworth. See Mary Bosworth and Emma Kaufman, 'Gender and Punishment', in Jonathan Simon and Richard Sparks, eds, *The SAGE Handbook of Punishment and Society* (London: Sage Publications Ltd, 2012), pp. 186–204. Here and elsewhere, I refer to 'feminist and queer theory' to acknowledge the contributions of both bodies of writing.

[45] See Judith Butler, *Bodies That Matter: On the Discursive Limits of Sex* (New York, NY: Routledge, 1993); Judith Butler, *Excitable Speech: The Politics of the Performative* (New York, NY: Routledge, 1997); Judith Butler, *Gender Trouble: Feminism and the Subversion of Identity* (New York, NY: Routledge, 1999); Judith Butler, *Undoing Gender* (New York, NY: Routledge, 2004); Eve Sedgwick, *Epistemology of the Closet* (Berkeley, CA: University of California Press, 1991); Eve Sedgwick, *Touching Feeling: Affect, Pedagogy, Performativity* (Durham, NC: Duke University Press, 2004); Warner, *The Trouble with Normal.*

Taking Nella Larsen's famous novel as an example, these scholars assert that the effort to appear white, or for that matter heterosexual or British, is a theatrical performance of belonging. Passing is a movement across social norms, one that demonstrates the porousness of identity categories. While it testifies to the power of norms, passing also opens space to imagine new modes of belonging.

Building from this account, scholars of punishment might read prisoners' attempts to pass as instances of resistance to migration control. When prisoners act out Britishness for prison and immigration authorities, they resist the boundaries set out in penal policies. These prisoners actively refuse to participate in border control, and in doing so, insist that they can define their own identities. This is a pragmatic and deliberate response to the laws imposed on non-citizens. Passing is an assertion of agency in a regime that tells prisoners that cannot decide who they are.

Passing is also a way to challenge the link between citizenship and race. In practice, prisoners' efforts to 'seem British' illustrated that citizenship is in some fundamental sense about the performance of social norms. One prisoner, Roland, told me that he understood how to enact 'British behaviour' in prison because he had experienced life as a black migrant in Great Britain. Originally from Nigeria, Roland said that he had 'gone through a lot of what I could call a racist life' in the United Kingdom, and as a result, had learned to be sensitive to how those in power wanted him to behave. He explained:

> I went through a racist life... I'm very good at playing tennis. I was playing and I won, and one guy comes up to me and says where did I come from. He could see I'm from Africa, and he was white. He asked if I'm a gangsta. He said I have to pretend that I don't know how to play tennis when I'm with gangstas. He said he's free to tell me this because this is his country, he was born here, it's not my country.

Interactions like these taught Roland that fitting into British society involved behaving in certain ways, namely, ways that align with racist and xenophobic assumptions. Drawing on that lesson, Roland attempted to pass as British. In faking Britishness, Roland adapted to the pressures of migration control. He also made a claim to British culture.

In the context of testimonies like these, the prison begins to look like a place where prisoners debate, negotiate, and rework the relationship between race and nation. When prison and immigration staff members try to identify the 'real' citizens in the prison population, they produce the borders of citizenship and affirm normative assumptions about Britishness. Conversely, when prisoners pretend to be British, they parody those norms. Drawing on the basic flexibility and instability of identity, prisoners perform acts of national belonging that 'allegorize' the border controls to which they are subjected.[46] Through performances of belonging, prisoners insist that national and racial identity cannot be as fixed as penal policies demand.

Passing was not the only instance of performative belonging I witnessed. Prisoners also responded to hubs and spokes with heightened claims of gender conformity. In interviews, foreign national prisoners consistently told me how important it was to 'behave like a real man' and to protect women from harm. Prisoners often emphasized their heterosexuality, announcing that they would be friends 'with everyone except the gays'. When I asked about making friends across racial and national lines, one prisoner responded, 'oh, it doesn't matter as long as you aren't gay'. Another prisoner said that he was 'friends with anyone', including 'any kind of foreigner', unless that person was a 'sex offender'. These claims highlight the relationship between gender and nationality and the complicated link between homophobia and the stigmatization of sex offenders.

One of the most prominent themes in foreign national prisoners' testimonies was that men and women are inherently different. Many prisoners told me that men who hurt women were 'the worst off' in prisons, or that any prisoner who had touched 'a woman or a child' would be isolated. Prisoners also said that men have a duty to protect women and children. They cited this duty to justify discrimination against sex offenders:

> If a foreigner is in for rape, we wouldn't be friends. They're most likely to get killed in prison. They have to be on the secure unit. Sex offenders don't go on normal location.

This testimony situates 'the sex offender' as a particularly marginal prisoner, one whose deviance unites the rest of the prison community. Specifically, sex offenders have contravened the dictate that strong, 'real' men, the only kind of men welcome in the

[46] Butler, *Bodies That Matter*, p. 237.

prison, should protect women. This chivalrous discourse assumes that women are in need of protection. The stigmatization of sex offenders can be understood as an iteration of patriarchy.

The prisoners I interviewed also advanced a set of claims about sexuality. In general, prisoners were reticent to discuss sexuality in explicit terms and instead expressed their views as a kind of sweeping homophobia. When I asked what rules were the most important in prison, one prisoner told me, 'in prison, you can't be gay'. During another interview, a prisoner assured me, unsolicited, that 'we all like women here'. Rus, a South Asian prisoner, explained that sexuality mattered to his daily interactions more than any other category of identity. As he put it, 'nothing matters as long as you're not gay'. On the whole, prisoners described a penal culture in which heterosexuality was a deeply ingrained social norm.

This norm made life extremely unpleasant for prisoners who identified as homosexual. One prisoner offered this account:

> Being gay in prison is hard. People taunt you, staff take the piss. They're verbally abusive, call you a fag. You get a sausage and they say, 'You can come to mine and get fresh sausage'...'Give us a blow job', and then somebody pulls their penis out. People force themselves on someone...it's been known.

This prisoner was the only openly gay person I interviewed in a year of fieldwork. He spoke about forms of discrimination that many prisoners downplayed or dismissed. His comments depict the violent realities of a penal regime structured on compulsory heterosexuality.[47]

It is difficult to parse the relationship between gender and sexuality in these narratives. Prisoners' claims about what it is like to be gay in prison are conceptually distinct from their comments about the importance of protecting women or shaming sex offenders. Homosexuality, rape, and paedophilia, ideas that prisoners often invoked and conflated when describing the norms of prison life, are three different concepts. Considering them in tandem, even in the context of an academic book, threatens to obscure the distinctions between homosexuality, violent non-consensual sex, and sex

[47] The late feminist poet Adrienne Rich developed the term 'compulsory heterosexuality' in her work on lesbian existence in a heteronormative society. Adrienne Rich, *Blood, Bread, and Poetry: Selected Prose 1979–1985* (New York, NY: W. W. Norton & Co, 1994).

between adults and minors. Scholars should be wary of reproducing the same stigmas we critique.

Yet, at the same time, the slippage between homosexuality, rape, and paedophilia suggests the scope and depth of gender conformity in men's prisons. The notion of a sex offence has long been used to demarcate and construct the line between deviant and acceptable forms of sexual behaviour.[48] By linking sex offences to sexuality, prisoners implied that homosexuality is aberrant in prison. By insisting that they always protect women, prisoners reinforced a masculine gender norm. These claims are two sides of the same coin: they are both expressions of what it means to be a man. Sexism and homophobia are parallel modes of gender conformity and both shape prison life.

Again, it is crucial to emphasize that prisoners articulated these ideas to me, a woman, in the highly charged space of the prison interview. It is not clear that people I met subscribed to sexist and homophobic ideas outside of our discussions, nor even that these prisoners meant what they said when we spoke. There is no clear truth to these testimonies, at least not a truth that I could discover as an ethnographer with a subjectivity of my own. Yet assertions of heterosexuality and chivalry had real currency in prisoners' representations of the penal environment. Comments about protecting women, being straight, and hating sex offenders appeared with consistency and inflexibility in prisoners' depictions of their incarceration. Gender conformity did important rhetorical work as prisoners described their daily lives to me.

The question is what sort of work these ideas do. Criminologists have long been interested in the connections between punishment, gender, and sexuality. Beginning in the 1990s, scholars began to explore the role that gender norms play in the creation and enforcement of penal discipline. In one strand of writing, criminologists

[48] See Michel Foucault, *The History of Sexuality, Volume I: An Introduction*, trans. Richard Hurley (New York, NY: Vintage Books, 1978); Thomas Laqueur, *Making Sex: Body and Gender from the Greeks to Freud* (Cambridge, MA: Harvard University Press, 1993); Patrick Singy, 'Il Caso "Sade"', *Rivista Sperimentale di Freniatria* 130 (2006): pp. 83–102; Patrick Singy, 'What's Wrong with Sex?', *Archives of Sexual Behavior* 39, no. 6 (December 2010): pp. 1231–3; Patrick Singy and Kevin Lamb, 'Perverse Perversion: How to Do the History of a Concept', *GLQ* 17, no. 2–3 (2011): pp. 405–22.

argued that prison hierarchies hinge on the performance of 'hyper-masculinity'.[49] In another, feminist theorists asserted that prison policies create visions of good femininity and masculinity, which prisoners enact and reinforce.[50] Mary Bosworth has expanded the latter critique in recent years, arguing that gender conformity is a 'paradoxical resource' for prisoners. [51] Bosworth explains that prisoners' 'ability to reap the full benefits of masculinity is...held in check by the authority of prison staff', who control the minutia of prisoners' lives.[52] In this account, prisoners employ gender to regain agency in an institution that renders them dependent. Gender conformity is a response to the prison's challenge to individual subjectivity.

There is also a collective dimension to prisoners' claims about gender. In an interview with a man named Said, I asked how new prisoners find friends. Said explained:

> You learn about other prisoners over pool, table tennis, cards. They talk to each other. When you see someone who stays in his cell you ask, 'why is he not coming out of his cell? Is he gay? Is he scared?' That guy is either gay or scared.

Said portrayed a regime in which homosexuality is a failure, or perhaps a refusal, to take part in prison life. As he described it,

[49] See Joe Sim, 'Tougher than the Rest? Men in Prison', in Tim Newburn and Betsy Stanko, eds, *Just Boys Doing Business? Men, Masculinities and Crime* (London: Routledge, 1995) pp. 100–17; see also Lee Bowker, *Masculinities and Violence* (London: SAGE Publications Ltd, 1997); James Messerschmidt, *Masculinities and Crime: Critique and Reconceptualisation of Theory* (Totowa, NJ: Rowman & Littlefield, 1993); Tim Newburn and Betsy Stanko, eds, *Just Boys Doing Business?*

[50] See Mary Bosworth, *Engendering Resistance: Agency and Power in Women's Prisons* (London: Ashgate, 1999); Adrian Howe, *Punish and Critique: Towards a Feminist Analysis of Penality* (New York, NY: Routledge, 1996); see also Eamonn Carrabine and Mary Bosworth, 'Reassessing Resistance: Race, Gender, and Sexuality in Prison', *Punishment and Society* 3, no. 4 (October 2001): 501–15; Dana Britton, *At Work in the Iron Cage: The Prison as Gendered Organization* (New York, NY: New York University Press, 2003); Eamonn Carrabine and Brian Longhurst, 'Gender and Prison Organization: Some Comments on Masculinities and Prison Management', *The Howard Journal* 37, no. 2 (May 1998): pp. 161–76; Kathleen Daly, *Gender, Crime and Punishment* (New Haven, CT: Yale University Press, 1994); Kelly Hannah-Moffat, 'Feminine Fortresses: Women-Centered Prisons?', *The Prison Journal* 75, no. 2 (June 1995): pp. 135–64.

[51] Bosworth and Kaufman, 'Gender and Punishment', p. 190.

[52] Bosworth and Kaufman, 'Gender and Punishment', p. 190.

sexuality is a way to distinguish members from outcasts in the prison community. Said's questions—Is he gay? Is he scared?—cast homosexuality as a border in the prison environment. The prisoners on one side of that border were not full members of the penal collective. The 'gay and scared' were the foil against which a shared prisoner identity became clear. This account suggests that gender norms are a resource for prisoners seeking membership in a contested social space. However true to a person's actual beliefs or actions, the claim to be a straight man is one way for prisoners to show that they belong.

In the context of hubs and spokes, gender norms also became a way to assert national belonging. Several prisoners described gender as an integral part of their national identities. In our first interview, one prisoner told me that 'in prison you can't be gay'. When he came into our second meeting, I began the discussion, as I usually did, by asking him how his day was going. I did not expect his response:

> Jesus Christ, I'm worried about the gays. Today, someone said to me, 'you look good'...If you are gay, unlike in America, you are a dead man. They will beat the shit out of you...In England, it's all about macho this, macho that...And because this is a hold prison with short sentences...rapists and paedophiles? I stab them every day if I have to. I feel a victim of this.[53]

This prisoner framed homophobia as a form of self-defence. The self in his testimony was part of an implicit prisoner collective, and moreover, was a distinctly *English* self. 'Unlike in America', he stressed, 'in England, it's all about macho this, macho that'. Resisting his classification as a foreigner, this prisoner sought to demonstrate that he 'really knew' what English culture was, and in this sense, was in fact an English person. He invoked homophobia to lay claim to a British national identity.

Prisoners often drew these sorts of connections between sexuality and nationality. One man identified himself as British and then matter-of-factly informed me that 'Britain is a country where they never liked the gays'. Another prisoner explained to me, as an American, that homosexuals were 'not tolerated' in British prisons. Such rhetoric was not confined to claims about the United Kingdom, though my identification as an American did tend to

[53] The term 'hold' prison refers to a remand facility that incarcerates prisoners pending trial.

draw out sweeping claims about the nature of British culture. In a parallel narrative, a Jamaican prisoner named John described homophobia as a defining feature of his national identity:

> In the Caribbean, we kill gay people over there. We have them, but they undercover. Gays do not belong to the country. In my country, they prefer lesbians. Man on man, they shoot him. Over here them got gay rights. If any gay man come up to me, step off.

John's testimony drives home the gendered aspect of much homophobia. For John, it was not simply homosexuality but *male* desire that was particularly threatening and objectionable. As he described it, homophobia was both an expression of prisoner solidarity and a way to situate himself outside the country in which he was incarcerated. John argued that heterosexual norms are part of what it means to be Caribbean. Like other prisoners, he used homophobia to distinguish the place he called home.

These practices of conformity reflect the impact of hubs and spokes. Across the prison system, a new policy on 'foreigners' has introduced deep anxiety about citizenship and nationality into prisoners' lives. Confronted with this anxiety, non-citizens attest to their membership in an imagined community.[54] Prisoners contesting their deportation assert their Britishness, while those who identify as foreign describe why they represent and prefer their home countries. In both versions of the nationality narrative, homophobia and sexism surface as powerful vehicles for belonging. Gender conformity, already used to establish the borders of the prison collective, becomes a way to identify the nation's borders as well.

Conclusion

Empathy, parody, and conformity are only three of many reactions to hubs and spokes. In every interview, prisoners described different ways that the new policy on non-citizens had affected their friendships and coping strategies. Incarcerated foreigners were keenly aware that hubs and spokes existed and that prison officials cared, more than ever before, about their citizenship status. They

[54] Benedict Anderson, *Imagined Communities: Reflections on the Origin and Spread of Nationalism* (New York, NY: Verso, 2006).

responded to that pressure with creative, surprising, and in some cases disconcerting modes of compliance and resistance.

This snapshot of policy in practice illustrates how live prisons are. Penal institutions are supple and responsive spaces. They are small and highly regulated institutions where people wake, sleep, work, and survive. Prisons are also places that exacerbate and warp the contours of identity. Anxieties that shape the outside world become particularly acute under the weight of incarceration. Concerns about what it means to be black or British permeate prisons and affect how prisoners interact with each other and view themselves. When a policy as broad as hubs and spokes is introduced into this environment, it has ripple effects on every aspect of identity, from the meaning of race to the experience of sexuality and the expression of gender.

A study of prison policy is thus always a study of identity. Often, issues like race, gender, ethnicity, and sexuality become niche topics of criminology and law, subjects of a single report or scholarly inquiry. This approach flattens the exchange between identity and imprisonment and misses a deeper point about how penal power works. Because prisons are used to craft and contest subjectivity, it is impossible to write about them without addressing the role that identity plays in determining the boundaries of punishment.

On paper, the hubs and spokes policy aimed to isolate one category of identity—nationality—and to incorporate it into the organization of the prison system. But nationality cannot be so confined, for citizenship is bound to beliefs about how prisoners look, speak, and express belonging in a social collective. Whether or not prison officials intended it, the hubs and spokes system has become a powerful framework for the identity construction that plays out in every prison. In a matter of a few years, the new policy has altered the dynamics of race, ethnicity, gender, and sexuality inside prisons. In this sense, hubs and spokes is as much about race and gender as it is a policy on where prisoners are born. As we shall see in Chapter 6, the hubs and spokes approach is also an explicit attempt to distinguish contemporary Britain from its colonial past.

6

Political Amnesia

JB was born in Lagos. He grew up in a Christian family and attended church every week. One day, approximately ten years ago, JB came home to find his house burned to the ground. 'Me, war', he told me:

Me no father now, no brother. No sister, no brother. They kill my family. Me found my family. They put house on fire. Dead.

After finding his family's charred bodies, JB joined the sectarian violence. 'Me fight then too with my Christian brother. Revenge back', he explained. Leaning across the square table between us, JB pulled up his sleeve to reveal a deep scar along his right bicep. He turned each of his palms up and traced his finger along scars that ran from his middle knuckles to his wrists. 'These people want to kill me', JB said. He wrapped his hand around an imagined blade and banged his fist down on the table, hard. 'So I leave.'

To flee Nigeria, JB enlisted a 'British white man' who lived in Lagos. He became that man's driver and, after several months, asked for help coming to England. At age 27, JB got on a flight to London, hoping to leave Nigeria for good. He repeated the date of his arrival over and over, punctuating our interview with its rhythm: '2003, May, eight; 2003, May, eight'.[1] When he first got to the United Kingdom, JB lived on the street. 'Five years, sleep on street, wash clothes for hand cash', he recalled. Eventually, a friend helped him find a job at Sainsbury's, where he worked on the false passport for which he would ultimately be arrested. JB told me that he was a hard worker at Sainsbury's, made good money there, and was thankful for his job. He said that the job helped him support his girlfriend, and later, to pay bills for their infant son Matthew.

[1] This date has been changed at JB's request but the form of his testimony remains the same.

When I met JB, Matthew had just turned five and his partner had recently given birth to two more children, twin girls. One of those girls died in the hospital shortly after her birth. The other survived, though with a heart condition that required an emergency operation. JB and his partner decided to name their surviving baby after the cinema where he had seen his first images of life in England. JB loved films, he told me. So he called his daughter Odeon.

JB's narrative begs questions about where foreign national prisoners come from and why they choose to move to Britain. His experience of migration, aided by a 'British white man' and motivated by images of British life, highlights an enduring link between colonization and punishment. JB was born in a former British protectorate. He migrated to England, named his child after the largest British cinema chain, and wound up in prison for forging a document that said he belonged in the United Kingdom. When describing twenty-first-century punishment, criminologists have to contend with stories like these.

This chapter delves into the legacy of British imperialism. In studying this history, scholars have noted that terms like colonial and postcolonial obscure as much as they illuminate.[2] Stuart Hall writes that attempts to define the postcolonial period typically 'take us on a detour through a conceptual labyrinth from which few travellers return'.[3] Without treading too far down that path, it is crucial to acknowledge, as Hall and others have, that studies of postcolonialism often imply too clean a temporal break.[4] Hall writes:

[2] See, e.g. Homi Bhabha, *The Location of Culture* (London: Routledge, 1994); Paul Gilroy, *The Black Atlantic: Modernity and Double Consciousness* (Cambridge, MA: Harvard University Press, 1993); Derek Gregory, *The Colonial Present: Afghanistan, Palestine, Iraq* (Oxford: Wiley-Blackwell, 2004); Stuart Hall, 'Conclusion: The Multicultural Question', in Barnor Hesse, ed., *UN/Settled Multiculturalisms: Diasporas, Entanglement, Transruptions* (London: Zed Books, 2001), pp. 209–41; Edward Said, *Orientalism* (New York, NY: Random House, 1978); Gayatri Spivak, 'Can the Subaltern Speak?', in Cary Nelson and Lawrence Grossberg, eds, *Marxism and the Interpretation of Culture* (Champaign, IL: University of Illinois Press, 1988), pp. 271–317.

[3] Hall, 'Conclusion', p. 213.

[4] Hall, 'Conclusion', p. 213; see also Dipesh Chakrabarty, 'Postcoloniality and the Artifice of History: Who Speaks for "Indian" Pasts?', in Bill Ashcroft, Gareth Griffiths, and Helen Tiffin, eds, *The Post-Colonial Studies Reader* (Abingdon: Routledge, 1995), pp. 340–44; Graham Huggan, *The Postcolonial Exotic: Marketing the Margins* (London: Routledge, 2001).

[T]he 'post-colonial' does *not* signal a simple before/after chronological succession. The movement from colonization to post-colonial times does not imply that the problems of colonialism have been resolved, or replaced by some conflict-free era.[5]

This chapter follows Hall's logic. When mentioned, the term colonialism refers both to historical processes of economic and political subordination and to discursive patterns of 'ideological formation'.[6] The concept of colonialism describes not only a political history, but also a sociological relationship between different cultures. The term postcolonial, on the other hand, refers to the period after World War II when anti-colonial movements and war debts contributed to the decline of the British Empire.[7] As I use it, 'the postcolonial' does not imply an end to the 'problems of dependency, underdevelopment and marginalization' that defined the high colonial period.[8] Rather, 'the post-colonial marks the passage of one historical power-configuration . . . to another'.[9] This chapter examines that power configuration as it surfaces in the prison. Drawing on prisoners' testimonies and Home Office statistics, I explore how the management of foreign national prisoners constructs a post-imperial British national identity.

This inquiry builds from a wide and challenging body of writing on colonialism. In the past forty years, scholars such as Homi Bhabha and Gayatri Spivak have pushed theorists to consider how colonial ideologies shape their respective fields.[10] Biko Agozino,

[5] Hall, 'Conclusion', p. 213.

[6] Stephen Slemon, 'The Scramble for Post-Colonialism', in Chris Tiffin and Alan Lawson, eds, *De-Scribing Empire: Post-Colonialism and Textuality* (London: Routledge, 1994), p. 15.

[7] See Judith Brown, *The Oxford History of the British Empire, Volume One: The Twentieth Century* (Oxford: Oxford University Press, 1998); Niall Ferguson, *Empire: The Rise and Demise of the British World Order and the Lessons for Global Power* (London: Basic Books, 2004); Randall Hansen, *Citizenship and Immigration in Post-War Britain* (Oxford: Oxford University Press, 2000).

[8] Hall, 'Conclusion', p. 213.

[9] Hall, 'Conclusion', p. 213.

[10] Bill Ashcroft, Gareth Griffiths and Helen Tiffin have compiled a collection of some of the most famous critiques of colonialism, including Homi Bhabha's *The Location of Culture* (1994), Gayatri Spivak's 'Can the Subaltern Speak?' (1988), Frantz Fanon's *The Wretched of the Earth* (New York, NY: Grove Press 2005) and Edward Said's *Orientalism* (1978). See Bill Ashcroft, Gareth Griffiths, and Helen Tiffin, eds, *The Post-Colonial Studies Reader* (Abingdon: Routledge, 1995).

Chris Cuneen, and others have brought this critique to the study of punishment, providing a much-needed 'postcolonial perspective' in criminology.[11] At the same time, criminological writing on colonialism remains underdeveloped. While criminologists have explored colonial power dynamics, it has most often, though not always, been to assess justice systems in former colonies.[12] Criminologists tend to examine the conditions in once colonized spaces rather than applying postcolonial critiques to British institutions. This approach can eclipse the changes that globalization and decolonization have wrought on more traditional sites of criminological analysis. It also threatens to reproduce the marginalization that postcolonial theory seeks to upend.

This chapter begins and ends in Britain's prisons. The first section presents a close reading of the language British media outlets use to describe foreign national prisoners. Returning to the scandal of April 2006, which Chapter 3 explored in detail, the first part of the chapter traces reports on the 'foreign prisoner problem' to a tradition of anti-immigrant rhetoric that dates back to the end of the British Empire. The second part of the chapter contrasts colonial rhetoric with prisoners' own narratives of British rule. Many of the foreign national prisoners I interviewed spoke at length about the effects that colonialism had on their decisions to migrate to the United Kingdom. The second section recounts these narratives and connects them to a set of critical claims about what Stuart Hall calls 'collective amnesia'.[13]

Hall, perhaps the most trenchant critic of British imperialism, argued that British national identity is made possible by a wilful

[11] See Biko Agozino, 'Crime, Criminology, and Post-Colonial Theory: Criminological Reflections on West Africa', in James Sheptycki, ed., *Transnational and Comparative Criminology* (New York, NY: Glasshouse Press, 2005), pp. 117–34; Harry Blagg, *Crime, Aboriginality and the Decolonisation of Justice* (Annandale: Hawkins Press, 2008); Chris Cuneen, *Conflict, Politics, and Crime: Aboriginal Communities and the Police* (Sydney: Allen and Unwin, 2001); Chris Cuneen, 'Postcolonial Perspectives for Criminology', in Mary Bosworth and Carolyn Hoyle, *What Is Criminology?* (Oxford: Oxford University Press, 2011), pp. 249–64.

[12] See, e.g. Agozino, 'Crime, Criminology, and Post-Colonial Theory'; Blagg, *Crime, Aboriginality and the Decolonisation of Justice*. There are notable exceptions to this trend, including Ben Bowling's writing on British policing. See Benjamin Bowling, 'Transnational Policing: The Globalization Thesis, a Typology, and a Research Agenda', *Policing* 3, no. 2 (April 2009).

[13] Hall, 'Conclusion', p. 219.

effort to forget the country's past. Building from his analysis, this chapter explores how penal policies sever ties between the prison population and historical patterns of domination and migration. Drawing on statistics and interviews, media reports, and prison policies, I examine how penal practices mediate and suppress the history of British conquest. Ultimately, I argue that punishment is a mechanism for the production of a postcolonial present.

The Problem Is Still with Us

Chapter 3 tracked the emergence of the foreign prisoner scandal, which reached its apex in 2006. In April of that year, the British Home Secretary, Charles Clarke, announced that his agency had permitted more than a thousand non-citizens to be released from prison without being considered for deportation. Clarke's announcement, which led to his resignation, prompted a wave of media reports on the threat posed by 'foreign criminals'.[14] Without missing a beat, headlines linked Clarke's statement to a crisis in British national identity.[15]

The *Daily Mail* led the charge. In the days after Clarke's announcement, the tabloid released an editorial titled, 'It's Not Only the Foreign Criminals Who've Vanished, But Also Any Pretence that Britain Controls its Borders or, Indeed, Its Very Destiny'.[16] Describing prisoners as 'manifest undesirables', the editorial declared that the released non-citizens 'should have been at least considered for deportation twice over'.[17] The authors linked

[14] See, e.g. 'Foreign Criminals "Not Deported"', *BBC News*, 25 April 2006, <http://news.bbc.co.uk/1/hi/uk_politics/4942886.stm>; 'Home Office Blunders Left Foreign Rapists in UK', *Daily Mail*, 26 April 2006, <http://www.dailymail.co.uk/news/article-384183/Home-Office-blunders-left-foreign-rapists-UK.html>; Philip Johnston, 'Veil Escape "Exposes Chaos in Border Controls"', *Telegraph*, 21 December 2006, <http://www.telegraph.co.uk/news/uknews/1537514/Veil-escape-exposes-chaos-in-border-controls.html>; Philip Johnston, 'We May Never Find Foreign Murderers, Says Home Office', *Telegraph*, 27 April 2006, <http://www.telegraph.co.uk/news/uknews/1516747/We-may-never-find-foreign-murderers-says-Home-Office.html>.

[15] See, e.g. 'Foreign Criminals "Not Deported"', *BBC News*; 'Home Office Blunders Left Foreign Rapists in UK', *Daily Mail*; Johnston, 'Veil Escape "Exposes Chaos in Border Controls"'; Johnston, 'We May Never Find Foreign Murderers'.

[16] 'It's Not Only the Foreign Criminals Who've Vanished', *Daily Mail*.

[17] 'It's Not Only the Foreign Criminals Who've Vanished', *Daily Mail*.

trends in migration 'since the EU's borders were thrown open' to an increase in crime and 'gross overcrowding' of the prison system.[18] They argued that prison statistics reflected a 'crisis in national identity', one that could only be solved through a more aggressive detention policy.[19] The editorial concluded on a reflective note: 'Alas, the problem is still with us.'[20]

While the *Daily Mail* represents the dramatic end of a spectrum, it captures a common refrain. In the aftermath of the prisoner scandal, many newspaper reports underscored the danger of 'improperly' releasing non-citizens into the United Kingdom.[21] Outlets from the BBC to the *Daily Telegraph* questioned whether foreign national prisoners could ever be found once released.[22] *The Sun* asked how many new crimes 'Clarke's bungle' would beget.[23] Concerns about the nature of Britishness lay just below the surface of these articles. In more and less explicit terms, news reports positioned the release of non-citizens as a failure to defend the British polity from the dangers of migrants who have 'flooded' into the United Kingdom and overwhelmed it with crime.[24]

[18] 'It's Not Only the Foreign Criminals Who've Vanished', *Daily Mail*.

[19] 'It's Not Only the Foreign Criminals Who've Vanished', *Daily Mail*.

[20] 'It's Not Only the Foreign Criminals Who've Vanished', *Daily Mail*.

[21] See, e.g. 'Foreign Criminals "Not Deported"', *BBC News*; 'Home Office Blunders Left Foreign Rapists in UK', *Daily Mail*; 'It's Not Only the Foreign Criminals Who've Vanished', *Daily Mail*; Johnston, 'We May Never Find Foreign Murderers'.

[22] 'Foreign Criminals "Not Deported"', *BBC News*; Johnston, 'We May Never Find Foreign Murderers'.

[23] Michael Lea, 'Clarke's Bungle Ends in Rape', *The Sun*, 3 August 2007, <http://www.thesun.co.uk/sol/homepage/news/46603/Clarke-bungle-ends-in-rape.html>.

[24] Margaret Malloch, Elizabeth Stanley, and Rosemary Sales have written about the historical connotations of the term 'flooding' when used in reference to migrants. See Margaret Malloch and Elizabeth Stanley, 'The Detention of Asylum Seekers in the UK: Representing Risk, Managing the Dangerous', *Punishment and Society* 7, no. 1 (January 2005): pp. 53–71; Rosemary Sales, 'The Deserving and the Undeserving? Refugees, Asylum Seekers and Welfare in Britain', *Critical Social Policy* 22, no. 3 (August 2002): pp. 456–78. It is worth noting that the released prisoners posed very little threat under the 'risk assessment' tool used by the Prison Service. The *Vine Report*, the most recent and comprehensive review of the management of imprisoned non-citizens, found that only 36 of the 1,023 prisoners released during Clarke's tenure had committed offences classified as 'most serious'. John Vine, *Thematic Inspection of How the UK Border Agency Manages Foreign National Prisoners: February–May 2011* (London: HMSO, 2012).

These reports reflect and renew a history of xenophobic sentiment. For years, scholars have documented the conflict between tabloid perceptions of the nation and Britain's actual population.[25] While the *Daily Mail* and other media outlets tend to present Britain as a clearly defined and culturally homogenous place, the presence of migrants in the United Kingdom is not new and the country's borders have always been ambiguous.[26] Britain is and has for centuries been a nation with significant levels of immigration and a fraught relationship to its own boundaries. Moreover, as Stuart Hall notes, 'there have always been many different ways of being "British"':

> Most national achievements—from free speech and a universal franchise to the welfare state and NHS—were won as bitter struggles between one kind of British person and another. Only retrospectively were these radical differences smoothly reintegrated into the seamless web of a transcendent 'Britishness'.[27]

Hall argues that 'the so-called homogeneity of Britishness as a natural culture has been considerably exaggerated'.[28] This observation is particularly poignant in contemporary London, where residents from at least 179 countries speak over 300 different languages.[29] While the capital does not represent the country as a whole, it does offer one picture of British reality. As Steven Vertovec puts it, 'diversity is endemic to Britain'.[30]

This diversity flows directly from the country's history. Hall explains:

[25] See, e.g. Paul Gilroy, *Postcolonial Melancholia* (New York, NY: Columbia University Press, 2006); Colin Holmes, 'Cosmopolitan London', in Anne Kershen, ed., *London: The Promised Land?* (Aldershot: Avebury, 1997), pp. 10–37; Steven Vertovec, 'Super-Diversity and Its Implications', *Ethnic and Racial Studies* 30, no. 6 (2007): pp. 1024–54.

[26] See Ferguson, *Empire*; Hansen, *Citizenship and Immigration in Post-War Britain*.

[27] Hall, 'Conclusion', pp. 217–8.

[28] Hall, 'Conclusion', pp. 217–8.

[29] Greater London Authority, *London, The World in a City: An Analysis of the 2001 Census Results* (London: Greater London Authority Data Management and Analysis Group Briefing 2005/6, 2005); see also Philip Baker and Yasir Mohieldeen, 'The Languages of London's Schoolchildren', in Philip Baker and John Eversley, eds, *Multilingual Capital* (London: Battlebridge, 2000), pp. 5–60; Vertovec, 'Super-Diversity and Its Implications'.

[30] Vertovec, 'Super-Diversity and Its Implications', p. 1025.

> Britain was...the centre of the largest *imperium* of modern times, governing a variety of different cultures. This imperial experience profoundly shaped British national identity and British ideas of greatness and its place in the world. This more-or-less continuous intercourse with 'difference', which was at the heart of colonization, has framed the 'other' as a constitutive element of British identity.[31]

In Hall's account, imperialism positioned interaction with foreign cultures as an integral aspect of national consciousness. Colonialism made difference and foreignness into defining features of Britishness.

British imperialism also established the linguistic and social bonds that gird contemporary configurations of urban space. Anthropologists, historians, and geographers have long documented patterns of migration into and out of Britain.[32] They note that the postcolonial period witnessed wide-scale immigration of people from many parts of the world, including, notably, South Africa, central Africa, and the West Indies.[33] Many of these immigrants held citizenship and initial rights of entry into the United Kingdom under postcolonial legal arrangements.[34] These arrangements contributed to the establishment of large Afro-Caribbean and South Asian immigrant communities, especially in British cities.

British racism mirrored these geo-cultural shifts. In the second half of the twentieth century, public discussions of race in Britain began to focus on the threat posed by 'foreign invaders'.[35]

[31] Hall, 'Conclusion', p. 218.

[32] See, e.g. Kathleen Chater, *Untold Histories: Black People in England and Wales during the Period of the British Slave Trade, c. 1660–1807* (Manchester: Manchester University Press, 2009); Hansen, *Citizenship and Immigration in Post-War Britain*; Panikos Panayi, *An Immigration History of Britain: Multicultural Racism Since 1800* (London: Harlow Longman, 2010).

[33] Hansen, *Citizenship and Immigration in Post-War Britain*; Panayi, *An Immigration History of Britain*; Vertovec, 'Super-Diversity and Its Implications'.

[34] Vertovec, 'Super-Diversity and Its Implications'.

[35] Paul Gilroy, *There Ain't no Black in the Union Jack: The Cultural Politics of Race and Nation* (Abingdon: Routledge, 2002), pp. 53, 101; see also David Killingray, '"A Good West Indian, a Good African, and, in Short, a Good Britisher": Black and British in a Colour-Conscious Empire, 1760–1950', *Journal of Imperial and Commonwealth History* 36, no. 3 (2009): pp. 363–81; Leanne Weber and Benjamin Bowling, 'Policing Migration: A Framework for the Regulation of Global Mobility', *Policing and Society* 14, no. 3 (September 2004): pp. 195–212.

In speeches and campaigns, politicians such as Enoch Powell cast migrants from the British Commonwealth as part of a dangerous national problem.[36] Crime played a pivotal role in this discourse, providing a concrete fear around which ideas about nationhood could cohere. Paul Gilroy explains that 'the gradual importation of statistics' on crime and immigration into official government rhetoric constructed 'the black presence…as a threat' against which a unified Britain had to protect itself.[37] In the years after the dismantling of the British Empire, public discussions of crime and migration reinforced the image of a clearly bounded and naturally white British nation. In the context of this history, the coverage of Charles Clarke's announcement reiterates a familiar narrative. The 2006 prisoner scandal was neither new, nor was it a crisis. It was the latest chapter in a long-standing conflict between British reality and the fantasy of national belonging that underlies British racism.

It would be a mistake, though, to say that the scandal was simply an outgrowth of colonial ideology. While the foreign national prisoner scandal grew from the history of British imperialism, it was also about newer forms of anti-immigrant sentiment, and in particular, ideas about migration that crystallized in the years leading up to the fall of the Soviet Union.[38] The late 1980s and early 1990s witnessed the opening of Eastern European borders and the start of the Yugoslav conflict. These developments transformed British immigration rhetoric.

Between 1989 and 1992, government policies and newspaper reports started to describe migrants from the Soviet Bloc, once

[36] In a 1968 speech to a meeting of the Conservative Political Centre in Birmingham, Enoch Powell criticized Commonwealth immigration. Referring to the future of Great Britain should the nation 'tolerate' migrants, Powell declared, 'As I look ahead, I am filled with foreboding; like the Roman, I seem to see "the River Tiber foaming with much blood"'. 'Enoch Powell's "River's of Blood" Speech', *Telegraph Online*, retrieved 1 October 2011, <http://www.telegraph.co.uk/comment/3643823/Enoch-Powells-Rivers-of-Blood-speech.html>.

[37] Paul Gilroy, 'Introduction', in *There Ain't no Black in the Union Jack*, p. 49; see also Stuart Hall, 'Racism and Moral Panics in Post-War Britain', in BBC, ed., *Five Views of Multi-Racial Britain* (London: Commission for Racial Equality, 1978); Nick Lynn and Susan Lea, '"A Phantom Menace and the New Apartheid": The Social Construction of Asylum-Seekers in the United Kingdom', *Discourse and Society* 14, no. 4 (July 2003): pp. 425–52.

[38] See Lynn and Lea, 'A Phantom Menace and the New Apartheid'; Panayi, *An Immigration History of Britain*.

considered asylum seekers fleeing communist regimes, as 'bogus' and 'undeserving' recipients of British aid.[39] Both the government and the media began to refer to immigrants as 'new asylum seekers', a different and implicitly less worthy group of people than those who sought refuge in the past.[40] This language propelled a series of restrictive immigration laws between 1993 and 1999.[41] It resurfaced in 2006 when reports on the prisoner 'crisis' ran alongside headlines such as 'UK Lets in More Poles Than There Are in Warsaw'.[42]

There are obvious parallels between headlines condemning 'bogus' asylum seekers and racialized discussions of 'New Commonwealth' migration. Both discourses reaffirm an exclusionary vision of British national identity and 're-inscribe the state' in the face of a perceived national crisis.[43] In the seventies, that crisis was a 'flood' of potentially criminal migrants from former colonies; in the nineties, migrants represented the dual 'problems' of European integration and the decline of the welfare state.[44] These discourses build from a shared assumption that immigration

[39] See Matthew Gibney, 'Refugees and Immigrants in the New Europe', in David Forsythe, ed., *Human Rights in the New Europe: Problems and Progress* (Lincoln, NE: University of Nebraska Press, 1994); Panayi, *An Immigration History of Britain*; UN High Commissioner for Refugees, *Die Lage der Flüchtlinge in der Welt (State of the World's Refugees)* (Berlin: UNHCR, 1994); Sales, 'The Deserving and the Undeserving?'.

[40] Lynn and Lea, 'A Phantom Menace and the New Apartheid'; Sales, 'The Deserving and the Undeserving?'.

[41] During the 1990s, Parliament passed three separate laws aimed at reducing the number of asylum applications. The first was the 1993 Asylum and Immigration Appeals Act, which restricted asylum seekers' access to housing and extended the 1987 Carriers' Liability Act, a law that made carriers liable for undocumented and incorrectly documented passengers. Three years later, the 1996 Asylum and Immigration Act further curtailed asylum seekers' access to welfare benefits. In 1999, the Immigration and Asylum Act tied the remaining benefits available to asylum seekers to dispersal and food voucher schemes.

[42] 'UK Lets in More Poles than Warsaw', *Mail Online*, 25 April 2006, <http://www.dailymail.co.uk/news/article-384121/UK_lets-Poles-Warsaw.html>.

[43] Mary Bosworth and Mhairi Guild, 'Governing through Migration Control: Security and Citizenship in Britain', *British Journal of Criminology* 48, no. 6 (Fall 2008): p. 715.

[44] See Bosworth and Guild, 'Governing through Migration Control'; Terri Given and Adam Luedtke, 'The Politics of European Union Immigration Policy: Institutions, Salience, and Harmonization', *The Policy Studies Journal* 32, no. 1 (February 2004): pp. 145–63.

threatens the British nation by increasing crime.[45] There is resonance between postcolonial and post-Cold War presentations of immigrant otherness.

Yet there are also tensions between these lines of thought. Most notably, rhetoric on new asylum seekers complicates the connection between xenophobia and racism. In the nineties, critics of migration policy tended to focus on 'white' migration, and specifically, on the threat posed by migrants who allegedly come to Britain for work and the welfare state.[46] These criticisms distort history: Britain's economy has always benefited from economic migration, and 'white' migrants—most obviously, the Irish—have long constituted a significant portion of the British population.[47] Nonetheless, post-Cold War rhetoric altered the link between racism and nationalism. As Paul Gilroy explains it, the emphasis on economic migration in the nineties 'dislodg[ed] the Caribbean from the centre of British blackness'.[48] Where before politicians like Enoch Powell railed against 'black settlement' from the New Commonwealth, now public figures warn of a more varied set of threats to the British nation.[49]

This rhetoric changes but does not eliminate the racial subtext of immigration debates. While claims about bogus asylum-seekers foreground 'white' migration, the language of non-racial refugees recodes racism by suppressing it in the language of pure statistics.[50] Leanne Weber and Ben Bowling argue

[45] In the aftermath of British Empire, the spectre of crime motivated distrust of Commonwealth migrants. See Gilroy, 'Introduction'. More recently, media reports have tied asylum-seekers to 'gang-warfare, drug trafficking, kidnapping, corruption [and] trafficking of people for the sex industry'. Malloch and Stanley, 'The Detention of Asylum Seekers in the UK', p. 54.

[46] See Malloch and Stanley, 'The Detention of Asylum Seekers in the UK'. See also Gilroy, 'Introduction'. The claim that immigrants come to Britain to enjoy or deplete the welfare state competes in popular discourse with arguments about economic migrants stealing 'British' jobs. See Malloch and Stanley, 'The Detention of Asylum Seekers in the UK'; Sales, 'The Deserving and the Undeserving?'. The conflict between these claims suggests that it is not migrants' goals but their mere presence in the United Kingdom that is at issue.

[47] See Chater, *Untold Histories*; Killingray, 'A Good West Indian, a Good African, and, in Short, a Good Britisher'; Panayi, *An Immigration History of Britain*; Vertovec, 'Super-Diversity and Its Implications'.

[48] Gilroy, 'Introduction', p. xiii.

[49] Gilroy, 'Introduction', p. xiii.

[50] Weber and Bowling, 'Policing Migration', p. 197.

that, while contemporary migration policies are 'justified in terms of *numbers*, the *origins* of these groups are central to the perception of them as a problem'.[51] Weber and Bowling explain that 'uncontrolled non-white migration embodie[s] public fears about the diminution of national sovereignty arising from the loss of Empire and the encroachment of the European Union'.[52] They conclude that the government's focus on migration statistics obscures the role that race continues to play in border control policy. From this perspective, actuarial discussions of migration, seemingly untethered from race, provide a new guise for old concerns about the nature of British identity.

Concerns about race also shape public discussions of multiculturalism. In the past two decades, British politicians have debated the merits and drawbacks of national, cultural, and ethnic diversity, a phenomenon the government calls 'British multiculturalism'.[53] This discourse has given rise to a new language of difference. Paul Gilroy writes:

> Today, Britain's black and other minority settlers still constitute a problem, but its dimensions have altered. As a result of major changes that occurred both inside and outside the country, 'race' is rendered differently.[54]

In a recent introduction to *There Ain't No Black in the Union Jack*, Gilroy argues that globalization has shifted discussions of racial difference away from the biological notions of the 1970s and towards euphemistic terms like 'taste and lifestyle'.[55] Stuart Hall concurs, noting that discursive shifts have encouraged a rapid 'subaltern proliferation of differences' along ever-more finely drawn lines.[56] Hall points out that the languages of culture and

[51] Weber and Bowling, 'Policing Migration', p. 197.

[52] Weber and Bowling, 'Policing Migration', p. 197.

[53] See, e.g. Foreign and Commonwealth Office, 'Kwame Kwei-Armah on Multicultural Britain' 28 March 2011, <https://www.gov.uk/government/news/kwame-kwei-armah-on-multicultural-britain>.

[54] Gilroy, 'Introduction', p. xii.

[55] Gilroy, 'Introduction', p. xii. Gilroy defines globalization as the regulation and expansion of financial markets, the growth of technologies, and the rise of 'the knowledge economy'. Gilroy, 'Introduction', p. xxv. Chapter 1 provides a more detailed discussion of the term 'globalization'.

[56] Hall, 'Conclusion', p. 214.

biology are not so distinct: 'biological racism and cultural differentialism...constitute not two different systems, but racism's two registers'.[57]

This account of race can strengthen critiques of punishment. In recent years, criminologists have focused on what David Garland calls the criminology of the other, an attitude towards crime that 'trades in images, archetypes, and anxieties rather than careful analyses and research findings'.[58] Garland and others position this criminology in the context of neoliberal policies that emphasize rational economic action and demonize the 'alien other'.[59] They argue that twenty-first-century crime control policies stigmatize communities whose 'culture and mode of life...is both alien and threatening'.[60] This argument helps to explain public responses to the foreign prisoner 'crisis'. Garland's work offers an illuminating way to think about how and why foreign national prisoners became the centre of a national scandal.

Yet the foreign national prisoner scandal is more than another case of exclusionary late modern logic. While the prisoner crisis reflects a 'criminology of the other', the fearful, dramatic response to the release of 1,023 foreign national prisoners finds its roots in beliefs about British national identity that have existed for centuries.[61] Debates over the foreign prisoner population are as much about colonialism and British decline as they are about transnational neoliberal trends. Accordingly, a study of British penal policy must look both to the late modern 'culture of control' and to the particular history of race and migration in the United Kingdom.[62] If the prisoner scandal is an instance of neoliberalism, it is also

[57] Hall, 'Conclusion', p. 214.

[58] David Garland, *The Culture of Control: Crime and Social Order in Contemporary Society* (Oxford: Oxford University Press, 2001), pp. 77–8, 135.

[59] Garland, *The Culture of Control*, p. 137; see also Malcolm Feeley and Jonathan Simon, 'Actuarial Justice: The Emerging New Criminal Law', in David Nelken, ed., *The Futures of Criminology* (London: Sage Publications Ltd, 1994), pp. 173–201; Eugene McLaughlin and Karim Murji, 'Lost Connections and New Directions: Neo-Liberalism, New Managerialism and the Modernisation of the British Police', in Kevin Stenson and Robert Sullivan, eds, *Crime, Risk and Justice* (Cullompton: Willan, 2000): pp. 104–22.

[60] Garland, *The Culture of Control*, p. 135.

[61] See Chater, *Untold Histories*; Panayi, *An Immigration History of Britain*.

[62] Garland, *The Culture of Control*.

embedded in an ongoing and in some sense very local debate about what it means to be British.

Colonial Amnesia

The people in British prisons bear witness to the enduring relevance of history. While prison officials I interviewed rarely mentioned colonialism, prisoners often offered opinions about the nation's history and place in the global order. People from the West Indies, India, and Nigeria regularly commented on the role that colonialism played in conditions in their 'home' countries and their decisions to migrate to the United Kingdom. Their testimonies highlight the problems that arise when governments use penal institutions to identify a 'foreign' population.

According to Home Office statistics, at the time of my research, incarcerated foreign nationals hailed from 161 different countries or disputed territories such as Western Sahara, which is counted as a distinct region in Prison Service polls.[63] Of those 161 countries, the top four represented in British prisons were Jamaica, the Irish Republic, Poland, and Nigeria, three of which were at one point under British rule.[64] The over-representation of the British imperium persisted in

[63] Ministry of Justice (MoJ), *Offender Management Caseload Statistics 2009* (London: Ministry of Justice, 2010). These statistics on the foreign national prisoner population are fluid—the prison population changes daily—and are probably slightly inaccurate given the difficulty of determining prisoners' nationalities, which Chapters 4 and 5 explore. Hindpal Bhui has written about the problems with data collection in prisons. See Hindpal Singh Bhui, *Going the Distance: Developing Effective Policy and Practice with Foreign National Prisoners* (London: Prison Reform Trust, 2004).

[64] At the time of my research, the precise numbers were: Jamaica (865), the Irish Republic (683), Poland (670), Nigeria (649). The list continued: Vietnam (536), Pakistan (435), Somalia (433), Lithuania (404), Romania (400), India (374). MoJ, *Offender Management Caseload Statistics 2009*. In addition to noting these numbers, it is worth examining gender disparities. Males make up the vast majority of the foreign national prisoner population. Of the top four countries represented in the prison system, only one, Nigeria, has a significant number of female prisoners. Females account for 13 per cent of the total population of Nigerian prisoners. In contrast, only 3 per cent of the prisoners from the Irish Republic and Poland are female, and 5 per cent of prisoners from Jamaica are female. MoJ, *Offender Management Caseload Statistics 2009*. However, in some cases, countries with relatively low numbers of total prisoners have a relatively high percentage of female prisoners. South Africa (13 per cent), Ghana (12 per cent), Germany (12 per cent), and Bulgaria (31 per cent) are among these countries. While this particular study focuses less on such statistics and more

the larger prison population: of the approximately 11,000 foreign nationals imprisoned during my fieldwork, nearly half, and possibly more, were born in countries with colonial ties to the British state.[65] Many of these prisoners—particularly those who were raised in the United Kingdom, possessed British passports as colonial subjects, or were educated in British colonial schools—conceived of themselves as British.

One prisoner told me that he had become British by attending schools in India. This man, who asked to remain anonymous, explained that he had grown up in India and had migrated to England in his late teens. He described how the experience of life in India had affected his sense of national identity:

> I went to British school. I think of myself as British. If tomorrow they went to war with India, I'd fight on this side. All my family is here.

Not so long ago, some prisoners classified as foreign were encouraged to see themselves as part of the British state. Moreover, some 'foreign' prisoners technically *were* British subjects at one point. Gus, for example, was born in St Lucia, which was a British colony until 1958 and is now a member of the British Commonwealth. When he was born, Gus received a British passport, which he used to migrate to Britain with his grandmother in 1968. Gus attended Catholic schools in London while his grandmother cared for him and worked as a maid. In a strong British accent, he told me that he 'read history and religion' for his O levels and always thought of himself as a British person. 'I've never seen anything but a British passport', Gus explained. 'I remember my mum saying, "you're a citizen of this country"'. Gus's story hints at the complexity of difference in a country that once governed a quarter of the world's population.[66]

on the individual testimonies of incarcerated foreigners, further studies might explore why women from particular countries are over-represented in prisons, or how these statistics have changed since they were first recorded in the early 1990s.

[65] Hall, 'Conclusion', p. 218. See note 5 of the Introduction to this book for a breakdown of the claim that there were 'approximately 11,000' incarcerated foreign nationals and note 10 of the Introduction for the claim that nearly half of these prisoners were born in countries with colonial ties to the British state. See also Bhui, *Going the Distance*.

[66] See Angus Maddison, *The World Economy: A Millennial Perspective* (Paris: OECD Publishing, 2001), pp. 97–8, 242; see also Brown, *The Oxford History of the British Empire*; Ferguson, *Empire*.

Statistics on foreign national prisoners also underscore the irony of British nationalism. According to the government study commissioned in response to the 2006 prisoner scandal, the Prison Service began gathering figures on foreign nationality in 1993.[67] This claim is slightly inaccurate—1993 is actually when statistics on Commonwealth prisoners began to be reported, with varying degrees of consistency, to the Immigration and Nationality Directorate. In other words, 1993 is not when prisons began documenting nationality; it is when the Prison Service began to identify migrants from the British Commonwealth as foreigners. Statistics on non-Commonwealth prisoners existed years earlier. In July 1988, the Secretary of State for the Home Department reported the numbers of non-Commonwealth prisoners, but stated that 'the recording of nationality for citizens of Commonwealth countries, Pakistan and Eire is not sufficiently reliable for estimates of their numbers to be given'.[68] Trends in recording prisoners' nationalities reflect discursive shifts in the conception of national difference. Prison statistics track Britain's relationship to its former empire.

Ultimately, whether or not prisoners are foreign nationals depends on whether the Prison Service counts them that way. The Prison Service is not alone in this determination; the agency is under external pressure from multiple directions when it collects information about the prison population. The UKBA defines the term 'foreign national' and instructs prison officials on how to keep statistics on non-citizens.[69] Prison statistics also derive from laws such as the 2007 UK Borders Act and the 2009 Borders, Citizenship, and Immigration Act, which determine the contours of citizenship. Straightforward claims about the number of

[67] Home Office, *A Review of the Failure of the Immigration and Nationality Directorate to Consider Some Foreign National Prisoners for Deportation* (London: Home Office, 2007), p. 33; see also Gavin Berman, *Prison Population Statistics: Notes for the Members of Parliament, 7 November, 2011* (London: MoJ, 2011).

[68] Douglas Hogg, *Hansard*, 15 July 1988, Col. 399. In interviews, Prison Service officials did not recall the year that prisoners' nationalities were first recorded.

[69] See Ministry of Justice (MoJ) and UK Border Agency (UKBA), *Service Level Agreement to Support the Effective and Speedy Removal of Foreign National Prisoners* (London: Ministry of Justice and United Kingdom Border Agency, 2009); see also the *Vine Report*.

imprisoned foreign nationals can obscure these contingent aspects of data collection. The Prison Service is one co-author in the current narrative of British colonialism.

Prisoners contested this narrative. In interviews, prisoners regularly reminded me that colonialism had affected their lives in tangible ways. Some people invoked colonial ties to explain their decisions to migrate to the United Kingdom, such as the prisoner who told me, 'we have a connection to the UK because they were in Ghana'. Another prisoner, GW, was born in Zimbabwe and had lived in England for ten years. He shook his head when I asked why he had come to England:

> My country is how it is because of the British. We all know the truth ... The British people know exactly what they've done to Zimbabwe.

GW was visibly upset about being 'flagged' for deportation when the British government had colonized his country. Many prisoners shared his anger. A man who was born in Guyana and had lived in London for several decades asked me:

> How is it possible for people from British colonies to be here? I've been here since I was twelve years old. I'd go to my country now, they'd call me a foreigner.

These claims capture just how counter-intuitive and arbitrary migration control measures can feel to prisoners who identify with Britain.

Prisoners also wondered aloud about how the government could categorize them as criminals given the history of British colonialism. In one conversation, Scott reflected on the practice of identifying foreign nationals:

> England is a racist country. They don't even like Scottish, Irish, people from Europe. They say we're taking their jobs. But Jamaica was a British colony. They don't take their history into consideration. They don't look back where they're coming from. People from the Caribbean...coming here in the fifties and sixties and long before that.

Senator also invoked England's long history of conquest and xenophobia. 'Remember, England used to have the first thirteen states', he told me:

> The mentality of England is they go to your country and take you over. But when you come here they don't like you. Look at Africa. Look at the big diamond the Queen is wearing. It came from Ethiopia.

The Queen's jewels came up in several conversations. In an interview in the same prison several weeks later, a prisoner who asked to be called System said:

> The fucking Queen have the biggest fucking diamond in the world. It was stolen from India. Why is it that other people can't handle stolen goods, but she can?

Side by side, these testimonies demonstrate that the Queen, and the national history she represents, plays an important symbolic role in prisoners' understanding of their treatment in the prison system. Whether the royal jewels in question came from Ethiopia or India, foreign national prisoners perceived a strain of hypocrisy in their confinement. Prisoners questioned how they could be imprisoned for crime when the British government had routinely 'stolen' jewels and land during the period of colonial expansion. One prisoner, who asked to remain anonymous, articulated this critique in particularly explicit terms. He drew a direct analogy between colonialism and criminality:

> The British people are the biggest thieves...They took half the world. America, Jamaica, India...you name it. I learned to be a criminal from this country.

This prisoner, who was born in Jamaica, was raised in England from the age of fourteen. When I met him, he had lived in the United Kingdom for thirty-seven years and had held a British passport for his entire life. At reception to the prison, an officer misidentified him as a foreign national 'because', as he put it, 'I'm black'.

These testimonies situate the policy on foreign nationals as a case of what Stuart Hall calls 'collective amnesia'.[70] In his critique of British nationalism, Hall argues that the postcolonial condition is marked by a 'disavowal of "empire"', which is framed as 'a new beginning' but realized as a widespread and more or less purposeful bout of amnesia about Britain's colonial past.[71] Hall describes this 'Cloud of Unknowing' in a powerful essay on 'the multicultural question':

> The old relations of colonization, slavery and colonial rule, linking Britain with the empire for over 400 years, marked out the pathways these migrants followed. But these historic relations of dependency and

[70] Hall, 'Conclusion', p. 218.
[71] Hall, 'Conclusion', p. 218.

subordination were *reconfigured*—in the now-classic post-colonial way—when reconvened on domestic British soil... Most British people looked at these 'children of empire' as if they could not imagine where 'they' come had come from, why, or what possible connection they could have with Britain.[72]

In this apt formulation, postcolonial Britain is shaped by an ironic sense of surprise at the resurgent, embodied remnants of its past.

In his writing on British history, Hall is concerned with the re-inscription of colonial dynamics in contemporary British society. He argues that amnesia is the contemporary manifestation of an ongoing relationship between colonizer and colonized, and more to the point, between the different cultures involved in the project of British imperialism. Hall concludes that colonial histories play out in the present through a systematic and collective process of memory loss. This reading of colonialism emphasizes the structures and practices, intentional or otherwise, that reproduce colonial subject relations in the twenty-first century.

Many scholars have taken a similar approach to 'the "question" of... colonialism'.[73] Literary theorist Stephen Slemon notes that colonialism was not simply an 'economic and political structure of cross-cultural domination', but was also, crucially, a process of 'ideological or discursive formation'.[74] Slemon argues that colonialism was 'an apparatus for constituting subject positions through the field of representation'.[75] In his account, analysing the aftermath of colonialism involves more than structural economic critique, though that line of thought is relevant. Studying colonialism also means exploring current cultural attitudes towards migrants and British history.

[72] Hall, 'Conclusion', p. 218.

[73] Slemon, 'The Scramble for Post-Colonialism', p. 15; see also Chinua Achebe, 'Named for Victoria, Queen of England', *New Letters* 40, no. 3 (1973): pp. 15–22; Homi Bhabha, 'The Commitment to Theory', *New Formations* 5 (Summer 1988): pp. 5–23; Gareth Griffiths, 'The Myth of Authenticity: Representation, Discourse, and Social Practice', in Chris Tiffin and Alan Lawson, eds, *De-Scribing Empire: Post-Colonialism and Textuality*, pp. 70–85; Benita Parry, 'Problems in Current Theories of Colonial Discourse', *Oxford Literary Review* 9, no. 1–2 (July 1987): pp. 27–58.

[74] Slemon, 'The Scramble for Post-Colonialism', p. 15.

[75] Slemon, 'The Scramble for Post-Colonialism', p. 15.

Such studies are relatively absent from criminology. In his recent writing, Chris Cuneen points out that 'the criminological enterprise lacks a coherent theoretical understanding of colonialism and postcolonialism'.[76] Cuneen calls on criminologists to advance a 'postcolonial perspective':

> A postcolonial perspective in criminology does not need to eschew evaluative approaches or empirical research but it should proceed from a critical and reflexive framework . . . A postcolonial vision for criminology can engage with public policy formulations and debates, but it does so from a theoretical grounding that recognizes the importance of history, particularly through understanding the long-term impact of colonization and imperialism, and it does so through an analysis of the structures of sentiment and ideology that determine the intersections of race, crime, and punishment.[77]

Cuneen argues that criminologists ought to map the 'structures of sentiment and ideology' that shape contemporary criminal justice institutions.

This goal requires recognition of the parallels between colonial amnesia and prison policy. The 'old relations' of colonialism not only established migration pathways; these relationships also fueled the 'structures of sentiment' that make incarcerated foreign nationals feel British.[78] Many prisoners who identify with British culture do so because in their lifetimes, and for a much longer period, the British governed their home countries. These people went to British schools; they have British relatives; they grew up with an image of British culture in their minds. The idea of British society has played a significant role in many 'foreign' prisoners' lives—how else to describe JB's decision to migrate to the United Kingdom and name his daughter Odeon?

Many incarcerated 'foreigners' feel British for a reason. Yet at reception into the penal estate, they become non-citizens. In the process of identifying foreigners, border agents and prison staff collectively reconceive national belonging, suggesting, in effect, that the government has no idea why or how non-citizens came to live in Britain. This process obscures the simple fact that

[76] Cuneen, 'Postcolonial Perspectives for Criminology', p. 251.
[77] Cuneen, 'Postcolonial Perspectives for Criminology', p. 252.
[78] Hall, 'Conclusion', p. 218; Cuneen, 'Postcolonial Perspectives for Criminology', p. 252.

imperialism has motivated migration patterns for centuries. Every day, local representatives of the British state, acting in the name of punishment, negotiate the boundary between the British present and the country's imperial past.

Foreign national prisoners resist this revisionist process by talking about colonialism. In interviews, prisoners spoke about colonial rule to describe their incarceration, to represent themselves and the histories of their cultures, and to situate themselves as subjects in both British society and the country's prisons. The concept of colonialism surfaced in many conversations, more than I expected at the outset of my research. I did not enter any particular prison expecting to speak about the postcolonial condition, nor did I mention British imperialism before prisoners did. Yet time and again, I wound up listening as prisoners told me that their incarceration, and especially their classification as foreign nationals, was illegitimate in light of British history. Prisoners' desire to discuss colonialism was one of the more evident forms of resistance to the amnesia of migration control.

Damien articulated this desire. During one of our first interviews, he chafed at the government's decision to classify him as a foreigner. Shaking his head, Damien asked me:

> How do you say I'm much different when Jamaica was colonized by the British, when my government is British? I don't see how they even try to give an answer for what they're doing.

Here, the amnesiac quality of imprisonment comes into full focus as a government policy disconnects Britain from its current commonwealth *and formerly domestic* Jamaican soil.[79] In the context of history, Damien's testimony contests the immigration policy that confines him and the prison begins to look like a key mechanism for the country's coordinated effort to forget its past. Moreover, the paperwork on which this effort unfolds and depends—reception questionnaires, visas, deportation orders—starts to become legible

[79] When it was a British colony, Jamaica was in an important sense a British domestic space. Prior to the Immigration Act of 1971, British subjects had a right of abode within the United Kingdom and British police forces acted on Jamaican soil. During the 1940s, for instance, MI5—the intelligence organization responsible for 'internal security'—operated in Jamaica. See Christopher Andrew, *The Defence of the Realm: The Authorized History of MI-5* (London: Allen Lane, 2009); see also Bowling, 'Transnational Policing'.

as the banal mode of expression for a contentious national project. This reading was not lost on Damien. He put it as a question: 'why does it take a visa to come here when your forefathers didn't need one to come rape my country?'

In the reverb of Damien's powerful claim, it is important to note that not all foreign national prisoners come from former British colonies. Many of the non-citizens most routinely forgotten in discussions of imprisonment are those from Eastern Europe and East Asia, who tend to face greater language barriers than prisoners who learned English in British colonial schools. While I interviewed men from Vietnam, China, Moldova, and Romania, I generally found that prisoners born in or identified with the British Commonwealth better understood my questions and were more willing to share personal information. For the most part, I also better understood English-speaking prisoners' answers. With non- and limited English-speaking prisoners, I resorted to communicating through translators and through the gestures and fragments that characterize language gaps. In these instances, the residue of colonialism shaped the possibilities of my research. While I strived to get many perspectives and to build my account from prisoners' words, this book would be very different if I had interviewed predominantly Chinese prisoners or had better understood the Vietnamese people that I met. The omissions of this book are just as significant as the narratives it contains. Both illustrate the relevance of identity.

Power dynamics between prisoners also complicate the relationship between colonialism and punishment. In practice, colonialism leaves an uneasy legacy on penal hierarchies. Given their familiarity with English, prisoners educated in British colonial schools were in some ways better situated to navigate prison than migrants from Eastern Europe, East Asia, and other parts of the world. Prisoners from former colonies often found it easier to communicate with prison staff, and at least in some cases, had established ties to the United Kingdom that supported their claims against deportation.[80] Geographer Derek Gregory notes that we

[80] Prisoners who have established families and other ties to the United Kingdom are in theory better situated to appeal their deportation under Article 8 of the European Convention on Human Rights, which protects the right to family life and a private life. That Convention became United Kingdom law in the 1998 Human Rights Act. Human rights considerations are the most common grounds for the court to grant prisoners' appeals of their deportation orders. See the *Vine*

live in a complex 'colonial present', one that recasts imperialism in new and constantly changing forms.[81] In British prisons, that present involved unevenly distributed language barriers, nuanced relationships between 'old' and 'new' migrants, and the evolving pressures of a migration control policy aimed at all 'foreigners'.

Each of these facets of prison life is connected to history. Prisoners' angry insistence on the relevance of colonialism, their heated exchanges with immigration officials, and prison staff members' frustrated responses to non-English speakers all serve as a reminder that imprisonment has an irreducibly historical dimension. Penal policies eclipse this history and divorce the prison from its wider social context. The problem of colonial amnesia, though concrete and crucial, is also a metonym for a larger concern about the prison's systematic capacity to detach penal institutions from the politics in which penality takes root.

The term politics has multiple meanings here. The claim that prison is de-politicized refers not only to public debates about migration and penal policy, but also to the very personal politics of how prisoners define themselves.[82] Penal policies suppress not only the partisan debates that lead to laws like the UK Borders Act of 2007, but also the charged politics of identifying as British, foreign, or something in between. This suppression occurs on a minute scale, in local interactions that come together to efface the political nature of prison life. If Coretta Phillips and Rod Earle are right that 'dehumanizing othering' is the prison's 'principal social accomplishment', it appears that political amnesia is its principal means to that end.[83]

Report, p. 19. However, while prisoners from former colonies may have stronger, or at least more recognizable, ties to the United Kingdom, these prisoners will not automatically, or even likely, be allowed to remain in the country. Ties to family do not preclude a prisoners' deportation.

[81] Gregory, *The Colonial Present.*

[82] Feminists and critical race theorists have long argued that identity formation is a political process. See, e.g. Shulamith Firestone, *The Dialectic of Sex: The Case for Feminist Revolution* (London: Bantam Books, 1970); Meredith Tax, Joreen, Ellen Willis, Suzie Olah, Pamela Kearon, Carol Hanisch, Bonnie Kreps, Barbara Mehrhof, Irene Peslikis, and Kate Millet, *Notes from the Second Year: Women's Liberation, Major Writings of the Radical Feminists* (New York, NY: Firestone and Koedt, 1970).

[83] Coretta Philips and Rod Earle, 'Reading Difference Differently? Identity, Epistemology and Prison Ethnography', *British Journal of Criminology* 50, no. 2 (March 2010): p. 375.

Managerialism and Memory Loss

Colonial amnesia is one strand of a broader tendency towards memory loss in prison. Empirical prison scholars have noted that the interior life of the prison is chronically disconnected from questions about who gets incarcerated, how, and why we choose to punish people.[84] The daily operation of penal institutions involves classifying prisoners, managing staff, serving food, and running education courses. At least in my experience, these practices do not include reflection on the topics that motivate critical prison scholarship, such as power, history, and inequality. To the contrary, imprisonment often seems like an exercise in confining and controlling people who 'just happen' to come through the prison's gates.

It is worth thinking about how incarceration becomes so routine. From day to day, prison officials tend to focus with myopic intensity on the rules and regulations of prison life. In the facilities I visited, prison and immigration staff concentrated on the provisions of the new foreign national prisoner policy. Staff explained in detail how the instructions for filling out paperwork on non-citizens had changed since the introduction of hubs and spokes. One line officer told me that 'foreign nationals take more time' than other prisoners. He explained, 'it's the problem of prison interpreters, and then they have medical issues, but there's the confidentiality issue. There's different rules.' Another officer said he wished that regulations on foreign nationals were more 'like a conveyor belt'. A third staff member told me, 'being an officer now is less interacting with them and more about the paperwork'.

At times, prison officers, particularly those who worked most with foreign nationals, asked philosophical and ethical questions about the confinement of non-citizens. Some staff members worried about what would happen to prisoners after they had been deported. Others wondered why the government held some people in prisons rather than immigration detention centres. For the most part, though, these concerns fell beyond the scope of the penal institution. When staff raised broad concerns, they quickly returned to claims about 'the reality of the situation' or the daily demands of the job. One policymaker exemplified this pattern in

[84] See, e.g. Alison Liebling, *Prisons and Their Moral Performance: A Study of Values, Quality, and Prison Life* (Oxford: Oxford University Press, 2004), p. xix.

a discussion about prison capacity. Halfway through our conversation, the official paused and asked, 'should they ever be held in prison? There's a question there, really.' After a moment, he continued, 'but there's a constant focus on numbers. It's £110 a night to keep someone in an I[mmigration] R[emoval] C[entre], and £130 in prison.' In another exchange, a foreign national coordinator spoke with a governor-grade prison official who had come to oversee that day's immigration surgery. 'How many are you getting rid of?' the official asked the coordinator. 'You're not supposed to put it like that', she responded. He replied, 'That's what it's about, isn't it? Move them out. It's the taxpayer's money. Move them out and open new prison spaces up.'

This approach to incarceration, while concerning, is not something that prison scholars should criticize without acknowledging the difficulties of running a prison. Imprisonment is an enormous bureaucratic undertaking and prisons are complex ecosystems. Still, it is clear that a near-obsessive focus on numbers has affected the tone of confinement.[85] The British government's strict focus on populations, deportation dates, and 'pure' statistics has encouraged an amnesiac institutional culture. Prison officers and border agents often made claims that seemed willfully dissociated from their political context. One immigration official explained in a placid tone that the UKBA caseworkers who make deportation decisions 'had to' work outside prisons because they 'simply couldn't' interact with people they might deport. 'I couldn't go on the wing if I made the decisions', she told me. 'If I made the decision and went on the wing, I'd be lynched.' Describing the form she filed to detain a prisoner beyond his criminal sentence, another border agent said, 'the IS 91 is a godsend'.

These claims are tied to particular people and politics—the term lynching has acute racial connotations—but staff articulated them as commonplace concerns. This was typical. In my experience, policymakers and staff usually operated with a flat affect when describing their jobs. In each of the five prisons I visited,

[85] For a discussion of actuarialism, see Malcolm Feeley and Jonathan Simon, 'The New Penology: Notes on the Emerging Strategy of Corrections and its Implications', *Criminology* 30, no. 4 (November 1992), pp. 449–74; and Malcolm Feeley and Jonathan Simon, 'Actuarial Justice: The Emerging New Criminal Law', pp. 173–201.

staff spoke about punishment, suicide, and self-harm in terms of specific forms, deadlines, and key performance indicators. These metrics turned the highly emotional act of locking people in metal rooms, sometimes indefinitely, into a curiously monotonous exercise. In my field notes one day, I wrote, 'how can this be so boring? If I made a documentary about incarcerating foreigners, people would fall asleep.' During another visit, a Rwandan prisoner told me that he had tried to commit suicide. I asked him what had happened afterward and he replied, 'they made a report'. In these moments, paperwork subsumed the politics of imprisonment.

Eamonn Carrabine calls this the 'dull compulsion' of prison life.[86] Damien called it torture:

> The paperwork they're using is just a bunch of words with no meaning. The only difference from Guantanamo is that you've got people lost in the system. You know Guantanamo exists. This type of torture is covered by paperwork.

As a matter of historical truth, paperwork is not the only difference between British prisons and the American detention centre at Guantanamo Bay Naval Base.[87] Detainees at Guantanamo 'arrived soaked in their own urine' and are held in 'steel-mesh cages, open to the elements, ringed by a razor-wire fence'.[88] The conditions in British prisons are much less severe than those at Camp X-Ray. Nonetheless, Guantanamo plays a symbolic role in prisoners' accounts of their treatment. Damien's words highlight the degree to which the government's routine approach to prisoners' lives becomes its own 'pain of imprisonment'.[89]

[86] Eamonn Carrabine, *Power, Discourse, and Resistance: A Genealogy of the Strangeways Prison Riot* (Aldershot: Ashgate Publishing, 2004), p. 38.

[87] For an account of Guantanamo Bay, see David Cole, *Enemy Aliens: Double Standards and Constitutional Freedoms in the War on Terrorism* (New York, NY: The New Press, 2003). Chapter 2 distinguishes between historical truth, which aims at an accurate depiction of events, and narrative truth, which represents a reality for the particular speaker. See Donald Spence, *Narrative Truth and Historical Truth: Meaning and Interpretation in Psychoanalysis* (New York, NY: Norton Publishing, 1984).

[88] Mary Bosworth, 'Reinventing Penal Parsimony: An Introduction', *Theoretical Criminology* 14, no. 3 (August 2010): p. 214; see also David Rose, *Guantanamo: America's War on Human Rights* (London: Faber and Faber, 2004), pp. 1–2.

[89] Gresham Sykes, *The Society of Captives: A Study in a Maximum Security Prison* (Princeton, NJ: Princeton University Press, 1958), p. 63.

The banality of the British penal project is central to the practice of political memory loss. When prisons are understood as routine spaces, prison staff and policymakers, and for that matter academics, do not have to explore questions about why only certain people are classified as foreigners, only some get deported, and many people see their nationalities and races in terms that clash with penal policy. The dullness of imprisonment conceals these lines of thought, each of which connects prisons to patterns of British conquest and migration. Ultimately, the bureaucratic approach to incarceration allows prisons to run without asking questions about how identity and punishment intersect.

Criminologists have commented on these issues in different forms. The phenomenon I observed as banality—the mechanistic approach to incarceration among officers and policymakers—is consistent with what other scholars call late modern managerialism.[90] Under this rubric, academics have critiqued a conceptual framework in which imprisonment becomes a problem of risk, one solved through audits, performance indicators, and regulations. Criminologists link this framework to neoliberal ideology.[91] Most recently, David Brown has argued that, in a neoliberal political culture, managerialism becomes an end in itself:[92]

> In relation to managerialism, the suggestion is that neo-liberal formulations of risk, KPIs and audit criteria, with their emphasis on narrowly defined notions of 'efficiency' and 'cost', increase the tendency for audit measures to become inward looking ends in themselves, eschewing more broadly defined social aims and outcomes that were and are aspirations under social democratic regimes. ...[93]

[90] See, e.g. Pat Carlen, 'Imprisonment and the Penal Body Politic: The Cancer of Disciplinary Governance', in Alison Liebling and Shadd Maruna, eds, *The Effects of Imprisonment* (Cullompton: Willan, 2005): pp. 421–41; Malcolm Feeley and Jonathan Simon, 'Actuarial Justice: The Emerging New Criminal Law', pp. 173–201; Eugene McLaughlin and Karim Murji, 'Lost Connections and New Directions: Neo-Liberalism, New Managerialism and the Modernisation of the British Police', in Kevin Stenson and Robert Sullivan, eds, *Crime, Risk and Justice* (Cullompton: Willan, 2000), ch. 6; Pat O'Malley, 'Volatile and Contradictory Punishment', *Theoretical Criminology* 3, no. 2 (May 1999), pp. 175–96.

[91] Garland, 'The Culture of Control'; see also David Brown, 'The Global Financial Crisis', in Mary Bosworth and Carolyn Hoyle, *What Is Criminology?* (Oxford: Oxford University Press, 2011), p. 87.

[92] Brown, 'The Global Financial Crisis'.

[93] Brown, 'The Global Financial Crisis', p. 86.

Brown's argument draws on Pat Carlen's critique of managerialism. In her writing on British prisons, Carlen contends that 'too often, rules are eventually cherished and embellished as being ends in themselves—at which point they become "disciplinarities"'.[94] For Carlen, the motivating concern is that criminal justice, along with the rest of government, has drifted away from social welfarist aims over the last thirty years.

There is little question that the imprisonment of foreign nationals unfolds in a consumerist, managerial discourse. The hubs and spokes agreement divides prisons into gold, silver, and bronze 'levels of service', each of which corresponds to a different amount of interaction between prisoners and staff.[95] Prisoners who receive gold service see staff the most and have better access to information, while those relegated to bronze service know less about their futures. Meanwhile, the Prison Service distributes flowcharts of UKBA protocol and a 2009 agreement between the Prison Service and the Border Agency describes shared data as a better way to 'monitor and measure performance'.[96] Managerialism is an accurate way to describe these practices.

The question is whether we might also think of them as instances of memory loss—as examples of an attitude that, in effect, detaches the prison from its political context. Casting managerialism in this light underscores the import of prison culture. It is difficult to describe how banality becomes a way of life, yet no feature of punishment has a more visceral effect on prisoners' experiences. Managerialism is not only a neoliberal language for success. It is also a way that prison and immigration staff cope with their jobs and societies relate to the fact that we confine and deport other human beings. Framing managerialism as institutionalized memory loss foregrounds the consequences of this approach. Over time, the counting, recording, and reporting that happens inside prisons creates a regime of rigid, dissociated presentism. This regime mediates history and suppresses the very live politics of incarceration. Through its prison system, the British government sorts citizens from foreigners, and its present from the past.

[94] Carlen, 'Imprisonment and the Penal Body Politic', p. 430.

[95] MoJ and UKBA, *Service Level Agreement*, pp. 20–3.

[96] MoJ and UKBA, *Service Level Agreement*, p. 5; see also Her Majesty's Prison Service (HMPS), *Prison Service Instruction 21/2007: Immigration and Foreign Nationals in Prison (Amended Version)* (London: MoJ, 2007).

Conclusion

At the end of our interview, I said goodbye to JB and wished him luck. I then walked across the hall, where I met the border agent who managed JB's case. She told me that JB would be deported to Nigeria directly from the prison, likely in a matter of weeks. It was too bad, she said, because she liked him. JB was agreeable and kind. She mentioned JB's son Matthew and his newborn daughter Odeon. They would be separated, she acknowledged, and then she shrugged, 'but that's the way it goes'.

This chapter has explored how situations like JB's become the way it goes. In the twenty-first-century British prison, deeply contested practices, such as deporting migrants who were once British subjects, become a routine aspect of running the nation-state. Choreographed interviews and detailed forms make sense of the 'structures of sentiment' that flow through prisons, confusing prisoners' allegiances.[97] There is no easy answer to questions about whether and where to draw the boundaries of a nation. But those questions matter: prisoners from former colonies invoke history to resist their incarceration; others dispute their criminality or struggle to communicate. The prison pulses with the politics of identity, and yet it is also remarkably dull.

British prisons thus operate on two different registers, one highly emotional and political, the other managerial and banal. The gap between these registers is notable as a sociological matter—rarely is there such a clear window into the consequences of bureaucratic culture. Perhaps more to the point, the dual registers of imprisonment raise ethical questions about the purpose of prison scholarship. One of the broader goals of this book is to grapple with the line between curiosity or voyeurism and a richer kind of engagement with punishment. The proposition underlying this chapter, which begins from Stuart Hall's work on amnesia, is that academics are implicated in the production of knowledge about prisons. Those who study prisons play an active role in outlining the borders of punishment. Academics create the context of imprisonment as much as Prison Service orders and penal policies.

From this perspective, the banality of prison life presents an opportunity to imagine punishment as a less dissociated practice. In using the term 'amnesia', Stuart Hall pushed his readers to

[97] Cuneen, 'Postcolonial Perspectives for Criminology', p. 252.

acknowledge their part in a collective past—in a word, to remember. Applying his term to prison is a way to ask what and who is being forgotten when the prison becomes another site for the calculation of risk. Scholars of punishment are situated to recollect the histories that reception questionnaires and performance metrics suppress. As people who write about prisons rather than running or living in them, sociologists of punishment are positioned to contextualize punishment and to challenge its basic assumptions. Chapter 7 considers how that project might begin.

7

The Bodily Remainder

In Britain, people awaiting trial walk through prisons in their own clothes and shoes. Sentenced prisoners and prison officers wear uniforms. Prison staff members prod prisoners' limbs and orifices looking for drugs. Prisoners classified as foreign—identified, often, by how they look and sound—live in separate facilities, apart from the rest of the prison population. These material acts give life and form to penal power. Punishment becomes real on human bodies.

Bodies also realize the limits of punishment. Black British citizens who are misidentified as 'foreigners' embody racialized assumptions about the meaning of Britishness. Detainees who linger in prisons beyond the end of their criminal sentences demonstrate that the terms of punishment fail to match the realities of mass mobility. In the face of these conflicts, prisoners struggle to survive: some turn to friendship, to faith, or to education; some place razors in their mouths or threaten self-harm. The prison is an institution flooded with feelings of pain, regret, fear, and hope.

Chapter 6 examined the flat affect of much penal policy and practice. Taking the legacy of British colonialism as a starting point, I argued that daily actions in prisons—filling out forms, checking boxes, completing risk assessments—come together to obscure the context of imprisonment and to promote what I called political amnesia. This chapter recasts that argument in different terms. Drawing on prisoners' testimonies, I contend that political amnesia is at its base about ignoring bodies. The body plays an integral and overlooked role in the creation of state power. Through symbols and euphemisms, prisons translate the act of keeping people in metal cages into state-sanctioned punishment. This chapter examines that translation process and calls for a more phenomenological approach to penality.

The chapter begins by exploring feminist writing on embodiment. Scholars such as Judith Butler, Elaine Scarry, and Eve

Sedgwick have made compelling arguments for studying the relationship between bodies and power.[1] The first part of the chapter asks how feminist and queer theories of power apply to the study of prisons. I then turn to British prisons, and specifically, to foreign national prisoners' testimonies about the material aspect of incarceration. The second part of the chapter presents prisoners' accounts of life inside a cell, from the body language prisoners use to communicate to their descriptions of self-harm and the feeling of time. I trace themes in these testimonies and connect them to a political critique of the prison's purpose.

Ultimately, this chapter links feminist scholarship to classic questions about the 'pains of imprisonment'.[2] For half a century, criminologists have examined the physical, psychological, and emotional tolls of incarceration.[3] Since Gresham Sykes wrote *The Society of Captives* in 1958, empirical researchers have documented the substantive, often deteriorating effect that incarceration can have on a prisoner's mental health and sense of self. [4] In a different but related vein, Michel Foucault transformed criminology with his insight into the relationship between discipline, embodiment, and subjectivity.[5] This chapter returns to ideas that

[1] See Judith Butler, *The Psychic Life of Power: Theories in Subjection* (Palo Alto, CA: Stanford University Press, 1997), p. 92; Elaine Scarry, *The Body in Pain: The Making and Unmaking of the World* (Oxford: Oxford University Press, 1985); Eve Sedgwick, *Touching Feeling: Affect, Pedagogy, Performativity* (Durham, NC: Duke University Press, 2004).

[2] Gresham Sykes, *The Society of Captives: A Study in a Maximum Security Prison* (Princeton, NJ: Princeton University Press, 1958), p. 63.

[3] See, e.g. Stan Cohen and Laurie Taylor, *Psychological Survival: The Experience of Long-Term Imprisonment* (New York, NY: Vintage Books, 1974); Timothy Flanagan, *Long-Term Imprisonment: Policy, Science and Correctional Practice* (London: Sage, 1995); Kimberly Greer, 'Walking an Emotional Tightrope: Managing Emotions in a Women's Prison', *Symbolic Interaction* 25, no. 1 (February 2002): pp. 117–39; Alison Liebling, *Suicides in Prison* (London: Routledge, 1992); Alison Liebling and Shadd Maruna, *The Effects of Imprisonment* (Cullompton: Willan Publishing, 2005). Elaine Crawley has also written about the emotional consequences of incarceration for prison officers, who receive less attention from academics than prisoners do. Elaine Crawley, 'Emotion and Performance: Prison Officers and the Presentation of Self in Prisons', *Punishment and Society* 6, no. 4 (October 2004): pp. 411–27.

[4] Sykes, *The Society of Captives*, p. 63; see also Cohen and Taylor, *Psychological Survival*; Liebling, *Suicides in Prison*.

[5] Michel Foucault, *Discipline and Punish: The Birth of the Prison*, trans. Alan Sheridan (New York, NY: Vintage Books, 1977).

Foucault and Sykes introduced to the study of penal institutions. Drawing on literature and philosophy, I imagine a criminology that begins and learns from the corporeal dimensions of prison life.

Feminist Critiques of Power

Feminists pioneered the study of bodies. While debates about the connection between body and mind date to before Plato, twentieth-century feminists are responsible for a sea change in the way scholars think and talk about materiality. After books like *The Feminine Mystique* and *The Second Sex*, it was no longer possible to write about bodies without acknowledging their relationship to power.[6] Feminists established that bodies express and contest social inequality.

Elaine Scarry brought the feminist critique of power to her now canonical treatise on violence, *The Body in Pain*.[7] Over the course of five challenging chapters, *The Body in Pain* explores how humans make sense of physical discomfort. The thrust of Scarry's argument lies in a close reading of two acts: torture and war. Scarry examines both practices, asking, as she puts it, how the 'real pain' involved in violence gets 'converted... into the fiction of power'.[8] This question grounds a critique of the disembodied language of weapons, damage, and defence.[9] How, Scarry wonders, do humans lose sight of the fact that 'the main purpose and outcome of war is injuring'?[10] She continues:

> With the exception of periodic body counts or 'kill ratios', the intricacies and complications of the massive geographical interactions between two armies of opposing nations tend to be represented without frequent reference to the actual injuries occurring to the hundreds of thousands of soldiers involved: the movements and actions of the armies are emptied of human content and occur as a rarified choreography of disembodied events... The crossing of a river is not now an event enacted by many individuals—some of whom know how to swim and others of whom do not, some vulnerable to wet and cold and some relatively immune... but is rather enacted by a

[6] Simone de Beauvoir, *The Second Sex* (New York, NY: Vintage, 2011); Betty Friedan, *The Feminine Mystique* (New York, NY: W. W. Norton & Co., 1964).

[7] Scarry, *The Body in Pain*.

[8] Scarry, *The Body in Pain*, p. 1.

[9] Scarry, *The Body in Pain*, p. 65.

[10] Scarry, *The Body in Pain*, p. 63.

single integrated creature who, if named, takes the name of a division or of the commander...If such descriptions were sustained over pages or even whole paragraphs, the text would become a mythology of giants lumbering across rivers and stalking through forests....[11]

Scarry argues that the metaphorical rendering of war effaces the body from an essentially embodied exercise. As she points out, war is premised on the vulnerability of human—and most often working-class male—flesh. War depends on the very literal possibility of injuring particular people's bodies. This reality makes it especially notable that discussions of war unfold in mythological terms, with little if any reference to the actual bodies at issue. Scarry concludes that the use of euphemism 'assists the disappearance of the human body from accounts of the very event that is the most radically embodying event in which human beings ever collectively participate'.[12]

This account of war highlights the importance of rhetoric. One of Scarry's most notable contributions to the study of power is her attention to the rather simple fact that wars are staked on 'actual (hence woundable) human tissue'.[13] The force of this claim lies in its obviousness.[14] Scarry reminds her readers that violence is made possible by the frailty of human flesh, and more to the point, by the adoption of rhetoric that suppresses the body's key role in power relations. *The Body in Pain* demonstrates that power depends on bodies, yet emerges from the practice of ignoring them.

Prison scholars could make a similar observation about incarceration. While policymakers and academics often describe prisons in terms of risk, we rarely reflect for more than a few lines on the fact that imprisonment is the act of forcing certain people to live inside a metal box.[15] In practice, punishment involves putting

[11] Scarry, *The Body in Pain*, p. 70.

[12] Scarry, *The Body in Pain*, p. 71.

[13] Scarry, *The Body in Pain*, p. 71.

[14] Scarry uses these terms to describe the process by which bodies get effaced from public discourse. In 'The Structure of War', she writes that the link between the body and the state 'can be overlooked by being too obvious'. Scarry, *The Body in Pain*, p. 111. She notes, for example, that 'one's citizenship ordinarily entails physical *presence* within the boundaries of that country'. Scarry, *The Body in Pain*, p. 111.

[15] Pat Carlen's critique of the resistance literature, in which she emphasizes the harsh physical realities of imprisonment, provides an exception to this claim. Gresham Sykes's writing on 'the pains of imprisonment' and David

on certain trousers, submitting to physical searches, and going to bed in a cage. Prisons would not make sense without the bodies held inside them, but discussions of punishment develop in largely metaphorical terms. Policymakers speak of crime and punishment in a bureaucratic tone—on any given day, you could pick up a new Prison Service order to find references to risk management, security levels, or speedy removal.[16] This discourse suggests that punishment is a matter of service provision and technical calculation.

Prisoners rarely conform to the categories articulated in penal policy. In the case of regulations on nationality, a prisoner's physicality and affect—the way he looks, how he talks, how he presents himself and feels—often contrasts with the official understanding of foreignness. A prisoner's mere presence in the penal institution can also reveal the tone deafness of penal rhetoric. Take, for instance, time-served detainees, the small but notable population of prisoners who remain in penal institutions after the end of their criminal sentences. These prisoners' existence in prisons demonstrates the limits, assumptions, and consequences of penal discourse.

Garland's early work on the prison also address material realities. See Pat Carlen, *Women's Imprisonment: A Study in Social Control* (London: Routledge, 1983); Pat Carlen, 'Carceral Clawback: The Case of Women's Imprisonment in Canada', *Punishment and Society* 4, no. 1 (January 2002): pp. 115–21; Pat Carlen and Anne Worrall, *Analysing Women's Imprisonment* (Cullompton: Willan, 2004); David Garland, *Punishment and Modern Society: A Study in Social Theory* (Chicago, IL: University of Chicago Press, 1990); Gresham Sykes, *The Society of Captives*. A body of criminological writing on mental health in prison, and in particular on conditions of solitary confinement, also focuses on the physical effects of imprisonment. See, e.g. Jo Borrill and Donna A. Taylor, 'Suicides by Foreign National Prisoners in England and Wales 2007: Mental and Cultural Issues', *Forensic Psychiatry and Psychology* 20, no. 6 (Nov. 2009): pp. 886–905; Craig Haney, 'Mental Health Issues in Long-Term Solitary and "Supermax" Confinement', *Crime and Delinquency* 49, no. 1 (January 2003): pp. 124–56; Alison Liebling, *Suicides in Prison*. These are important exceptions to my general claim about the tone of theoretical criminology and the relative dearth of research on the affective life of the prison.

[16] See, e.g. Her Majesty's Prison Service (HMPS), *Prison Service Order 4630: Immigration and Foreign Nationals in Prison* (London: MoJ, 2006); Her Majesty's Prison Service (HMPS), *Prison Service Instruction 21/2007: Immigration and Foreign Nationals in Prison (Amended Version)* (London: MoJ, 2007); Ministry of Justice (MoJ) and UK Border Agency (UKBA), *Service Level Agreement to Support the Effective and Speedy Removal of Foreign National Prisoners* (London: MoJ and UKBA, 2009), p. 1.

Time-served prisoners sit in prisons because they fail to fit any appropriate category of penal or migration policy. Some of these prisoners remain in prison due to sheer bureaucratic incompetence, because of delayed requests, under-staffing, or misplaced forms.[17] Others live behind bars because they have no legal citizenship status. These prisoners are the aftermath of border-focused prison policies. They reside in prisons because government policies leave little room for a man without a name, or with several names, or without a nationality. These prisoners literally, physically embody the ambiguity in discussions of punishment, citizenship, and nationality. Every minute of their lives illustrates that policies do not align with the world as it actually is. Instead, prison policies carve out the world as the British government wants it to be. The clash between that normative vision and the realities of globalized life results in hundreds of people sitting and waiting to be deported, or perhaps more likely, eventually released onto British soil.[18]

Time-served detainees are, in this sense, a daily reminder that penal and border control policies have human consequences. These prisoners remind us, in person, that contested borders in the Western Sahara or the Gaza Strip and conflicts in Rwanda, the Congo, Nigeria, and Sri Lanka have effects thousands of miles away, and moreover, that those effects take the form of real people living difficult lives in institutions that taxpayers build, fund, and govern. These prisoners are what, following Judith Butler, we might call the 'bodily remainder' of decisions about the purpose of the prison and the boundaries of the nation-state.[19]

The term 'bodily remainder' is worth examining in detail. Butler uses it in passing in the context of a broader exploration of Michel Foucault's work on prison regimes.[20] In *Discipline and*

[17] The *Vine Report* outlines various rationales for the continued incarceration of prisoners beyond their criminal sentences and describes situations in which prisoners cannot be deported. The report cites a lack of identity documentation, prisoners' appeals of their deportations on human rights grounds, and a lack of 'accuracy' in the referral process as three reasons why a foreign national would ultimately be released into Great Britain. See John Vine, *Thematic Inspection of How the UK Border Agency Manages Foreign National Prisoners: February–May 2011* (London: HMSO, 2012).

[18] Chapter 6 explores grounds for deportation and the likelihood of release into Britain.

[19] Butler, *The Psychic Life of Power*, p. 92.

[20] See Butler, *The Psychic Life of Power*, p. 89.

Punish, Foucault famously argued that prisoners become subjects through exposure to the disciplinary rituals of the penal institution, which include 'inspection, confession, and the regularization and normalization of bodily movement and gesture'.[21] Foucault claimed that these processes create prisoners as juridical selves.[22] He asserted that prisoners become identifiable subjects when they are subjected to the power relations embedded in the penal environment.

Butler develops Foucault's account into a critique of embodiment. In *The Psychic Life of Power*, she rejects the idea that bodies exist as blank material canvases onto which power is written.[23] Instead, Butler explains, bodies are knowable only after power relations create the conditions for us to see someone as a prisoner, a foreigner, a man, or a woman. Wearing a uniform, walking in a line, waking to a bell, and writing a number after your name—these acts make 'the prisoner' an intelligible category of being. The subject thus appears, as Butler puts it, 'at the expense of the body'.[24] Yet the body also lingers as a sign that identity is impossible without power relations. Butler writes:

> The bodily remainder survives for such a subject in the mode of already, if not always, having been destroyed, in a kind of constitutive loss. The body is not a site on which a construction takes place; it is a destruction on the occasion of which a subject is formed....[25]

This critique captures the corporeal aspect of power. The essence of Butler's argument is that bodies bear witness to the operation of power. Bodies provide a constant reminder that the terms of subjectivity are political and contested. In providing this living reminder, bodies reveal not only the pains of imprisonment, but also the scope and depth of penal power.

[21] Foucault, *Discipline and Punish*; see also Butler, *The Psychic Life of Power*, pp. 84–5.

[22] Foucault, *Discipline and Punish*; see also Butler, *The Psychic Life of Power*, pp. 84–5.

[23] Butler, *The Psychic Life of Power*, p. 92. Butler's claims build on her writing on performativity, which is discussed in Chapter 5, and on a Freudian vocabulary of sublimation and consciousness. *The Psychic Life of Power* includes an explicit reflection on Freud's influence on Butler's critique of Foucault. Butler, *The Psychic Life of Power*, pp. 91–2.

[24] Butler, *The Psychic Life of Power*, pp. 91–2.

[25] Butler, *The Psychic Life of Power*, p. 92.

Butler's scholarship dovetails with feminist writing on emotion and sentiment. The late literary theorist Eve Sedgwick, an interlocutor of Butler's, argued that there is an inextricable relationship between embodiment and affect.[26] In her last book, *Touching Feeling*, Sedgwick explained that bodies and sentiments are interdependent; as she wrote, 'a particular intimacy seems to subsist between textures and emotions... even to talk about affect virtually amounts to cutaneous contact'.[27] According to Sedgwick, the critical account of embodiment has to include a phenomenological inquiry into the expression and reception of emotion.

Together, Scarry, Butler, and Sedgwick provide a roadmap for revisiting classic criminological themes. These scholars demonstrate that writing about bodies, which also means writing about sentiment, is one way to ask how power works in practice. Feminists and queer theorists link the anxiety of life inside institutions to theoretical questions about how those institutions come to exercise social control. Feminist theory challenges scholars to consider whether power develops at the expense of the body—whether, in other words, influence flows from the suppression of the corporeal and affective qualities of social life. The feminist question is what happens to bodies, and to the people constituted by them, as power comes to pass. If we start from that question, a critique of power is incomplete if it fails to recognize the embodied dimension of concepts like punishment, retribution, and time served.

Body Language

The prison is an institution structured on hope, homelessness, and fear. In the course of a year, I interviewed hundreds of prisoners, some for fifteen minutes, others for hours. Many spoke about the material aspects of incarceration. The people I met explained what it was like to sleep in a cell each night. They described forging

[26] Eve Sedgwick, *Touching Feeling: Affect, Pedagogy, Performativity* (Durham, NC: Duke University Press, 2004). Sedgwick's claims about affect and performativity are an explicit response to Judith Butler's work. In the introduction to *Touching Feeling*, Sedgwick lists Butler's *Gender Trouble* as one of the four 'difficult texts' to which her book responds. Sedgwick, *Touching Feeling*, p. 2.

[27] Sedgwick, *Touching Feeling*, p. 17.

emotional relationships with each other and navigating charged interactions with prison and immigration staff. Prisoners also articulated the feeling of home and the experience of sensing time's passage. In some cases, prisoners described using their limbs and voices to cope with confinement or resist authority. Bodies surfaced in nearly every conversation.

The relationship between affect and power was clearest in my interviews with people whose feelings about themselves had changed as a result of imprisonment. Many foreign national prisoners said that confinement altered their sense of who they were. Chapter 4 introduced Damien, who 'realized he wasn't British' after he entered the penal institution. Other prisoners had similar experiences. Gus reported that 'being English... you can just feel it, hear it'. Deno, a time-served prisoner, said:

> Me not feel like a British person, understand? Everyday me wake up and write letters. Sometimes me smoke... Right now depression tablets. So much stress upon me head.

Thomas, another ex-prisoner incarcerated beyond his criminal sentence, felt he did not belong in the country because he was in prison. 'Would you say you're British?' I asked him. 'I understand them more', Thomas replied. 'But I don't feel British. I could never feel British in a place like this.'

These testimonies spring from material realities. Deno, who said he had a claim to citizenship as the husband of a British citizen, did not identify with Britain because he spent each day writing letters to a family outside prison walls. Taking depression medication, calling home, and waking up in a cell were not only morning events in Deno's life; these routines reinforced his sense that the borders of the nation-state were real and that he did not belong within them. The physical aspect of incarceration encouraged Deno to feel like a foreigner in a country where he once believed he belonged. The corporeal experience of imprisonment, with all its pills and pains and frustrations, shaped his belief that the nation-state was a concrete and bounded thing.

Prisoners often emphasized this link between feeling and power. Victor told me that handcuffs made him 'feel like I am a terrorist or a suicide bomber'. Roland insisted, 'I'm not a criminal', then added, 'of course you feel like one here. We hang together, do everything together.' A detainee named Patrick, who I interviewed several times, described the emotional shifts he weathered behind bars. In our first interview, Patrick said that he had viewed himself as a 'free British person'. After a period of incarceration, he began to see himself as a prisoner and a perpetual foreigner. 'In here I am frustrated', Patrick told me. 'I am scared about the prospect of going [to the Congo]. It's like dropping me on Mars or the moon.'

In our last interview, Patrick told me that imprisonment was a war of attrition: 'They try to break you down. I'm in a psychological war with the Home Office.' After four years of post-sentence detention, Patrick was released into the United Kingdom. Damien's narrative had a different ending: he was deported to Jamaica shortly after our last interview. Like Patrick, Damien felt that incarceration was at base a form of emotional 'warfare'. When we first crossed paths, Damien had swallowed a razor to protest his ongoing confinement.[28] The razor sliced open his stomach and caused internal bleeding. Damien was in pain when I met him, but he still wanted to appeal his deportation order. 'Physically I am broken', he said. 'Mentally I am not.'

These testimonies hint at the extreme emotional pressures of incarceration. For the prisoners I interviewed, the stress of prison life emerged not only from the psychological feeling of being classified as a criminal, but also from the sense of shame and hopelessness that accompanied imprisonment. 'I'm too embarrassed to have my son visit me in here', one prisoner said. 'That's my punishment being in prison. The best thing about my life became the worst.' Another prisoner, Noishime, said that the blankness of his cell's walls brought on a depression he constantly had to 'keep fighting'. Noishime reported that he had to leave his prison cell to stay sane:

> I'm not a citizen of any country...I'm blaming the system big time. All I need was...by the end of the day you end up with depression...If you stay in your cell, everything comes back. Stress, depression, your whole life starts coming in, you start getting more depressed.

The architecture of incarceration exacted a toll on many prisoners. Thomas, a long-time British resident who was born in Jamaica, said he could not identify with British culture when he lived out each day in a beige room with a toilet in the corner. Patrick told me

[28] Chapter 4 describes this incident in more detail. That chapter explores whether Damien's decision to put a razor in his mouth should be understood as a form of self-harm, as an act of protest, or as something else altogether.

that, 'for somebody who's never been to prison before, it's a foreign country. It can be very intimidating.' Both of these prisoners felt displaced by the impersonal qualities of the penal institution. These men felt—and became—foreign because they lived in a foreign, alienating space.

In these instances and others, imprisonment translates the look and feel of state power into ideas about identity. This translation process occurs on a small scale, in acts like raising a hand when an officer asks who needs to see an immigration solicitor or dialling the telephone to call a family member in Nigeria. Taken together, such acts constitute a form of communication—a body language—between the state and those subject to it. Local, material moments inside penal institutions turn incarcerated people into prisoners, detainees, citizens, and foreigners.

Yet, if body language confines identity, it also helps prisoners survive incarceration. Leon described how to make friends in prison:

> You read faces. It's about body language, facial expressions, how he talks and presents himself. Sometimes you don't even need to have a conversation with a guy to know.

Noishime said that he read prison officers' body language to determine if they were racist:

> You can tell...the guards give you the cold shoulder if you ask for anything. You see it in their eyes.

Another man, who asked to be called S, told me that body language helped him determine whether it was safe to speak to new prisoners. S explained:

> I'm good at judging by looking at other people's faces. The first and last impression is just a face. Your face tells a lot of stories. It's like love at first sight.

Love came up again several weeks later. This time, it was a description of relations between prisoners, offered by a man who chose to remain nameless:

> Criminals got a sense of love for each other. Criminals is one family, you know. Locked in the same cells, you develop what you call love.

These testimonies suggest that the hierarchies of the penal institution play out in the register of sentiment, and often, in sentiments like love and hope as well as fear and frustration. Physical cues, and the emotions they transmit, are crucial modes of communication in the intensely intimate environment of the prison.[29]

When introduced into this environment, new policies can have profound effects on prisoners' emotional lives. One result of the hubs and spokes policy, which isolates foreign nationals from the rest of the prison population, is that certain prisoners feel more alone and homeless than before they were singled out as non-citizens. In an attempt to talk about national and cultural belonging without relying on birthplace or legal status, I often asked prisoners where they felt at home. Many people told me 'Birmingham', 'London', or 'Jamaica'. Some said the concept of home no longer made sense to them. Deno paused for a long time after I asked him 'where is home?' Eventually he shook his head and shrugged, as if the question had no answer. 'Right now the only thing I'm interested in is my baby.'

A prisoner named Sam told me that he had no idea where he was at home. 'I don't know, to be honest', Sam responded. 'What I know is where my family is and they're here. This is the only place I'd fight to stay.' When pushed to identify his home, Sam turned to acts of his body—to fighting and to family—as the measure of belonging. These are notably gendered acts: Sam invoked fatherhood and his ability to fight 'as the man of his house' to explain where he belonged. For him, the concept of home was about what kind of body he had and what was happening to it in the prison.

Another prisoner, Victor, struggled to describe home. In our first interview, I asked Victor 'what is home?' intending to prompt a conversation about where he felt he belonged. He looked back at me for a moment and then replied, 'my mouth cannot describe it'. After a beat, he said it again: 'my mouth cannot describe it'. In this moment, the liminality of incarceration became a literal, physical barrier to speech. The pain of imprisonment registered on Victor's body as a failure to capture what he felt, or rather, could

[29] Physical cues are also key forms of communication in ethnography. My interviews often hinged on prisoners' physical responses to my questions—on whether they looked up at me when I asked where they were from or looked down and away from my face. In this sense, the way I felt and the way prisoners felt in interviews mattered a great deal to what being imprisoned actually means. See Chapter 2 for a more detailed discussion of the limitations and ethical implications of ethnography.

not feel.[30] I responded by asking Victor where his home was. He asked me, 'How do you define home? It's where you feel security. When someone chases you outside, home is where you run.'

These conversations illustrate the degree to which punishment alters 'structures of feeling'.[31] Imprisonment works by warping people's perceptions of home, nationality, and time. This process was especially poignant for ex-prisoner detainees, who described watching time pass without a clear release date. Thomas, who was born in Jamaica, came to London in his early twenties. He had three British children over the course of thirteen years and was incarcerated in 2003. When I met him in 2010, Thomas had been imprisoned for four months past the conclusion of his criminal sentence. He had signed a deportation order agreeing to return to Jamaica and said he was ready to go 'back home'. The problem was that Thomas had sent his passport to the Border Agency, which had lost it, and the Jamaican embassy would not accept his return without official travel documents.[32] So Thomas was stuck in prison, waiting for his case to unfold.

This situation was visibly frustrating. Thomas recited from memory the message that plays on the Jamaican embassy phone line. During our interview, he repeatedly pulled out a photocopy of his Jamaican birth certificate and slammed it on the table. Thomas

[30] Jean-François Lyotard calls the gap between feeling and speech 'the differend'. Jean-Francois Lyotard, *The Inhuman: Reflections on Time*, trans. Geoff Bennington and Rachel Bowlby (New York, NY: Polity Press, 1981). For Lyotard, this term describes that which cannot be articulated in speech, that which is only ever realized on and in the body. This phrase has been used to analyse survivor accounts of the Holocaust. See Aleida Assmann, 'History, Memory and the Genre of Testimony', *Poetics Today* 27, no. 2 (2006): pp. 261–74; Michael Frisch, *A Shared Authority: Essays on the Craft and Meaning of Oral and Public History* (New York, NY: SUNY Press, 1990); Marianne Hirsch and Leo Spitzer, *Ghosts of Home: The Afterlife of Czernowitz in Jewish Memory* (Berkeley, CA: University of California Press, 2010). In this context, the differend is a helpful way to understand Victor's incapacity to describe the feeling of home.

[31] Raymond Williams uses the term 'structures of feeling' to describe the lived, experienced, cultural aspects of a particular historical moment. Williams's term brings accounts of lived experience into a broad and originally Marxist discussion of power relations. See Raymond Williams, *Marxism and Literature* (Oxford: Oxford University Press, 1978).

[32] UKBA officials told me that lack of official identity documentation is a common barrier to a prisoner's deportation. The *Vine Report* verifies this claim. See the *Vine Report,* pp. 19–22.

said that he had been a relatively calm prisoner during the ten years of his criminal sentence, but now he was anxious and angry:

> I think they find me easy to deal with so I get put to the side. So I'm planning to go to the block on Monday. I'll refuse to bang up, maybe see the governor, protest. When I was doing my time I was relaxed. I have to be in their face every day now because I have to go. I'm that guy now.

The change in Thomas's attitude stemmed from his experience of indefinite detention. 'Ten years is a long time', I said, referring to Thomas' criminal sentence. He replied:

> Time stop, innit. Six and half years feels like one. When I came here in February, I thought I'd be leaving in two weeks... It's harder without a date. I know I'm not going this month, so you put it on the next month... When I'm doing my time, I'm fine. But my time finished and I need to go.

Several prisoners told me that it was harder to serve indefinite time than a concrete prison term. Patrick, who had been detained on and off for nearly four years post-sentence, explained:

> All I can do is just sit here. If I do anything else, I'll go mad. In prison, you have something to look forward to. You have a date. It's harder now. You see people born in England going home and you're still here. You think to yourself, hold on, my crime was eight years ago. I've done the full sentence. I'm doing extra time, for free.

The frustration of doing 'extra time' is why so many post-sentence prisoners end up being what prison staff called 'difficult' or 'challenging' members of the prison population. Time-served prisoners have a distinct experience of incarceration. They are not counting down to a release date but are rather waiting in limbo, watching each day pass without any sense of when their imprisonment might end. For Thomas, this experience created hope for the future and then dashed that hope each day—so 'I just put it on the next month', he concluded. This cycle of hope and disappointment continues over and again, turning imprisonment into a particularly prospective and demoralizing exercise.[33] Deno described the

[33] Many scholars have commented on the malleable perception of time in penal institutions. More than three decades ago, Foucault mined records on prisoners' daily schedules to critique the structure of penal discipline. Foucault, *Discipline and Punish*. More recently, Greg Moses has written about 'lived time' and the need to view 'time as experience' inside the prison. Greg Moses, 'Time and Punishment in an Anesthetic World Order', in Mechthild Nagel and Seth Asumah, eds, *Prisons and Punishment: Reconsidering Global Penality* (Trenton, NJ: Africa

process: 'If them know they was not gonna take me out of the prison, them supposed to notify me. They build up me hope and then at reception them mentally play with my mind.'

The stress of this experience is realized on and in the body. Most of the time-served prisoners I interviewed reported that they were depressed, lethargic, and unhappy. Several had attempted suicide. Noishime, a Rwandan migrant, told me that he had tried to kill himself in 2004:

> I had just had enough. After my friend was taken [and deported from an Immigration Removal Centre] they said they were gonna force me to that. I said 'what's the point?'. But they don't do anything when you try to commit suicide...just put it in your record. I'm not gonna tell them. I have something to live for now, my kids.

Another man, who asked to remain anonymous, described his suicide threats:

> Me tell them I'm gonna kill myself if them not move me from the prison and carry me to immigration centre...me not gonna kill myself...I need the attention. I will never kill myself. The bible say you not supposed to kill yourself...So if them find me dead, it's the system that killed me, the prisoners and the authorities...It's them who made me get dead. Me not want to commit myself further, but they push me, push me, because they want to me to get mad and write a bad report.

This prisoner represented suicide as a form of communication to prison authorities and as the culmination of the trauma of incarceration. In another interview, a prisoner broke down in silent sobs when I asked him how he coped with life behind bars. We sat in the interview room together for half a minute until I broke the silence. 'I'm sorry', I told him. 'Thank you', he said quietly. This was a difficult shared moment, a window into the intensity of prison life. I encountered that intensity again when another prisoner told me

World Press, 2007), pp. 71–6. Criminologists have also commented on the shift towards more prospective and preventive modes of incarceration. See Andrew Ashworth, *Sentencing and Criminal Justice* (Cambridge: Cambridge University Press, 2005); Lucia Zedner, 'Security, the State, and the Citizen: The Changing Architecture of Crime Control', *New Criminal Law Review* 13, no. 2 (Spring 2010): pp. 379–403. Juliet Stumpf writes about this prospective shift in the particular context of immigration law. Juliet Stumpf, 'Doing Time: Crimmigration Law and the Perils of Haste', *UCLA Law Review* 58, no. 1705 (July 2011): pp. 1705–48.

that he had sewn his mouth shut—literally silenced himself—using what a prison officer called a 'housewife kit'.[34]

Thomas had not self-harmed in these ways, but the anxiety of indefinite detention surfaced on his body nonetheless. Over the course of our two-hour interview, Thomas seemed relatively relaxed, a fact which I mentioned to him. 'What can you do?' he said. 'The desire for revenge eats at you, makes you want to do something stupid.' Eventually, our conversation turned to standard ethnographic questions: what is the food like? How many people on your wing? How is the dental care? The last question prompted an unexpected reply. Thomas told me that the dentist was important to him because he had been grinding his teeth in his sleep:

> Because I am suffering in silence I grind my teeth. Down to the nerve. I asked the dentist to just pull my teeth because I couldn't eat. I need medicine to kill the nerves.

This embodied experience bears witness to the affective force of penal power. As he slept, Thomas's jaw registered the pain of detention without a clear end.

These accounts are worth sharing simply to give those outside prison walls a glimpse of what it is like to be inside a penal institution. They also ground prison theory in lived experience. The emotional and physical dimension of incarceration does not always come across in debates about penal policy or carceral power, but for the people who live in them, penal institutions are about dental care, food quality, and the feeling of seeing your family after a long time apart. The state's power to punish is a real thing because bodies respond to it. Thomas's teeth, Damien's stomach, the anonymous prisoner's tears—this bodily remainder bears the mark of, and makes possible, the construction of the state.[35]

The bodily remainder also raises thorny questions about agency. It is possible to view prisoners' embodied acts as forms of resistance to penal power. Just by being in prisons, time-served prisoners contest assumptions about the purpose of the prison and the clarity of national borders. These prisoners' bodies clash with

[34] The term 'housewife kits' connects prisoners' protests against deportation and incarceration to concerns about masculinity and normative gender roles. This gendered reference makes the fact that prisoners use sewing kits to self-harm, and to protest their incarceration, all the more complex.

[35] Butler, *The Psychic Life of Power*, p. 92.

the terms of penal policy. Others do as well—the bodies of foreign national prisoners who attempt suicide, for instance, and the corpses whose attempts do not fail.[36] Prisoners who sew their mouths shut, prisoners who pretend to be British by taking on accents, and prisoners who speak in 'the Queen's English' at reception: these are all instances of protest against the state's claim that particular bodies, and only those bodies, belong on British soil.[37] Yet the uneven flow of power in prisons also makes it difficult to find agency in confinement.[38] Prisoners are at once subject to penal power and the authors of its undoing.

Prisoners also use their bodies to protest in a more positive sense. In several interviews, prisoners insisted that border controls and prison hierarchies were irrational given our corporeality. Leon told me:

> At the end of the day I'd socialize with anyone... We eat and drink from the same cup. We both have fingertips, mouth, eyes, nose. So what's the difference between me and you?

Pointing to parts of his body as he named them, Leon explained that distinctions between people—the differences on which national boundaries depend—are arbitrary. He argued bodies exceed the limits of the nation-state. In a similar conversation, Gus told me that border control would ultimately fail because states

[36] Jo Borrill and Donna Taylor have documented suicide and self-harm rates in the foreign national prisoner population. Jo Borrill and Donna A. Taylor, 'Suicides by Foreign National Prisoners in England and Wales 2007: Mental and Cultural Issues', *Forensic Psychiatry and Psychology* 20, no. 6 (Nov. 2009): pp. 886–905.

[37] Chapter 5 describes prisoners' attempts to pass as British citizens by speaking in 'the Queen's English'.

[38] There is a robust body of writing on the relationship between agency and resistance in British prisons. That writing suggests that the options for agency in prisons are limited and fraught, but real. See, e.g. Robert Adams, *Prison Riots in Britain and the USA* (London: Macmillan, 1992); Mary Bosworth, *Engendering Resistance: Agency and Power in Women's Prisons* (London: Ashgate, 1999); Eamonn Carrabine and Mary Bosworth, 'Reassessing Resistance: Race, Gender, and Sexuality in Prison', *Punishment and Society* 3, no. 4 (October 2001): 501–15; Eamonn Carrabine, *Power, Discourse, and Resistance: A Genealogy of the Strangeways Prison Riot* (Aldershot: Ashgate Publishing, 2004); Liebling, *Suicides in Prison*; Liebling and Maruna, *The Effects of Imprisonment*.

cannot constrain bodies. He focused on the ways in which bodies resist social control:

> Sooner or later, race and borders won't matter, like Martin Luther says. Drug charges in prison…I think the solution is to legalize everything. Then you have to get rid of the borders. They can police the borders, but they can't police your body.

Another prisoner, Charles, emphasized that bodies are the basis for a shared humanity. 'For everything you find a word for in the dictionary, that thing must have happened', Charles said:

> That's my key philosophy: if you're feeling hungry it might be different in two different people. But crises, situations of pain? Those you feel the same.

Charles's testimony could be a line from *The Body in Pain*.[39] Like Elaine Scarry, he argued that the ability to feel pain is a defining feature of human experience. Charles tapped into that capacity in our interview, asking me how we could be individuated from one another if we could both be in crisis.

Scholars of embodiment have asked this question in different terms. In her writing on collective grief, Judith Butler explores moments of anguish that bring people beyond themselves, into an embodied communion.[40] For Charles, posing such questions was a way to understand himself and his identity outside the categories that prison had written onto him. Acknowledging the shared capacity for pain was a means to resisting penal power. In this sense, Charles's body not only contested definitions of nationality and citizenship. It also pointed the way towards a world that does not divide us into citizens and foreigners.

[39] Scarry, *The Body in Pain*.

[40] Butler's book *Precarious Life: The Powers of Mourning and Violence* re-examines her long-standing concerns about subjectivity in the aftermath and context of the 11 September 2011 attacks on the World Trade Center in the United States. Butler explores how the acts of public mourning and grief that ensued from that moment of extreme violence might beget not more violence, but rather a recognition of our shared humanity—or as she puts it, our capacity to be 'given over' to one another. Butler argues the capacity to feel one another's pain can ground an embodied ethics of non-violence. Judith Butler, *Precarious Life: The Powers of Mourning and Violence* (New York, NY: Verso Press, 2004).

Foreign Bodies

Up to now, this chapter has proceeded as if 'the body' is a self-evident term. I have used the word 'bodies' to describe prisoners' corporeal reactions to incarceration, acts of self-harm, and feelings about confinement. I have not distinguished prisoners' bodies from each other or from bodies outside prison. This is the traditional approach. In her critique of philosophical writing, Judith Butler worries that debates about mind and body stray too far from material realities:

> Those trained in philosophy, always at some distance from corporeal matters...invariably miss the body, or worse, write against it. Sometimes they forget that 'the' body comes in genders.[41]

Butler reminds her readers that bodies carry the mark of power relations. Bodies come in shapes and sizes, colours, styles, ethnicities, and genders. Bodies do not look the same; they look different, and those differences become the basis for social inequalities. The histories of racism, sexism, and xenophobia all revolve around the politics of classifying particular bodies in specific ways.

When scholars write about the interior life of penal institutions, we sometimes forget to ask whose material experiences are at issue.[42] We do not always pause to reflect on whose bodies—what kinds of bodies—are subject to penal power. The bodies in my research belonged to foreign national prisoners. They were often black prisoners. They typically had accents and spoke in English that sounded different than my own voice. They were male bodies; they were usually young bodies. These were bodies that exuded what a staff person called 'the tell-tale signs' of nationality. They were, in short, foreign bodies. These bodies, not others but especially these, wind up behind bars facing deportation.

Taking feminist and queer theory seriously means asking how and why these particular bodies become foreign under the law. This inquiry begins in prisons, where it is always and immediately clear that some bodies matter more than others in the late modern

[41] Judith Butler, *Bodies That Matter: On the Discursive Limits of Sex* (New York, NY: Routledge), p. ix.

[42] Alison Liebling uses the term 'interior life' in *Prisons and Their Moral Performance*. Alison Liebling, *Prisons and Their Moral Performance: A Study of Values, Quality, and Prison Life* (Oxford: Oxford University Press, 2004), p. 462.

nation-state. For me, this lesson emerged in immigration 'surgeries', the meetings in which border agents enter prisons to interrogate non-citizens. I visited many surgeries during my fieldwork, and in one, observed the differentiation of bodies up close.

The meeting took place in a hot room with no windows inside a Category A (maximum-security) prison. Several hours into the day, one prison staff member, a white woman, fainted and fell to the floor. Prison guards rushed to administer first aid. After several minutes, she regained consciousness and guards escorted her to the infirmary. Shortly afterward, a prison manager came into the room and led all the people who had seen her faint, except the prisoners and several line officers, into the chapel for a discussion of what had happened. I followed the group across the hall. There, surrounded by pamphlets about Islam and a large crucifix, the manager explained to us that it could be traumatic to watch someone faint. He welcomed and encouraged us to speak to a counsellor.

This was a professional suggestion, but it seemed particularly ludicrous coming from the room we had just left. Several paces away, I had been listening as foreign national prisoners described attempting suicide, watching their families get burned alive, and grinding their teeth to the gums. Immigration officers had been telling prisoners, to their faces, that they would be deported to war zones. Yet it was this woman's fainting that registered as noteworthy in the context of the surgery. In moments like these, there was a jarring contrast between the acute feelings of pain that circulate in prison and the 'dull compulsion' of prison life.[43] This episode raised urgent questions about why some experiences matter more than others.

These questions surfaced again during a different visit to the same prison. Typically, when I visited the Category A facility, I proceeded through security as a legal visitor in the same way a solicitor or a prison staff member would. My classification as a researcher meant that I had a lighter security check than a social visitor and that I stood in a separate, shorter line to enter the prison.[44] One time, however, a prison officer grouped me with the family members who stood outside each day to visit their partners, fathers,

[43] Carrabine, *Power, Discourse, and Resistance*, p. 38.

[44] See Her Majesty's Prison Service, *Prison Service Order 4410: Prisoner Communications, Visits* (London: MoJ, 2007).

and brothers. I waited, and when my turn came, took off my cardigan. I walked through the metal detector and stood on a box as an officer patted me down. I opened my mouth, arms wide, as she looked under my tongue. None of this was atypical of a social visit. It was, however, unusual for me, and I felt suddenly exposed. In penal institutions, bodies become the basis for a very specific language of inequality. Differences in class and power are expressed through the treatment of people's bodies, including my own.

Judith Butler has commented on these issues in a more strictly philosophical context. In *Bodies that Matter*, Butler explores why certain bodies, and only those bodies, get counted when we think about gender.[45] Butler asks, for example, why transgender bodies are so rarely recognized as 'bodies that matter' to mainstream society.[46] She examines the fate of bodies that fail to conform to dominant norms:

> It will be as important to think about how and to what end bodies are constructed as it will be to think about how and to what end bodies are *not* constructed and, further, to ask after how bodies which fail to materialize provide the necessary 'outside', if not the necessary support, for the bodies which, in materializing the norm, qualify as bodies that matter.[47]

Butler argues that non-conforming bodies provide 'the necessary "outside"' against which societies determine the contours of subjectivity.[48] She develops this argument in *Precarious Life*, a book on public mourning written after 9/11. In that text, Butler explores whose lives societies consider worth grieving and protecting by law.[49]

All of this writing coheres around an interest in the creation and contestation of power structures. Whether focused on gender or grief, Butler is concerned with how people get counted or ignored in social institutions. Criminologists can apply this inquiry to the study of prison practices. Whose bodies count as foreign in prisons? How do certain bodies come to matter more than others? Prison staff treated my body—a white, female body with an American accent in a professional-looking black suit—differently

[45] Butler, *Bodies That Matter*, p. 16.
[46] Butler, *Bodies That Matter*, p. 16.
[47] Butler, *Bodies That Matter*, p. 16.
[48] Butler, *Bodies That Matter*, p. 16.
[49] Butler, *Precarious Life*.

than the bodies they viewed as 'really foreign', or as one UKBA official put it, 'you know, *foreign* national'. Governments track only a very particular set of people for prison statistics and deportation rates. These choices constitute migration control and enable both political campaigns and my own visa.[50]

There is, in other words, a charged politics to recognizing certain bodies. There is also a politics to acknowledging affect. The people I interviewed often had strong emotional reactions to incarceration. 'I cry, believe me, every night', one Romanian man said. Another prisoner, who was facing deportation to Nigeria, told me, 'That's one of the things I'm going through . . . not able to call anybody . . . Nevertheless, I know there's a purpose to everything. I believe. . . . ' His voiced trailed off. Then, in a whisper, as he began to cry, he finished: 'I might not understand, but the future will tell.' These prisoners, like so many others, were traumatized by incarceration and the prospect of deportation. Yet, in an important sense, their emotional lives did not get to be part of the process of punishment and 'removal'. The penal institution absorbs prisoners' experiences, turning pain into legal sanctions.

This process is inextricably connected to identity. In the criminal justice system, only some pains become the basis for punishment. Legal systems prioritize particular feelings, such as my fear of crime, and suppress others, such as Patrick's sense of alienation.[51] The bodies inside prisons do not simply happen to be black, or white, or male, or female, or born in former colonies. Patterns of migration, conquest, and inequality create the conditions for certain bodies to count. History clings to bodies, giving them meaning and giving rise to systems of power. Paying attention to the way that people look and feel, and asking how those feelings come or fail to be recognized by actors cloaked in state power, is a crucial part of the criminological project. To understand the relationship between punishment and construction of the modern state, we

[50] Chapter 2 describes the political campaign that motivated the British Prison Service to introduce a new policy targeted at non-citizens. Throughout the course of this research, I lived and worked in the United Kingdom on a five-year student visa.

[51] Butler uses the term 'expendable' in her accounts of which bodies matter. See Butler, *Bodies that Matter*, p. 16; *Precarious Life*; see also Judith Butler, *Undoing Gender* (New York, NY: Routledge, 2004).

have to ask what happens to bodies behind bars, and whose bodies are really at issue.

Conclusion

When criminologists write about politics, they typically mean the process by which collectives structure and express their preferences. The classic study of politics involves partisan battles and divergent models of social organization, from two-party democracies to authoritarian regimes.[52] Criminologists have advanced strong critiques of politics in this sense of the term. Scholars such as Ian Loader, Jonathan Simon, and Nicola Lacey have developed insightful arguments about the connection between political processes and the operation of criminal justice institutions.[53] These thinkers have contributed to a rich body of writing on the 'governance of punishment' in liberal democracies.[54] They have also explored the link between governance and penal excess.[55]

[52] See Adrian Leftwich, ed., *What Is Politics? The Activity and its Study* (Cambridge: Polity Press, 2004).

[53] See, e.g. Ian Loader, 'Plural Policing and Democratic Governance', *Social and Legal Studies* 9, no. 3 (September 2000): pp. 323–45; Ian Loader, 'Fall of the "Platonic Guardians": Liberalism, Criminology and Political Reponses to Crime in England and Wales', *British Journal of Criminology* 46, no. 4 (Oct. 2005): pp. 561–86; Ian Loader, 'For Penal Moderation: Notes toward a Public Philosophy of Punishment', *Theoretical Criminology* 14, no. 3 (August 2010): pp. 349–67; Ian Loader and Richard Sparks, 'Contemporary Landscapes of Crime, Order, and Control: Governance, Risk, and Globalization', in Mike Maguire, Rod Morgan, and Robert Reiner, eds, *The Oxford Handbook of Criminology*, 4th ed. (Oxford: Oxford University Press, 2007), pp. 44–78; Jonathan Simon, 'Megan's Law: Crime and Democracy in Late Modern America', *Law and Social Enquiry* 25, no. 4 (October 2000): pp. 1111–50; Nicola Lacey, *The Prisoner's Dilemma: Political Economy and Punishment in Contemporary Democracies* (Cambridge: Cambridge University Press, 2008). See also Vanessa Barker, 'The Politics of Punishing: Building a State Governance Theory of American Imprisonment Variation', *Punishment & Society* 8, no. 1 (January 2006): pp. 5–33; Michael Cavadino and James Dignan, *Penal Systems: A Comparative Approach* (London: Sage, 2006); Kevin Stenson and Robert Sullivan, *Crime, Risk and Justice: The Politics of Crime Control in Liberal Democracies* (Cullompton: Willan, 2001).

[54] Frank Zimring and David Johnson, 'Public Opinion and the Governance of Punishment in Democratic Political Systems', *The Annals of the American Academy* 605, no. 1 (May 2006): p. 266.

[55] Zimring and Johnson, 'Public Opinion and the Governance of Punishment in Democratic Political Systems', p. 266.

For feminists and critical race theorists, the word politics also refers to the principles that structure subjectivity. Scholars concerned with race and gender treat politics as a way to study the terms of recognition, dignity, and respect in a shared social space. This inquiry—into the politics of identity rather than governance—is not as well developed in criminology. While criminologists have explored particular aspects of identity, most notably race, scholars have spent less time than we might examining how normative beliefs about identity become structural principles of imprisonment.[56] For the most part, criminological scholarship does not focus on the way that gender, sexuality, class, race, and nationality shape prison life.[57]

The concept of 'shaping' is crucial here. This verb shifts attention away from the representation of particular groups in the prison population and towards the way that beliefs about foreignness, masculinity, race, and sexuality affect the prison experience. While demographics matter, prison scholars have offered a relatively robust account of statistical trends in incarceration.[58]

[56] For examples of the criminological account of race, see Robin Alfred, *Black Workers in the Prison System* (London: Prison Reform Trust, 1992); Martin Bulmer and John Solomos, eds, *Racism* (Oxford: Oxford University Press, 1999); Kimmett Edgar and Carol Martin, *Perceptions of Race and Conflict: Perspectives of Minority Ethnic Prisoners and of Prison Officers*, RDS Online Report 11/04 (London: Home Office, 2004); Loraine Gelsthorpe, 'The Experiences of Female Minority Ethnic Offenders: The Other "Other"', in Sam Lewis, Peter Raynor, David Smith, and Ali Wardak, eds, *Race and Probation* (Devon: Willan, 2005); Paul Gordon, *White Law: Racism in the Police, Courts, and Prisons* (London: Pluto, 1983); Kathleen McDermott, 'We Have No Problem: The Experience of Racism in Prison', *New Community* 16, no. 2 (1990): pp. 213–28; David Wilson, '"Keeping Quiet" or "Going Nuts": Some Emerging Strategies Used by Young Black People in Custody at a Time of Childhood Being Re-constructed', *Howard Journal of Criminal Justice* 42, no. 5 (December 2003): pp. 411–25.

[57] Those exceptions include Bosworth, *Engendering Resistance*; Mary Bosworth and Jeanne Flavin, eds, *Race, Gender, and Punishment: From Colonialism to the War on Terror* (London: Rutgers University Press, 2007); Carrabine and Bosworth, 'Reassessing Resistance'; Rod Earle and Coretta Phillips, 'Con-viviality and Beyond: Identity Dynamics in a Young Men's Prison, in Margaret Wetherell, ed., *Identity in the 21st Century: New Trends in Changing Times* (Basingstoke: Palgrave MacMillan, 2009), pp. 120–38; and Adrian Howe, *Punish and Critique: towards a Feminist Analysis of Penality* (New York, NY: Routledge, 1996).

[58] See, e.g., Leonidas Cheliotas and Alison Liebling, 'Race Matters in British Prisoners: towards a Research Agenda', *British Journal of Criminology* 46, no. 2

In contrast, criminologists rarely ask how punishment forges and reifies the belief that heterosexuality is normal or that Britishness looks white. Prison scholars do not always consider whether concepts like foreignness and citizenship could exist without the penal institution. Scholars also tend to overlook the powerful 'structures of sentiment and ideology' that are the prison's most lasting creation.[59] These intellectual trends turn features of identity such as race, gender, and nationality into discrete subtopics of prison analysis. Mainstream criminologists—that is, scholars who do not explicitly identify as critical race theorists or feminists—usually treat gender as if it matters in women's prisons, masculinity as one of many issues in men's prisons, and race as a theme that applies to research on people of colour. These academic mores suppress the degree to which the politics of feeling are infused in every aspect of imprisonment.

Even a brief glimpse of prisoners' testimonies demonstrates that the body is always involved in debates about punishment. Penal power operates not only through rules and regulations, but also through the formation of emotions, affects, and ideologies. Prisoners' narratives remind those outside penal institutions that imprisonment is a material practice and that it is actual raced, gendered, classed, feeling bodies that we punish and expel. Ultimately, the narratives inside prisons suggest that academics concerned with the stratifying effects of incarceration ought to be thinking more about how state power feels in practice. This line of thought will encourage a more politically explicit criminology. It might also push criminologists to rethink the purpose of our work.

(March 2006): pp. 286–317; Elaine Genders and Elaine Player, *Race Relations in Prison* (Oxford: Clarendon Press, 1989); Marc Mauer, *The Race to Incarcerate* (New York, NY: Free Press, 1999); Michal Tonry, *Malign Neglect: Race, Crime and Punishment in America* (Oxford: Oxford University Press, 1996).

[59] Chris Cuneen, 'Postcolonial Perspectives for Criminology', in Mary Bosworth and Carolyn Hoyle, eds, *What Is Criminology?* (Oxford: Oxford University Press, 2011), p. 251.

Conclusion

Prisoners' narratives do not end when a researcher leaves prison. Many of the people I met continue to live and work in British penal institutions. Some have been transferred to immigration detention centres or deported. The truth is that I do not know what happened to most of the people who shared their stories with me. Prison research is ephemeral, transient, and truncated. At the end of a year of interviews, I had the freedom to walk away, to leave these issues behind and write about them rather than living them each day. In the face of that freedom, this book concludes with a few thoughts on the purpose of prison scholarship.

This book began from a sense that the most provocative thinking about what it means to put people behind bars is articulated in mythological terms. The sharpest critical writing on prisons has a decidedly metaphorical bent. Accounts of the carceral state, the punitive turn, and the culture of control are challenging and inspiring.[1] They are also relatively disconnected from empirical questions about punishment. Often, scholarship on penality represents the prison and the nation-state in the kind of disembodied language that Elaine Scarry identified in public discussions of war.[2]

[1] See Ulrich Beck, *World Risk Society* (Cambridge: Polity Press, 1999); David Garland, *The Culture of Control: Crime and Social Order in Contemporary Society* (Oxford: Oxford University Press, 2001); Paul Gilroy, *Postcolonial Melancholia* (New York, NY: Columbia University Press, 2006); Pat O'Malley, 'Volatile and Contradictory Punishment', *Theoretical Criminology* 3, no. 2 (May 1999): pp. 175–96; Joe Sim, *Punishment and Prisons: Power and the Carceral State* (London: Sage, 2009); Jonathan Simon, *Governing through Crime* (Oxford: Oxford University Press, 2007); Loïc Wacquant, *Punishing the Poor: The Neoliberal Government of Social Insecurity* (Durham, NC: Duke University Press, 2009).

[2] Elaine Scarry, *The Body in Pain: The Making and Unmaking of the World* (Oxford: Oxford University Press, 1985).

The politics of metaphor are clear in Scarry's work—she suggests that a euphemistic rendering of war enables wide-scale violence.[3] In the case of the prison, the political implications of thinking in metaphor and myth are slightly less obvious, but are equally real. Chapter 1 mentioned these politics when it introduced Lucia Zedner's 'appreciative critique' of David Garland's *The Culture of Control*.[4] There, I noted that Zedner is critical of a trend towards what she calls 'grand narratives' of criminological theory. Such narratives present the prison and penal policy in sweeping, symbolic terms. Zedner describes Garland's book:

> *The Culture of Control* is painted on a large canvas and the schematic overview of changes in crime problems, penal ideas, penal politics and institutional forms it describes is masterly. To shift the metaphor slightly, the book has the character of a vast tapestry in which myriad, diverse strands are woven together with great skill and care.[5]

Zedner's reading of Garland, though admiring, is only half a step from Scarry's description of the 'lumbering giants' in war narratives.[6] Zedner identifies the 'vast', 'schematic', and 'myriad' qualities of Garland's theory.[7] Like Elaine Scarry before her, she is worried about the effects that such 'grand' language has on the topics—and the people—it describes.

In particular, Zedner is concerned that grand narratives promote a dystopic vision of criminal justice. She explains this problem in 'Dangers of Dystopia in Penal Theory', a companion piece to John Braithwaite's powerful article, 'What's Wrong with the Sociology of Punishment?'[8] According to Zedner, books like *The Culture of Control* set out to debunk 'the myth of the sovereign state', and in doing so, situate the criminologist as a 'vigilant watch, the witness to the multiple, shifting dangers that attach to late modernity'.[9]

[3] Scarry, *The Body in Pain*.

[4] Lucia Zedner, 'Dangers of Dystopias in Penal Theory', *Oxford Journal of Legal Studies* 22, no. 2 (Summer 2002): pp. 341–66; see also Garland, *The Culture of Control*.

[5] Zedner, 'Dangers of Dystopias in Penal Theory', p. 342.

[6] Scarry, *The Body in Pain*, p. 70.

[7] Zedner, 'Dangers of Dystopias in Penal Theory', p. 342.

[8] Zedner, 'Dangers of Dystopias in Penal Theory'; see also John Braithwaite, 'What's Wrong with the Sociology of Punishment?', *Theoretical Criminology* 7, no. 1 (February 2003): pp. 5–28.

[9] Zedner, 'Dangers of Dystopias in Penal Theory', p. 364.

Grand criminology aims to locate and deconstruct the state. This goal figures the state as a metaphor, a protagonist in the narrative of contemporary social control. It also places the academic in an explicitly descriptive stance: our mission is to track the state, to recount its workings, and to expose it behind and beneath the machinery of criminal justice.[10] Zedner warns that this descriptive vantage point delivers a fatalistic approach to state power. She argues that deconstruction becomes a dystopic and self-fulfilling enterprise, for it leaves little room to imagine the possibility of change.

Zedner's critique springs from a close reading of *The Culture of Control*, but her insight extends well beyond the boundaries of that book. At its base, Zedner's point is that sociologists of punishment have lost sight of the political implications of our writing. Zedner argues that Garland's account entails 'the abandonment of a larger political vision and smack[s] of capitulation to the "hyper-modern, flexible, neo-conservative, economic politics" that are the very subject of [his] analysis'.[11] She contends that there is a latent politics to the 'apoliticism' of contemporary writing on punishment and society. In Zedner's view, the assiduous effort to deconstruct the state has divorced critical criminologists from the normative and political purpose of our research.

The goal, then, is to advance a more normative and politically explicit account of punishment. That does not mean scholars have to be less theoretical, but it does mean that critics of imprisonment need to frame incarceration, and our own work on prisons, as a political act. To resist the dystopia of penal theory, academics need to explore the ways in which the state is not a monolith but the product of continuing and contingent interactions between bureaucrats, officers, and prisoners. Scholars also have to ask whether and why certain penal practices, such as the racialized identification of foreigners, are right or wrong. Zedner does not

[10] I wrote about Zedner's critique of Garland, and began to develop this conclusion, in a chapter on gender composed with Mary Bosworth. See Mary Bosworth and Emma Kaufman, 'Gender and Punishment', in Jonathan Simon and Richard Sparks, eds, *The SAGE Handbook of Punishment and Society* (London: Sage Publications Ltd, 2012), pp. 186–204.

[11] Lucia Zedner, 'Dangers of Dystopias in Penal Theory', pp. 364–5; see also van Swaaningen, *Critical Criminology: Visions from Europe* (London: Sage Publications Ltd, 1997), p. 194.

fill in the details of this normative criminology, but she does prioritize concerns about *why* academics study justice. This is an important conceptual move. Zedner's critique of grand narratives implies that the shortcomings of critical criminology spring from academic methods. She suggests that scholars should shift away from deconstruction and towards new ways of thinking about state power.

On one level or another, each of the past seven chapters has explored this suggestion. The critique that runs throughout this book is epistemological: we have set ourselves up to find and out the state behind penal practices, and as a result, have limited what we can find within the prison. In the prevailing intellectual framework, the way criminologists know the truth about prisons is to identify the state at work beneath ordinary penal practices. But the meaning of prison lies not only in its connection to power. The prison's force also rests its resilient humanity, in the stories told by Charles, Damien, Patrick, and Noishime. These stories may or may not be true—Chapter 2 argued that academics ought to care slightly less about their truth and more about the people telling them. Rather than asking which narratives are verifiable, or where the state surfaces, criminologists could learn about punishment by asking how prison feels. In a study less committed to outing the state, there is more space to explore the insights that live in the affective remainder of the penal institution.[12]

Literary theory paves the way for this critical work. In the last book she wrote before she died, Eve Sedgwick encouraged her fellow literary scholars to move away from deconstruction, and in particular, away from a practice she called 'paranoid reading'.[13] Sedgwick argued that writing about literature had become a paranoid exercise, one in which the good critic 'unveils' or 'reveals' the knowledge beneath the novel.[14] 'This novel is really about x!', the paranoid scholar proclaims, 'and now we can understand it'. Sedgwick worried that this approach to literary criticism had

[12] Judith Butler, *The Psychic Life of Power: Theories in Subjection* (Palo Alto, CA: Stanford University Press, 1997), p. 92. See Chapter 7 for a description of Butler's use of the term 'remainder'.

[13] Eve Sedgwick, *Touching Feeling: Affect, Pedagogy, Performativity* (Durham, NC: Duke University Press, 2004), p. 126; see also Bosworth and Kaufman, 'Gender and Punishment'.

[14] Sedgwick, *Touching Feeling*, p. 126.

developed into a normative epistemology in which only one kind of reading—the paranoid kind—is right, smart, and worthwhile. Scholars of punishment could voice a similar concern about paranoid criminology. According to Sedgwick, one thing that happens in paranoid studies of the novel is that scholars end up writing and reproducing the same story over and again.[15] In faithfully finding and outing the state, critical criminologists threaten to do the same—and as Lucia Zedner might add, we reproduce a deeply dystopic picture of contemporary society.

To resist these problems, Sedgwick suggests a turn towards phenomenology, or as she puts it, towards the practices of touching and feeling.[16] Sedgwick wants scholars to tune into the affective dimensions of literature, to the ways that touch, sound, and emotion surface in the novel. She argues that such an approach, which she describes as an openness to texture, will produce less rigid and repetitive scholarship and will open lines of thought that challenge existing accounts of 'agency and passivity'.[17] Sedgwick writes that 'texture seems like a promising level of attention for shifting the emphasis of some interdisciplinary conversations away from the recent fixation on epistemology ... by asking new questions about phenomenology and affect'.[18] Translating that hope into the language of prison studies, criminologists could redirect theoretical accounts of punishment towards the systems of sentiment in penal institutions.

Throughout this book, foreign national prisoners' embodied experiences have pointed the way towards a set of questions that flow beyond the nation-state—questions about the construction of citizenship, the nature of national belonging, and the 'structures of feeling' that motivate conduct inside prisons.[19] Chapter 4 explored how, in practice, the concept of nationality becomes a debate about what it feels like to be recognized as a full member of a polity. Chapter 6 argued that claiming to 'feel British' is one way to contest legal definitions and borders. In Chapter 5, prisoners' racial, ethnic, and national identifications vacillated along

[15] Sedgwick, *Touching Feeling*, p. 124.

[16] Sedgwick, *Touching Feeling*.

[17] Sedgwick, *Touching Feeling*, p. 14.

[18] Sedgwick, *Touching Feeling*, p. 17.

[19] The term 'structures of feeling' belongs to Raymond Williams. See Raymond Williams, *Marxism and Literature* (Oxford: Oxford University Press, 1978).

the politics of belonging, as did discrimination on each of those grounds. These accounts put monolithic versions of the state into relief, and more to the point, shift attention away from the revelation of the state by suggesting that punishment is, at its base, a problem of feeling.

This book has argued that feelings have a political dimension. It is worth noting, in conclusion, that feelings can also provide the foundation for a more normative approach to prison studies. For decades, feminist theorists have demonstrated that studying emotion, embodiment, and identity is a normative project. Feminists who write about the body—people like Judith Butler, Kimberlé Crenshaw, and Eve Sedgwick—are rarely presented as moral theorists, but their work has a normative dimension.[20] These thinkers document the body's part in power relations; they explore how the material, gendered, raced body shapes social hierarchies. The point of this writing is not simply to identify cultural norms. Feminist writers are also crucially interested in changing the dynamics of culture, in making the world less sexist, less racist, less homophobic, less violent.

The purpose of emphasizing bodies, in other words, is not only to explore what identity means in cultural context. It is also, quite explicitly, to acknowledge the people constituted by those bodies and to make those people count in a world where they are otherwise objectified, oppressed, and ignored. Judith Butler wants to 'challenge . . . the symbolic hegemony' in a way that 'forces a radical rearticulation' of what qualifies as a life 'worth protecting'.[21] Kimberlé Crenshaw works to 'locate' women of colour in a discussion about criminal justice from which they have been effaced.[22] Many other feminist authors write with similar motivations.[23] Feminists, critical race, and queer theorists turn to the body to

[20] See Judith Butler, *Bodies That Matter: On the Discursive Limits of Sex* (New York, NY: Routledge, 1993); Kimberlé Crenshaw, 'Mapping the Margins: Intersectionality, Identity Politics, and Violence against Women of Color', *Stanford Law Review* 43, no. 6 (July 1993): pp. 1241–99; Eve Sedgwick, *Epistemology of the Closet* (Berkeley, CA: University of California Press, 1991); Sedgwick, *Touching Feeling*.

[21] Butler, *Bodies That Matter*, p. 16.

[22] Crenshaw, 'Mapping the Margins'.

[23] For a longer genealogy of gender in criminology and prison studies, see Bosworth and Kaufman, 'Gender and Punishment'.

'connect their activist goals with their academic work'.[24] Their aim, as Butler puts it, is to make bodies matter.[25]

Taking a cue from this strategy, criminologists can turn to the body to highlight the normative dimension of writing on the prison. Asking questions about the material experience of incarceration is not merely an effort to acknowledge the bodies behind bars. Foregrounding the materiality of prison life is also an attempt to direct criminological attention towards the painful aspects of incarceration and towards the fundamental interconnectedness, and sense of possibility, that springs from lived experience. In Chapter 7, a prisoner named Charles pointed out that bodies are capable of feeling pain, and as such, are the foundation for empathy, sympathy, and hope. In *Undoing Gender*, Judith Butler argued that sentiments expose our 'constitutive sociality'.[26] She claimed that feelings of 'passion, grief, and rage…tear us from ourselves, bind us to others, transport us, undo us, and implicate us in lives that are not our own….'[27] The question is whether prison studies can begin from recognition of this shared capacity for feeling.

Over the course of the last seven chapters, I have argued that prisons are de facto sites for border control. This book has tracked a transformation in the use of British penal institutions—specifically, a shift away from twentieth-century conceptions of punishment, which assumed and constituted a bounded polity, and towards the goals of nationalism and migration control. In offering this account, I hope to disrupt a narrative in which incarceration has a static purpose. One goal of this study is to ask when, if ever, custody is an appropriate practice. My other goal is to insist that penal institutions are human places, capable of change. Nowhere is the humanity and incoherence of punishment clearer than inside prison walls. Focusing on prisoners' sentiments, feelings, and flesh reveals deep tension in concepts like rehabilitation, retribution, state, and nation. Penal narratives suggest that imprisonment does not have to be as it is.

The concluding call of this book is thus to turn with a phenomenological eye towards the 'bodily remainder' of the nation-state, particularly as it comes to life in prisons.[28] Emphasizing

[24] Bosworth and Kaufman, 'Gender and Punishment', p. 196.
[25] Butler, *Bodies That Matter*.
[26] Judith Butler, *Undoing Gender* (New York, NY: Routledge, 2004), p. 19.
[27] Butler, *Undoing Gender*, p. 20.
[28] Butler, *The Psychic Life of Power*, p. 92.

embodiment is an effort to incorporate feminist writing into prison studies and to better address the shifts that globalization has prompted inside penal institutions. It is also a return to Foucault and to the lines of thought from which critical criminology began. For it was Foucault who argued that:

> In our society the systems of punishment are to be situated in a certain 'political economy' of the body: even if they do not make use of violent or bloody punishment, even when they use 'lenient' methods involving confinement or correction, it is always the body that is at issue—the body and its forces, their utility and their docility, their distribution and their submission.[29]

More than thirty years ago, Foucault argued that imprisonment is always about the body, whether it is tarred and feathered, incarcerated, or electronically tagged.[30]

Today, attending to the bodily remainder of penality is a way to think politically, normatively, and empirically about what is happening—to prisoners, to prisons, and to the concept of citizenship—in British penal institutions. Never sufficiently identifiable within the official rubric for nationality, nor ever fully dissociated from the politics of identity, foreign national prisoners embody the irreparable gap between the fixed identity categories that citizenship demands and the lived realities of a postcolonial, globalized world. These prisoners' experiences suggest that the prison is not only a space in which national identity is constructed, but also one in which the limits of citizenship are realized every day.

[29] Michel Foucault, *Discipline and Punish: The Birth of the Prison*, trans. Alan Sheridan (New York, NY: Vintage Books, 1977), p. 25.

[30] I first used this phrase in Bosworth and Kaufman, 'Gender and Punishment', p. 196.

Postscript

In an ending too fitting to omit, I received the following letter as I typed the last lines of this manuscript from New York:

Important Notice from the Home Office: Decision to Curtail Leave

Dear Miss Emma Moffat Kaufman,

Curtailment of Leave

You were granted leave to enter as a Tier 4 General Student until 08 August 2015 in order to undertake a course of study with your sponsor. However, the Home Office was informed by your sponsor on 23 July 2012 that you ceased studying with them.[1]

Home Office records have been checked and there is no evidence that you have made an application to change your sponsor or made a fresh application for entry clearance, leave to enter or leave to remain in the United Kingdom in any capacity. Therefore . . . your leave is curtailed under paragraph 323A(a)(ii)(2) of the Immigration Rules. . . .

We would also like to take this opportunity to remind you of the Immigration Rules that govern the way in which applications to enter the United Kingdom are treated from persons who have previously breached the UK's immigration laws. In accordance with paragraph 320(7B) of the Immigration Rules, any person who previously overstayed for more than 90 days will have their application refused unless they meet one of the exceptions set out in the Rules. Those who have breached the UK's immigration laws could see applications to re-enter the UK refused for the following periods:

- 1 year if, following the breach, they left the UK voluntarily at their own expense;
- 2 or 5 years if, following the breach, they left the UK voluntarily at public expense;
- 10 years if they were removed or deported from the UK following their breach.

[1] This is a slightly condensed version of a longer letter. I have omitted descriptions of the UK Immigration Rules and my right to appeal.

[Y]ou should make your own arrangements to leave the UK before your leave expires.

Help and Advice on Returning Home

You can contact Choices, the UK's assisted voluntary return service, who can assist you in a voluntary return. ... Choices will provide you with practical support to help organise your departure from the UK.

Yours Sincerely,

A. Ahmed
Tier 4 Curtailment Team
UK Visas and Immigration
On Behalf of the Secretary of State

Building a Safe, Just and Tolerant Society

I wrote back to Mr. Ahmed to say that I had left the country more than three years earlier. I hope I will be able to return.

Index